MW01233330

Comatized 3

Lipstick Wearing Liberal Lesbian

By

Missy C Luckett

Printed   by CreateSpace, an Amazon.com company

ISBN-13:978-1545207611
ISBN-10-:1545207615

Individual sales may be purchased at
Missy's "Out of the Way" Café.
860 Horseshoe bend Road
Raywick Kentucky 40060

ACKNOWLEDGMENTS

Dedicated to the land and the people of Kentucky....

INTRODUCTION

Welcome back Y'all:

I'm still just writing stories on how to kick drama in the ass and tie them together like connective tissue. It's free conscience writing, so I hope you don't judge me as harshly as my aunt Beverly.

My child is grown and I've given her many memories, and I hope to give her many, many, more. I tell myself to try and write when I'm happy and giddy, so the story doesn't take a turn for the worst. "Let it marinate." I have to be in a certain state of mind, even though this life stays in distress most of the time. I will try to keep this story as light hearted as possible, I promise. I mean I use to see every ending as a new beginning. It's becoming much harder these days, and it takes much more thought and dedication to make yourself move on, like la-te-da... I'm realizing that it may come with more age. Most of the time, all it takes is a good joke at the end of the day to make it all better. For example: Two gays guys were sitting at the bar. One of the waitresses who was new to the Thursday evening crowd, handed them their ticket and said, "you're on top and you're on bottom." Yep! That's all it took to make the day great again.

I myself, just want to share my life with that special person whom I can adapt my life to. I haven't written any of my love/relationship stories yet, in any of my books. I'm holding my cards close on this one at the moment. Why? Because I'm waiting on a happy ending. No can do! Just can't get it right. What is my happy ending? It is finding true love. Going on 50 and and still no such luck. DAMN! That sucked to say.. Boo hoo! Guess I will end up like dad. He seems content. No worries. Let's move along.

Mom walked into the Cafe and I immediately threw up my hands and asked. "Why am I writing! Why? Tell me!"

"Because there is something driving you."

"True. But I don't know if it's a passion or a curse. I'm barely scratching the surface of what I want to say. It's hard, hard as hell. I get all kinds of intense thoughts, then whoosh, into thin air they go. I can't keep them in my head long enough to even get them written down."

"Well, I bet your English teachers would be proud to know you are writing a long, long, long term paper."

"Yeah, but they won't be proud of my grammar."

$6+3=9$ and $4+5=9$. We all get to our destinations differently. These are a few stories about how I survived high school. There is not a back road around here that me, a friend or a family member hasn't put a stamp on. So just join me on these winding roads and take in the adventure.

April Fool's Day 2017, all revisions on my book are done and complete. (THRILLED) April 3rd, I delete all revisions. (PANIC). Luckily I had a PDF copy, but it has been a bitch converting back to my original. I keep looking for perfection when it comes to writing these series, but it's time for us all to accept, that it's never gonna happen. It's truly not gonna happen and it must be accepted or I'm gonna have a stroke, if I don't.

WARNING...... Flaws ahead.

Just a reminder: Readers! Remember you are the readers. So when I say people, just know, I'm not talking about you. You will understand later.

Getting my first hard copy book in the mail was like Christmas Day for kids.

SUMMER OF '85

Let's see! Where do we begin? Or may I ask? Where did we leave off? Oh yes! I woke up and it was the summer of eighty-five. The night before was such a blur. A girl got arrested for trying to cut another girl's hair off. They got her for wanton endangerment. Just know that was the big news for that week. Hell someone just brought it up in the cafe the other day. We all agreed she wasn't wanting to cut her, she really just wanted to cut off her hair. It was definitely way more dramatic than when the girl got her hair cut off in the movie, *Sixteen Candles*. You guys remember that, don't you?

I find it hard spelling the word "definitely" today, because my dyslexia is acting up again. I can't even find the mistake when the word gets underlined in red. This is gonna be a tough journey, but here goes.

During this time of my life (Eighties) my priorities were pictures and alcohol. I didn't have my ducks in a row. I didn't even know there was any such thing. I had monkeys. Drunk monkeys. I suspended good judgment for many years. So did a lot of my friends. Just know we all survived the eighties and are all respectful, productive adults. Most of them with husbands and proud mommies. None of us are alcoholics. You will wonder how we aren't, after reading some of these stories. It's all *Cyndi Lauper's* fault. She never should have released that song, *Girls Just Wanna Have Fun*. Girls, they want. Want to have fun. Girls. They just wanna, they just wanna. Really want. Fun! Girls.

Speaking of girls, this is when I realized I may like them. You know, a different kind of like. I'm sure you have seen the movies about the friend having a crush on the other. Well, that's what happened to me when I started high school. When I met this one particular girl, I was

7

smitten. She came from the other junior high. (PAUSE) Maybe we might ought to get to that later. (PAUSE) Oh shit! Let's talk about it now. It was the first girl crush I had experienced and it was really weird to me. But she was all I could think about. She lived way out in the country, so I never got to go hang with her until I got my license. Before that I would hang out with her at parties. I don't really know what I was looking for. I just knew I liked hanging with her. I feel that most girls get a girl crush before they grow up, gay or not. It's odd that I never had a crush on a girl up until that point. Well, I did, but she was on the big screen. I'm talking about a real life one. I didn't have another crush on anybody else till my senior year, which is now, the stories I'm about to tell. But when it comes to this second crush, I will never tell. Just gonna let that dead dog lie. The first crush never knew, till many, many years later. I will enlighten you about all that in due time. That crush was hidden in the bushes like a stalker in the night. It was a feeling that stretched throughout the years.

At the time I was still living with Maw-maw, but I hung out at Kandy's house for most of the summer. She was a friend I had made when I entered high school. Kandy's normalcy makes her hard to describe, so I won't even try. Except that she was exceptionally smart, attractive and a good friend and lived way out in Saint Joe. She had two younger sisters, Michaela and Sarah. Loved them like they were my own little sisters. Kandy and I were addicted to the show *Miami Vice*, and used to always watch it in her basement. One night Sarah came down the steps to bug us. She was probably only four at the time. Out of the blue, she bit me. I thought you little shit! So I slightly bit her back, just to show her you don't do that. OMG! Dooms day was here! She went running and crying upstairs to her mom. I thought I was gonna get the death penalty for a moment. Her mom came strolling down the steps. The only

8

response I had, "I swear it wasn't hard."

I just wanted the little fart to know you don't do that. I'm sure in today's time, I would already be sitting in court and being sued. Not by her mom, but by the state or something. I swear you can't even look at a kid wrong these days without repercussions.

I never tried the bite back tactic with Summer. Oh wait! She never bit anyone. But Kaitlyn, Kristen's daughter, sure liked to bite. One time she bit Summer, and Summer just stood there with her feelings hurt. I said, "Summer! Bite her back. She shouldn't do that to you." Summer just shyly backed away. I have to say, Summer never went through that phase, that, or pulling hair. Kristen use to laugh and say, you will get yours at some point. I was like yeah right, and I waited and waited for years. Then it happened. I believe we're gonna have to discuss that, on a way later note.

Back to Kandy's house for a minute. We loved, I mean loved, loved the movie *"Breakfast Club."* We would crack up every time at the part where *Anthony Michael Hall* got high. "The chick can't hold her smoke." Then *Judd Nelson* knocked him across his forehead and out of his chair. I guess it was funny to us, because at that time we were piddling around with smoking a little pot ourselves.

So we were outside with Sara one evening and we put a fake joint in her hand and told her to say the chick can't hold her smoke. When she did, we busted out. I know, that's not good, but she didn't know and it was harmless. Honestly it was. Wish I had the pictures to show you how cute it was.

I guess like any other generation we were stuck on phrases. We came up with one word and we thought we had created the English vocabulary. Instead of saying okay, we would say, "O-ba-ta-ba." We even had shirts made that said it. Guess maybe we were smoking a little more weed than I thought. Maybe Trump got a hold of some of the same

9

shit with the new vocabulary he is creating. Words like bragadocous and bigly.

Kandy was a big Gnome collector. That's what I used to get her for her birthday almost every year, until she said, enough already. So anyway, we were riding around one night and fired one up. Well, actually we didn't fire it up. We didn't have any papers and we only had an itty bitty piece of weed. I'm not even sure where we got it, probably from an Uncle. Even if I had a paper, I wouldn't be able to roll it right. We would have weed flying down our throat and choking while saying, I hate them damn things. I couldn't roll then and I can't roll today. So we had to improvise. So I pushed in the lighter on the car. You remember those don't you? Dropped it right on there and we took a big smoky hit. It wasn't but a few minutes later, when we could have sworn we saw a Gnome sitting in a tree. We were actually seeing Gnomes, both of us. I have no idea what kind of shit we were smoking that night.

Kandy and Lisa

There was this one time when I went to ask her a question. "Do you remember?" Before I finished, she said "Yes!" I was like, "Whatever Kandy! I haven't even asked you what you remembered yet. You're making shit up already." Then she turned right around and started to talk about what I was gonna ask her. All I could do was look down and say with amazement, "Heavens to Betsy! What the hell did we just smoke?" That is some mind connecting shit. I had no idea it had powers like this."

TWO DOLLAR TIP

Kandy and I headed off to Florida with her parents for the summer. It was my second trip to Florida, thanks to my friend's family. A few guy friends also came down in a separate car, of course. I recently asked Kandy about the trip, but if you think my mind has trouble remembering things, just talk to her. I have a semi-fuzzy memory. She has no past! But at least she remembered us wearing outfits that looked like Miami Vice. You know, Tubs and Crocket. We had cool ass blazers, over T-shirts and wore our pants with no socks. Bright ass pastel colors, too. Now that I think about it, we didn't dress like Tubs. He wore for real suits and that just wasn't cool to us. But Crocket on the other hand, he was cool and so were we. But if I think about it real hard, it could have been a disaster. It's kind of the same as when Marybeth, Lynn and I dressed alike and we all know that went over like a lead balloon.

The only other thing I remember about that trip, is she and I going to eat with the guys. We were eating at a restaurant and when the waitress gave us the bill, he said he wasn't leaving her a tip because the food sucked. I even knew way back then, you're suppose to leave a tip, even if the food isn't very good. It's not the waitresses' fault, especially if she is jovial. When we were walking out the door the waitress spoke out with disgust. "A two-dollar tip on a hundred-dollar meal!" One of the guys yelled back. "More like a two-dollar meal, and a hundred-dollar tip."

I was slightly embarrassed and thought to myself, Shit man, tell em how you really feel. I wasn't paying for the meal, so I walked on out the door. I was a poor little girl without two pennies to rub together at the time. No excuse, I still should have stood up and spoke up. Sorry, girl, hope the next customer made up the difference.

The gang

When we got back from Florida, Kandy had to start practicing for Junior Miss, which happens right before school starts back. In recent years they have changed its title to, *Distinguished Young Woman.* It is a talent program that awards college scholarships and provides a once-in-a-lifetime experience, for us high schoolers. Especially the ones looking for something more than the backwoods life. All my friends were practicing their skills, so they could show them off in the spotlight and up on stage. They literally performed in front of the whole town. Even though I opted out of this program and wasn't going to participate, I still practiced with Kandy, night and day. We would practice in the pool, in the yard and anywhere we could. Mostly the pool.

Most of my friends were gonna be in it and everyone was wondering why I wasn't. I didn't feel I was up for standing in front of the whole town reading a monologue or something. What talent did I have? I refuse to speak in public and I definitely can't sing or dance. I guess I could've gotten up there and dribbled a basketball with one hand and had a drink in the other. That may have been a talent, but I don't think the school would have agreed. Plus, we all already know I hate captivated audiences.

I knew captivated audiences stressed me out way back when. I noticed it when I first started playing basketball. It sent my body into panic mode every time someone fouled me. Standing at the free throw line all alone made me nervous, and I could feel my little boney knees chattering. I was still good at it, but I didn't like the way it made me feel. Maybe that's how I got my knotty knees.

Summer didn't participate in Junior Miss either. Don't quite remember what her reason was. She likes to design clothes, so I guess that would be hard to pull off on stage. I just found out in recent years that the little shit can really sing, but she is too shy to do it in front of anyone. I just happened to catch her one day and was greatly impressed. So she had a talent, she was just hiding it.

Bobbi Jean ended up winning Junior Miss. She was a friend, but we didn't party together like several of my other friends, as you will see. But anyway, she was headed off to the state finals and we all decided we would skip school that Friday and head on down to Bowling Green, to cheer her on. We got so freaking hammered that weekend. Pictures of this occasion, I so desperately miss. I can remember the pictures, not perfectly, but I can remember. You could tell everyone of us was drunk, as we sat on our hotel room floors. Although I had thousands upon thousands of pictures, I had never had a picture of me where I looked so drunk. Drunk as a skunk, as they would say.

We had basketball practice that Sunday. I got up the nerve to call my coach and say I wasn't gonna make it. She said, "I better." But I told her, I can't, and basically won't. I have people with me. I drove people down here and I can't come back and I didn't. Well, I reaped the consequences. My second game in my lifetime I didn't get to play. At least I didn't have to play sick this time. My dad was in prison and there was no one there to watch anyway. I was my own cheerleader. Speaking of cheerleaders!~

This short story has nothing to do with nothing really. Except I was the protector of my cheerleading friend Rosemarie. Before the game started, I went into the bathroom and some black girls had my friend Rosemarie in the corner about to kick her ass. She was a cheerleader and for some reason the black girls always wanted to taunt her. Not sure why, but they did. Maybe they thought, she thought, she was goody two shoes. I'm also not sure why they left her alone when I walked in either. But they did, even though I was a scrawny, boney, little white girl. They would look at her like, "Girl! It's your lucky day."

It wasn't the only time I had to save her. You're welcome, Rosemarie.

Rosemarie and Jeff. Jeff wasn't always around to protect her.

But anyway, back to the game. We were playing Adair county and they were a really good team. My coach was chomping at the bit to put me in and I think she should have. She was trying to prove a point to me. We were getting our asses kicked and I was sitting there on the bench just staring at her, like you should really put me in, neither of us were liking how this was playing out. She would glance down at me every now and then and put her head down and shake it and kick the floor. We lost of course, and all I could think was, serves you right and I'm sure she was thinking the same thing. But the fact is, and the fact that pissed me off, is that previously, there were several other girls that missed practice. So I don't know why she decided to prove her point on me. Probably the smoking tree incident. Which reminds me, my smoking is out of hand and I need a severe intervention. It's my "Achilles heel" and is so very taboo.

At work dressed up for eighties night, 2005-6-7-8 or 9.

LAMP STORY

Let's talk about Maw-maw for a minute. Remember how I told you that she doesn't call you out on stuff right away. She has the patience to hold it in for as long as she feels fit. Well this is the perfect example. Time was drawing near for me to be purchasing my prom dress for senior prom. We little poor girls, who had prom dresses from the previous year, would sell them to someone else and get the money to put down on a new one. I was really needing the money for my new dress.

I came home from school one day and she was just chillin in her chair as usual, knitting an afghan. She looked at me and told me to go look in my room. I thought I had a surprise awaiting. I was so excited. So I ran to my room and looked all around and to my surprise, nothing new was there. So I came back down the hallway and looked through the door to the room Maw-maw was sitting and I said. "There is nothing there."

She said with a smirk, "Oh! You may wanna go look again. Maybe in your closet, see if something is missing."

I went back to look. I still couldn't figure out what the hell she was talking about. She done gone and lost her marbles. What the hell is she talking about? So I came back down the hallway again. "Maw-maw! What are you talking about?"

She grinned and clapped her hands. "I sold your prom dress. Let's call it even for the lamp."

My mouth dropped. "Are you serious?"

"Is the Pope Catholic?"

I had been caught with my pants down and I was totally butt hurt. There was absolutely nothing I could say. Why could I not say anything? Well, this is why I couldn't say anything. I came in drunk one night like a Weeble Wobble and knocked over the lamp in the guest bedroom.

Actually, I have no idea why I went to that bedroom, except for the fact I was drunk. When I woke up, I saw the broken mess. I panicked and cleaned it up quickly. I never said a word. As in if, I thought she would never notice. It was an antique lamp, so I should have known better. Lesson after lesson, "don't try to hide the truth." That's what I was learning. But it still took me a little longer to stop the drinking. Not much of a drinker these days though.

I remember the first time I drank beer. Trust me, it took me years to try that shit again. I came home that night and laid on the couch. The ceiling was spinning faster than the spin cycle on a washing machine. I went to put my foot down to stop it and whatever was in my stomach, screamed, I'm coming out. I dashed to the bathroom, but didn't have time to put the lid up. Maw-maw always kept those fuzzy things on them, so it didn't splatter too far. I was too sick to clean it up and went back to the couch. When I awoke, I awoke in a panic. I ran to the bathroom. But by this time Maw-maw was already frying up the bacon in the kitchen, well, not really frying, running it through the skillet. But anyway, I looked at the toilet, it was clean. Hummm! She never got me back for that one. Wonder why? I know she wasn't born yesterday, because she always told me she wasn't. Maybe sympathy? Jury is still out.

REAL TIME: Back flashes

Fall of 2016, is upon us and it's been a hell of a year for everyone. It's also been eight years since my house burnt to the ground. I was out cutting the grass, when images came flooding back and was realizing how much things have changed. I felt like I might cry when the smell of the freshly cut grass started to bring back memories of the old days. I started thinking about Maw-maw Luckett. That was the first place I ever cut grass. She was fancy smancy back in the day and had a riding lawn mower. But not for long, not after I took control of the wheel. The very first time I hopped on it, I raised havoc on it and I took it out with a tree. I really don't know how I could have been going fast enough to put it in its grave, but I did. So from that point on, it was push, push, push. She never bought another riding one.

Everyone should know by now, how I have been looking for pictures. Been on a quest for years. My friends and family have been pretty lame when it comes to finding any pictures for me. But I knew I had some doubles out there, lots of doubles. Why? Because I always had doubles made and handed them out to someone. Most likely to the people whom I was spending my time with. So, finally Chickie and Shannon, this is another Shannon, not the country, *Jamie Lee Curtis*, Shannon, set a date with me to come down and bring some pictures.

I had finished up mowing and was up here writing when they arrived. We were sitting upstairs when I opened the album. As I was rummaging through the pictures, it was a familiar feeling. A happy, sad feeling. I looked over at them. "Damn you bitches! These are all my doubles. All of them!"

"We know, we know. We wouldn't of had any pictures, if you hadn't taken these."

They weren't my lifetime of pictures, but they were the pictures of the times I spent with them. I met these two fine ladies once I started high school. The first few pictures were not very clear, so I won't be publishing them. They were of the 1985 graduation party, the one I was just telling you about. Then we came upon the cabin ones. Oh! The cabin! We went camping there several times. It's where Uncle Charlie lives now. But back then it was just an old beat up cabin that was old, old, and no one was suppose to go there. In the seventies and early eighties, it was a place for a few of the Corn Bread dealers to hide out and stay. I used to sneak all my friends up there, anytime I could convince them to go. Marybeth, the little chicken shit, never went.

Me, Chickie, Kathy and Shannon. (Jamie Lee) Shannon is taking the picture.

I have several stories from there, but I don't know exactly which night each happened. So I will combine them. Hell they may have all happened on the same night, who knows. We girls couldn't decide as

20

we were looking through the pictures. Chickie, brought up Kathy, a long time friend from grade school. "I ain't got near a one with Kathy. Shannon! How do you have all the ones with her?"

"Well, Chickie, you should. Don't you remember when Missy got doubles, we would go get prints made, too."

"Kathy was there. I do know that." I said with confidence. "Look! Here's the date and where we were."

"We were at the cabin and I wanna know what we were eating?"

"Who the hell knows. Probably spam on a stick." I replied.

Chickie took a quick ride down memory lane. "You remember throwing them firecrackers in the fire and they would blow out chunks of fire at me every time. I thought Kathy was doing it and I was cussing her out like a sailor. She kept saying, Chickie! I'm not doing it. I looked at her so mean and pointed at her. Don't you be lying to me! And as soon as I would turn around, them son bitches would start popping out at me again. Every time! Right at me. Why me? Missy, I had no idea you was doing it. I was about to beat Kathy's ass, like a rented mule."

"Trust me I was laughing my ass off the whole time, especially when you kept giving her the hairy eyeball."

"I figured it was Kathy. She would aggravate the balls right off a pool table."

Then I showed them the cover of my first book.

"I really liked your first book." As they both nodded their heads.

"Well, thanks girls. For this book, I'm gonna get a story from all you bitches. So let me turn on my recorder."

They both started shaking their head. "No! No!"

"Hold on, girls. Chill out! I'm just gonna get some of the conversation."

"I told Shannon on the way over here. Girl, my memory is shit."

"Tell me about it. You ought to sit up here at this computer with no pictures and try to remember shit. That's why you girls are here."

21

"I know! I know!" Shannon said.

"Look! Kandy can't remember nothing and Shannon can tell you what I wore to church every Sunday."

"Shannon Bradshaw?" Chickie asked.

"Yes!"

Shannon chimes in. "Look, there is your white Monte Carlo."

She really had it cut out and in her book.

I smiled. "That car was the shit. I ran that sucker off the road so many times, but it just kept going and it never got a dent put in it."

"Really, Missy? How many times did you wreck it?" Shannon asked

"A bunch. But don't tell Summer. One day I ran it off the road headed to the twin's house to watch *Santa Barbara*."

"Santa Barbara? Missy, you watched soap operas?" Chickie said with surprise.

"I watched that one! Wouldn't catch me dead watching one now! But anyway, I came around a curve and started spinning in circles. I hit the hill with every corner of my car, then I got stuck. But these guys pushed me out and I drove right on. Another time, I ran it off in a ditch going to Kandy's. I think I was listening to that damn *Saint Elmo's Fire*, instrumental shit and crying or something. That song, or let's say music, pulls my heart cords every single time."

"You cry?"

"Yes, I cry, you shit head, and I had to walk to Kandy's house. Don't remember who came and pushed me out. I also wrecked on Chrissy's road, but I won't get into that right at this moment."

"Damn, Missy, that car took a lickin and kept on tickin. It was the party car! I mean the party car!" Shannon said excitement.

"Yes and it even reminds me of the car in the movie, *Christine.*"

"Why, Missy? That wasn't an evil car."

"Why? Because it drove me home one night. Drove up the sidewalk and parked me right in front of Maw-maws front porch. Of course, I didn't know it did that for me, till the next morning. That car took really good care of me."

"Missy! Shit! Girl. You crazy. That car didn't drive you home."

"It makes me so sad. Listen! I wouldn't be writing none of this shit, if those pictures hadn't burned up."

"Yes, you would."

"The hell I would!"

"You got too many stories not to be writing."

Just like my dad would say no. I responded in an elongated, sarcastic monotone voice. "NOOOOOO! I would have gone straight to the big screen."

They started laughing. "Well, why don't cha?"

"No connections I guess. Listen, I was gonna put my senior year in the second book. Then I realized we did way too much freaking shit."

"We did, we did. Omg! We went everywhere in this county. This is the dag on picture! I love it! Oh my God! I love it! You guys are just getting down with the fire sticks."

Mindy, Chickie and Me

"Hey, wait a minute, I got on that senior jersey. So it has to be our senior year. I do, don't I?" Chickie said with excitement once more. She was on the edge of her chair the whole time.

Shannon asked with curiosity. "Didn't we go to the cabin more than one time? Boy I ain't been down memory lane in a long time Missy."

"Memory lane is fun ain't it." As they both nodded their heads yes, I started telling the girls about the Jake story and how I cut loose like a deuce, after we had sex. Told em I didn't have it again till I got out of high school. Found myself having it from time to time, cause everybody feels sexual at least once a year. Even though I had to close my eyes and think of England.

Chickie rolled her eyes. "Girl, you ain't right!"

"I will tell you what's not right. The time I drove Jakes car to see Josh."

"Eww, that ain't right, either." As we all laughed. Then they started to name real names. So we will have to skip that part. Then I was telling them about the day my pictures burnt up and I said they were melting right in front of me like the wicked witch. "I'm melting! I'm melting."

Shannon's thoughts sank for a moment. "I know... I know... I can't imagine losing everything I own."

"My shit was dated in my albums. Just like your shit here, but better and way, way more." I laughed. "When I got old, I was gonna sit in my little fucking rocking chair. I had just gotten through putting pictures in my albums, two weeks before it burnt."

"I know Missy. I hate that."

"Look! This is at Maw-maw Luckett's!" I said.

"I didn't know where some of those were." Shannon replied.

So we conversed about where the pictures were taken for a few minutes. Then I said, "OMG! I ran into Sam Fogle at Ham Days the other night. I walked up to him and some of his high school buddies and he just blurted out. "Yeah! I used to date Missy. But she liked some other boy." And then he said something or something, and I said. OMG! I wrecked your car and he smiled, "I don't care. You were so worried about it Missy, but I didn't care. You used to make me pick you up, then drive all over the county to pick up all your other friends." He smiled again and repeated. "But I didn't mind a bit."

Chickie sighed. "Oh. That's sweet. He was a sweetie."

"He said he had a blast doing it. Oh! Is that me? Look you guys. I told Summer the other day. I know I always wear my hair pulled up now, but back in the day, I wore it down. I fixed it with the times. She doesn't believe me." As we all started to laugh.

"Missy, do you remember going to the concert?"

"Which one? We went to so many."

"I don't know! Remember Jake needed to pee so bad his eyeballs were floating. He literally turned white in the face. We were on I-65 and they

25

were doing road work and we were stuck in traffic. I just felt so sorry for him, he about passed plumb slick out. Put that in your book."

"Its funny that you say that, because people say that to me every time they think they say or do something funny. "Put that in your book."

"Look at this picture." Shannon interrupted.

Chickie stared with confusion. "Is that you, Missy? You know who I thought that was? Bobby Jean!"

"Well, I will take that. She is a pretty girl. So Shannon! Which picture do you want me to put in there and which story?"

"I don't know! I was involved in all of 'em."

"Were you with us when we got pulled over and me and Rosemarie was stoned in the back seat?"

"I was the one driving y'all people, and y'all was just laughing and I didn't have any shoes on."

"I know, you told the cop you lost them at the creek. That was the day we had to actually drive across the creek to get to that old haunted house. When I drove across it, we about sunk. Like literally, water was coming in the windows and smoke was flying out from under the hood. We were in such a panic when we got to the other side, just staring at the car smoke, wondering how we was gonna get back across."

"Yeah, I know. Then someone decided it was a good idea to get stoned. We didn't even go in the haunted house, because we thought we were screwed. But we made it back across, when you floored it through and hydroplaned across it. Then you got out and said, drive bitch. I'm too stoned to drive any further."

"Omg, what is this picture? Did we think we were models? Who took these?" Chickie said.

"I did you fool. I had these pictures. I took these picture."

"But you had a bazillion more than we have."

Me, Kandy and Sharen, on some old back road.

"You know I got in trouble sometimes because I hung around different groups of you. I took the Loretto group to the cabin all the time."

Chickie said in a perky voice. "We all liked each other."

"Yes! Until someone liked someone else's boyfriend. That was always a mess."

We will delete this conversation. I ain't naming no names on this one.

"It brings back so many memories looking at these pictures." Chickie said with a smile.

"I know! It's like bam mother fucker! Bam! People try to say you don't need pictures to remember! Bullshit! Aw,,,,, I like this one."

Chickie started to chuckle. "Who is grabbing my ass? Is that you Missy?"

"Look at that. Look at me pinching butts already back then."

"You was doing it in another picture too."

"Started young I guess."

Me and Chickie

"Look at this one. We are eating again." Chickie said.

"I probably cooked it. Everything but that cheese. It tasted like cornbread rubbed down someone's ass."

"I don't remember the cheese, but you cooked for us, all the damn time, Missy. You were the only one that cooked. Oh Lord! We loved it."

"Here, pull this one out."

"They're stuck. They're thirty-years old." Shannon said.

"What did we eat? I wanna know what we ate?" Chickie kept asking.

"That I do not know. Deep fried possum maybe."

"Whatever Missy! We don't eat possum."

"Look at this one! Do I not look like a rock and roll star or what?"

"Look at us! Oh my god. I don't remember which night that was, but look at me. You can tell, you can tell I'm high. I was torn up." Chickie breathed real hard as if she was experiencing it all again.

"Oh Shannon! Do you have the pictures of Junior Miss down in Bowling Green. I was so wasted and I remember this one picture so well for some reason. We were on the steps and I had a Bellarmine sweat shirt on. I don't know where the hell it came from because no one in my family had gone to Bellarmine."

Shannon says with excitement. "Look, I have them! I have them!"

"Omg, you have them. Look! I was so wasted."

Chickie was screaming, "Oh girl, you know it. You look hurt up in that picture." She literally starts laughing like the devil. She knew she was a naughty girl that weekend.

"Y'all bitches got these pictures because of me." I said with a gloat.

Shannon, Me, Stephanie, Chrissy and Lynn.

Chickie sat back and laughed. "We went and got on birth control that day. Every time I peed I felt like a needle was coming out. What did that

29

son of a bitch do to us anyway? We played quarters all night long. They kept playing that song, *Addicted to Love*, every other minute. I liked it, but damn they wore it out."

And of course I changed the subject as soon as I seen another picture. "Oh! Why are we dressed up?"

"That's the smoking tree. Look at us. We ain't really dressed up." Chickie said.

"We were for that time in our life." I replied as we all busted out in laughter. I've already talked about the smoking tree and me getting in trouble with Miss Roby, but here is our picture.

Me, Shannon and Mindy. Where is the tree?

Chickie leaned toward the album. "Look at y'all's chicken legs."

Shannon pouted. "I never had chicken legs. They ain't mine."

"Y'all got some chicken legs there. Now I'm telling ya."

"That's my chicken legs. Remember we were jamming to *Jump,* by *Van Halen.* So I jumped over the fire. Hay ride! Hay ride! When was this? Thank God I gave you guys doubles."

"Revco, Revco! I went to Revco with you all the time. You remember Revco?" Chickie asked, as she was shaking her head up and down.

"Two extra dollars for doubles. I always got doubles. Who else has the doubles? Who is hoarding or too lazy to look?"

"Look at you looking over the pillow. That was on the way home from King's Island. I don't think you were very happy, Missy."

"I wasn't. I was hangin with a boyfriend."

We got to laughing so hard, when Shannon said. "Do you remember at the cabin, Missy, when we slept out in the lawn chair? Do you remember that? We slept out on the lawn chairs."

"Yeah, yeah!"

"So what was it that woke us up? It freaked us all out and we ran franticly into the cabin. Was it dogs or was it cows?"

I replied "Dogs! Wild dogs. Robbie had a few run-ins with them up there. He got chased to his truck by two and he shot one of them. He said he thought he was gonna die that day."

Chickie said, "See Shannon, I said dogs. But you kept saying cows. Who is afraid of cows?"

"I say dogs! It could have only been dogs, if we were afraid."

Chickie starting waving her arms all around. "It was, it was! Cause I remember you telling that story about people throwing pups into the Rolling Fork. The ones that survived would come out wild and crazy and would try and get ya! I was straight up freakin creeped out, that night."

Shannon said, "Well then! The wild dogs came and we all ran inside the cabin and slammed the front door. We really thought we were safe when we wiped our brows with relief. Then we looked around and there were no windows or doors on the back of the cabin. We really started to freak out."

"Oh! There wasn't no windows, was there? We were so scared that we had to go get in the car and sleep there till morning."

"You still don't think it was the cows?"

I looked over with a smirk. "Shannon, you fool! The cows could have been around us when we woke up, but it had to be the wild dogs through the night."

Chickie pointed over at her. "Yeah, cause it scared the shit out of us. We were freakin out. No lights! No windows! No back door. We were like! What the hell! There ain't even no damn windows in here. I said oh shit…. Shannon! Did your mom and dad even know where you was?"

"Hell no! They didn't know."

"Look at this picture! Me and this guy keep arguing on Facebook about Trump."

And yes we said his name. But I won't say your name here, Kevin. Oops. LOL. While writing this story and listening to our conversation,

I just realized what A.D.D. moments we are having. Insane A.D.D. moments. Hope you guys are keeping up. We may need an Adderall to calm our titties.

Then we saw a picture of the guy, who got shot by Cow Patty. You all remember Cow Patty, don't you? I will never forget her. She is the one who got me stoned out of my mind at the Club 68. Chickie covered her mouth and said. "You remember at the fair? When we was yelling, Chris! Chris! Get out of here. Cow Patty is here and she is gonna shoot you. We was scared back then, but that is some funny shit now."

"Yeah! Sometimes it takes a minute to comatize a story. You have to let it marinate for a minute. Kinda like the other day when I walked into the cafe. I was telling Kitty that I can't hardly get my stories written because you girls over here keep giving me enough to write about. Stuff like husbands shooting at wives. She looked up at me with shock. "Who got shot at?" I just stared at her with dismay. "Kitty! You got shot at." She started busting out laughing and said, "Oh yeah! That's right. I did get shot at." That girl is a mess. Oh! I remember this one. Sportsman Lake."

Chickie said, "I don't think I went with y'all. Oh yes I did, look there I am."

Shannon said, "See! Yes, you did. You were there. Here is the proof."

Chickie was laughing, "I swear I didn't think I went with y'all."

"You was there. The proof is in the pudding."

"Did you see that one of you and Jeff?"

"Well, dag on that boy, he was something else. That's the night we were egging cars."

"We did go egging that night. Did we egg the meat wagon? Is that what we called it?"

"Yes, we called it the Meat Wagon. And yes we egged it along with many other cars."

Marybeth, Jeff and me. Don't forget Marybeth's face. I will have a
story soon, about that same face. Just no picture.

Chickie said, "Look at Missy with that bow tie, and look at me at the
prom, with that flat ass hair. We some pretty good sights. Cigarette in
my damn hand. Jesus Christ! Yeah right, it looked like we were going
to the prom. Look like heathens. Oh Lord! Look at all the different
people that dated. What in the Sam Hell?"

"Look! Look! Does Jeff have a cast on?"

"I'm sure he does. Yep, he does. You know he broke his bones all the
time."

"Look! Jeff and Rosemarie and me in the back, looking off again."

"Oh! And them kissin."

"Is that a picture of you and Carl? Oh my Jesus! Did you date him?"
"Of course I did! I went to the prom with him."
"See, my damn brain don't remember shit."

Prom 1986

"Is that me? What am I doing? Not looking at the camera again. Never conform, never conform. I got to use that as a reference, non-conformative. That's me!"

"That's you!" Chickie replied and then said ever so sweetly. "Aw, look at that. Geralyn is in that one. That blue eye shadow. Lord, Lord. We look like a hot mess. I done look like I sweated like a pig."

"Speaking of pigs, cows, whatever farm animal you want, I use to go out to Geralyn's when I was at Saint Augustine. I would ride the bus out there. She always had to feed the cows buckets of grain. She filled up three of them and handed me one. "Here, you carry this." as she took off with the other two like she was carrying a loaf of bread. I went to pick up my bucket and about fell over. Here I was, way behind her dragging my one bucket on the ground with both hands, as it kept smacking my leg till I was bruised."

"She was built like a brick house." Shannon said.

"Yes, she was."

"Look cabin night again! There's old Jeff again? I swear we have more pictures of him than his momma."

"Oh my god! That's our five-year reunion. Y'all skipped from this to that. What the hell? You know what? Here's what happened. I disappeared out of your life, then I come back in. Boom! Pictures, I disappear out of y'all's damn life and look!"

"Oh my God." Chickie said as she rolled her eyes. "Look what happens four years later. Here we are." "Oh my Jesus."

"No wonder no one understood my devastation. Look at my hair! What the fuck?

Shannon said, "You probably had one of those banana clips in your hair."

"What am I doing?"

"You're saying, oh please don't take my banana clip out."

As I went on through the album, I soon realized, that when I stopped hanging with Shannon after college, her pictures abruptly stopped. I mean nada. Then they started again 4 years later when we had our five year reunion. Why? Because, my ass was there and I took the damn pictures. But I was tickled pink to have this smidgen of my life back. I am on a quest for more. Every time I find a picture, I get inspired to tell the story. I was telling Mom at the cafe about it. I was showing her a few pictures and she said. "How on earth did you take so many pictures, when you were always as drunk as you were?"

I just laughed, "because I lived with a camera in my hand. It was an extension of me. Kind of like *Edward Scissor Hands*. Everyone should be thankful."

Quote.....Time moves in one direction, memory in another.---
William Gibson

A little story about Blue

I just got back home from Jo Eddie's dad's funeral. It was a huge, memorial. It was beautifully sad. They had horses pulling an old time casket. His dad was way up in his nineties and boy do I have a few stories on him, but in due time. Well…. let's go ahead with a quick one. I was on the leaf ride with a friend. It was so cold that day, that we had to wrap up as tight as a burrito just not to freeze our asses off. Anyway, I accidentally ran us off in a huge mud puddle and we sunk up to our boobs as water penetrated down to our skin. We instantly became human popsicles. Luckily Mr. Clyde was there and gave me his overalls. When I reached in his pocket, there was a pair of women's panty hose. When I made him aware of what I had found, he just winked at me and smiled. He was an old bachelor and I will let you imagine the rest.

So anyway, I was exhausted from the funeral. When I got home, I decided I would finish off my day with mowing. It was a beautiful, breezy, perfectly blue, eighty-degree day and not a cloud in the sky. It was gonna be a time for reflection, but Blue, my husky, had something else in mind. Out of the corner of my eye, I seen him come running across the yard, with something in his mouth. At first I thought he had killed him another damn groundhog and was going to shred him in the yard. The last time he killed one, it was so big, he could barely carry it back to the yard. Damn! I'm gonna have to call Jimmy, (my pest control man)

But something was different. I noticed long leg dangling. I thought it might be a cat. Blue what have you done? So I chased him down across the yard with the lawnmower. As I got closer, I noticed it was a damn baby deer. I was distraught and my peaceful mowing turned into a, steal dinner, from Blue, kinda day.

Blue and I had begun our standoff. I was still on the mower, screaming, Blue! Blue! You little fucker. Put it down! Pulling up in front of him everywhere he tried to run. I finally jumped off the mower and ran toward him aggressively. I was still screaming, Blue! Drop it now! He dropped it, and stood their staring at me, like, I will drop it, but you're not getting it. I didn't know how far I could go to get his kill without getting bit. He has never bitten anyone, but I have never taken his kill away from him either. I mean I have, but not when he was looking.

I didn't have my phone with me to call for backup. I didn't want him to eat it. I could tell it was still breathing. So I hopped back on the mower and maneuvered Blue toward the house. As I had him cornered to the house, I jumped off the mower and I sprinted inside to grab my phone. I came flying back out within seconds and we raced back toward his catch.

I was in a panic for sure, as I hovered over the poor little thing. So I called Beverly. She was mad at Blue, but she was not in a position to come help. So I called Dad. No answer. Then I called Jimmy. He answered. I immediately asked. "Where are you?"

"With your daddy."

"Let me talk to him."

"Here, Buddy."

"Hello." Dad said.

"Dad, what are you doing?"

"Up here on the farm working."

"Can you send Jimmy down here immediately? Blue has a baby deer." I heard him laugh. "Baby deer. Ole Blue, got him a deer, did he?"

"Yes, I don't want him to eat it."

I hear Daddy say something else to Jimmy. "She doesn't want Blue to eat the deer." Then he had the nerve to tell me. "Just let him eat it."

"No, Dad! Send Jimmy down here now. I'm not moving from this spot till someone shows up."

So I waited and I waited. It was only around 20 minutes I think, but it seemed like an eternity. Especially when you're standing ground between your husky and a barely breathing baby deer. Then I saw the poor little thing take its last breath. I reached down and touched its foot. Don't think I ever touched a deer before. Yeah Yeah! I know this is deer hunting country, but I'm not one of them. So I kept looking at the poor little spotted thing. Then looking up the road. Then looking at Blue licking his lips. I was trying to figure out how I was going to pick it up and what I was going to do with it. Blue was ready to pounce. I was wondering if it was really safe to stay in between an animal and its dinner, no matter how tame they have been all their life. So I picked it up by all four legs. His little head fell back toward the ground. It was breaking my heart. I was walking across the yard when my dad finally pulled in. "Ole Blue got em a deer! Why don't you let him have it?"

"No, Dad. There is no way on God's green earth, I could watch Blue eat it."

"He's part wolf. That's what they do. The mama won't take it back anyway. Just put it on the back of the truck, I will take it somewhere. If Blue don't get to eat it, something will. That's how nature works." I gently laid it in the back of Daddy's truck, said thank you and I hopped back on the mower. As he drove away, I watched Blue sniff and search. When I got done mowing, Blue was still searching, running and sniffing back and forth, back and forth. He would run to Conrad's yard, then back over here with his nose to the ground. It continued the rest of the day. I started to feel guilty, that I had stolen his kill, especially after Daddy told me something else would eat it anyway.

43

Quote: *"I hope to have God on my side, but I must have Kentucky."—Sean M. Vandevander*

My plantation, that I created from scratch..

***Quote:** When I tell someone where I live and they're like "omg that's so far."*

Easy mate. I'm not inviting you over, so don't worry about your imaginary journey."

I love Kentucky. It is my stompin grounds. But I have to say my heart sank, when I seen that 70 percent of the people voted for a little handed 70-year-old tweeting, man baby. It was shocking! When it comes to him, I've stepped on better things. He scares the holy shit out of me. I almost had a cow, when I seen the results. I knew he would win Kentucky, but I had no idea the extent.

But anyway, I've thought about leaving Raywick, from time to time, but don't think I will actually do it. Unless the Alt right tries to run me out. I hope not! The needle of my nature points me to the country and I've hung my hat up here. Who knows how the rest of this game called life will play out.

There is so much to do here out in the wilderness. It makes me happier than a pig in mud sometimes.

Lots of mischief, lots of nature activities and lots of peace. Well, not sure about the peace thing, but maybe if you take away the Café, the stand offs, and the family and girlfriend drama. Oh shit! That leaves me with nothing. LOL. Just kidding, I still have horse rides, razor rides, canoe rides, kayak rides, fishing and what not. And lots of good fun loving friends to do it with. I could tell you some stories about these adventures, but we need to move along and get me the hell out of high school, so I can quit time lapsing you so much. I'm ready to be a grown up and get to some other people's stories.

Quote: *"Tough girls come from New York. Sweet girls, they're from Georgia. But us Kentucky girls, we have fire and ice in our blood. We can ride horses, be a debutante, throw left hooks, and drink with the boys, all the while making sweet tea, darlin'. And if we have an opinion, you know you're gonna hear it." ---- Ashley Judd*

Beaver Beach! PETA!

This picture proves how easy it is to Co-exist. Even when Zombies are biting your head.

Other Happenings in 1986.

Wow! It's been 30 years since I graduated. My uncle thought it was impressive that he was born in 46 and graduated in 64. Until I told him, well, I was born in 68 and graduated in 86. He seemed disappointed and said, Damn! I thought I was the only one who could flip the numbers. Was the statement important? No! No is wasn't. LOL. Maybe some of the next ones will be.

Remember when the shuttle broke into pieces after only 73 seconds into its flight, leading to the death of seven crew members? I have no idea where I was at the time, maybe climbing a tree or running from wild dogs. Who knows? I sure don't. I could have been taking 73 seconds to fall to the ground. I usually fall in slow motion and with grace. There have only been a few times, where it was a flat out, high speed splat!

Top Gun was the highest grossing film. Even though *Pretty in Pink* was my favorite. Did anybody ever catch the mistake in that movie when her daddy's hair kept changing? It bugs the hell out of me every time I watch that scene.

Rock me Amadeus by *Falco* was the #1 single of the year. And the *Cosby Show* was the top television show. Hey, Mr. Cosby, what a nice hypocritical example you have made.

I was also bagging groceries for 3.15 an hour. Actually I was the first girl in our town to do it. Only boys had done it up to that point. Breaking a glass ceiling anyone?

Lindsay Lohan was born. That could be good or bad for some of you.

Nasty Girl by Janet Jackson was a huge hit. Which is making its way back after Trump called Hillary a nasty woman. Guess I'm a nasty woman too.

9 ½ weeks. Hum! Gonna leave that one alone. Not gonna write no X-rated stuff, not now anyway. Maybe in due time.

Crimes of the Heart was a hit also. It starred, *Sissy Spacek, Diane Keaton, and Jessica Lange.*
    Miss Lange was my first crush. When I watched her star in *King Kong* back in 1976, she made me feel all fuzzy, especially when King Kong blew her out to dry. "ooh la la" Yes, I was only eight.

I've already told you about my biggest story of my basketball career. You know, Mom showing up on the court. The main thing I would have left to say about my career, is that it was exciting, fun and hard work.

A song by *Kool and the Gang* became our theme song for the year. We played it in the locker room before every game. You're gonna be shocked with what it was. "Ladies Night." Ha! Thought I was gonna shock you. Sorry! No shock there.

Ronald Reagan was president. I wasn't paying much attention to politics back then. I had no idea *Jane Fonda* had a feminist agenda and was trying to break the glass ceiling way back then. She was fighting so hard for equality for women. Thank you.

Why in the hell are we always having to fight for equal rights? What part does society not get? Is equality that hard to comprehend? Doesn't it say at the end of the pledge of allegiance, Liberty and Justice for all? Why do you want it back in schools, if you don't mean it? Like all of it.

I also didn't know till the other day we had a woman vice president nominee in 1984, when *Geraldine Ferraro* became *Walter Mondale's* running mate.

We also had our first women CEOs back then. Go ladies! But with what I'm seeing in 2016, looks like we may be heading back to the struggles of the 30's.

We must not let this happen!!!!!!

(Jamie Lee) Shannon getting ready for her adventure. She hasn't a clue about what's going to happen next.

Before we get into this story, lets talk about Shannon and her personality. She is the only friend I can describe as sunshine in a bottle, like for real. She has been this way since I have known her. She is bubbly, attractive and always pleasant to be around. She is the most agreeable person I've ever met. She doesn't like to make waves. But don't get me wrong, if she thinks you're wrong, she will come out and tell you, but in a very, very charming way. Like if your poop stinks, she will put the most positive spin on it as possible and say, at least it has a hint of flower smell.

She talks with her hands, smacks her hair around and always snorts and giggles, cute snorts that is and the sweetness oozes out. She reminds me of a miniature version of *Aidy Bryant,* from SNL.

So one time as we were planning to crash the cabin, I think we all got too drunk and maybe too high, to be doing anything. Not Shannon, but the rest of us. She was usually the drunk detective and kept an eye out for us. She was kind of the goody two shoes in our group. Not in a bad, snooty way, but a good mother hen kind of way. She would just sit back like an Orca whale, filing away memories. I'm guessing the Orca has a damn good memory, according to the movie I watched as a kid. Not sure if that is fact or fiction. Could be an alternative fact I made up in my head. I just remember that the fishermen killed the Orca's female mate and baby. Then he got them all back, chasing them down and killing them one by one. So he remembered, he sure did! I remember the part where the Orca crunched the girl's leg off and it had a cast on it. The sound and fright stuck with me through my childhood years.

Anyway, Shannon was always game for our adventures, even though she may have been wrapped too tight for this one. I decided I would take her on an adventurous 3-wheeler ride, while the other girls stayed at the cabin. Not sure who we conned into letting us borrow it, but I told Shannon to get on and across the cornfield we flew. Shannon gripped me tight, screaming, "Missy, you might wanna slow down." I kept hitting the gears higher and higher and faster we went. "Just trust me Shannon." There was a huge hill ahead of us and I was ready for the challenge. Shannon looked ahead and saw what was coming and starting smacking my back, "No Missy! No!" I just yelled, "Shannon, don't flake out on me now. Hold on!" I revved it up like a deuce in the night, as we took off up the hill. We were hitting ditches and rocks and bouncing all over the place. I had committed myself and there was no turning back. When I was nearing the very tip top of the hill, we were losing momentum. I tried to lower the gear back down and accidentally knocked it into neutral. This was not good, not good at all. I desperately tried to get it knocked back in the right gear, but to no avail. I was caught by the short hairs, when the 3-wheeler stalled and so did my face, and backwards we went. We were franticly trying to get off the three wheeler, as it rolled over. We flipped backwards and rolled down the hill along side it. Flipping and rolling, rolling and flipping, as our bodies and our hair flipped along the side, missing us with every flip. It felt like we were rolling as fast as a blown off wheel of a race car. When we finally came to a stop at the bottom of the hill, we laid there staring at the sky. I reached over and squeezed her shoulder. "Shannon, are you okay?" A smile filled her face. "We are alive!" When we stood up we were just fine, except our knees were shaking and our hair was filled with cockle burrs. Somehow we both came out unscathed.

Advice for the day: Just remember when you say "Watch this!" or "I will show you!" Rarely does it have a good outcome. But just know, when I say "Trust me!" You can trust me. The outcome might not be what you expected, but you can trust me. Ha-Ha!

53

FIGHT WITH SISTERS

So, let's see how this all went down. Kandy and I decided we would go riding around before we met up with all our buddies. We had pulled into the local convenient store. When I went to back out, another car was backing out right beside of me. I stopped and looked, to see if they were gonna keep going or if I was gonna keep going. All of a sudden the girl on the passenger side threw me the finger. I had never seen this girl in my life. Or let's say, I never noticed her in my life. You'll understand what I mean by that shortly. Anyway, Kandy and I just looked at each other like, what the hell? Who them bitches think they are? They pulled on out and took off. Well, not long after that, we were riding down the four lane and we came upon them. Kandy asked me if that was the car. I said, hell yeah it is! Let's give them the finger back. So we drove up next to them and that's what we did and sped on off. No biggie right? A finger for a finger.

So we pulled on down to the Club 68 like we always did, waiting on everyone else to show up. We were just sitting there listening to music in the car, when all of a sudden a car came around the club wide open and skidded right up to our ass. Doors flew open and three people came flying out. It was an ambush. The one girl grabbed Kandy's door and opened it. I noticed she was pregnant and so did Kandy, when she shrank back in her seat. Then the girl started slapping Kandy all around. Kandy would have protected herself I guess, if the girl hadn't been pregnant. So I jumped out of my side and ran around the car. The other girl stopped me and was dead up in my face. I screamed. "Get out of my way. What is she doing?"

"Why did you throw us the finger?" The girl yelled back. "Why did you girls throw us the finger?"

The idiot speaks again. "Because you was staring at us."

"I was staring at you…. Because! I was trying to see who was pulling out." The other girl had Kandy by the hair and they weren't doing any communicating. So I tried to push my way around the girl. All of a sudden she smacked my cigarette right out of my mouth. I just stood there in shock. Then she swung at me again and ripped my gold chain off. It flew through the parking lot. Yes, I had on a gold chain, wouldn't catch me dead in one today. But anyway, I thought hell to the naw! I felt my blood start to boil. I plowed right into her as we hit the ground and rolled a couple times. I landed on top of her like Nala did Simba, in the movie *Lion King.* I had her pinned to the ground. I was feeling like a proud attack dog protecting my friend. The girl was screaming. "When I get up from here, I'm gonna kick your ass." I was nervous as hell because there was still another girl standing there hovering over us. "Let me up. You're gonna die, when I get up from here."

My adrenaline was at its all time high. "I'm not gonna die as long as I have you pinned here." I just knew the other girl was gonna grab me at anytime. but she never did. The girl was still on the ground, diggin in the gravel with her feet, trying to get up.

The pregnant girl finally let Kandy out of the car and told the girl on the ground to give it up and come on. So I released her and stood up. As soon as she stood up, she came at me again and we did the same ole dance. And yes, I ended up back on top of her. The other girl kept telling her to calm down and she acted like she might. But she was a spit fire and I was concerned. By this time, I was exhausted and my throat was as dry as a biscuit when I swallowed and said. "I'm gonna let you up, but this better be the end of it!" So I let her back up and stepped backwards. She stared with evil eyes as she brushed the gravel from her clothes, and headed back to the car. When Kandy and I got back in my car, my legs were shaking like a fucked up washing machine. Then we went about our night as usual, except we had a crazy story to tell all of our friends.

I would like to say that was the end of it, but it wasn't. We soon found out they were all sisters and two of them actually went to school with us and one was married to my stepdad's brother at the time. Never knew, never knew them before this. The one girl that messed with me worked at the lunch room at school, and one day when I was sliding my tray down the line, she looked at me and started to growl. All I could think was. "Wow!" Winked at her and walked away.

I thought that was the end of it, but it wasn't. This girl was obviously hell-bent on kicking my ass. I was at the Golden Horseshoe one night when some more shit went down. She and her sister were there and I was with some of my friends minding my own business. I'm sure maybe, we threw each other the stink eye, a time or two, but that was it. The club's bathroom had a lounge in it. You know with a couch and some chairs. When I came out of my stall, with my Long Island Tea in hand, the girl was standing down at the other end of the couch. She looked like a Toro bull ready to attack the matador. Trust me when I say I hadn't trained for this position. She yelled. "What are you doing calling me and my sister queers?"

"What? Why would I do that? You're sisters! Not queer. Maybe a psycho bitch." That's all the words that got to come out of my mouth when she started to charge. I raised my drink back in my hand and gave it a sling as hard as I could. Of course this did not stop her and we ended up on the couch. The bouncer came in and grabbed her and threw her out. When I looked over in the mirror, it looked like I had been slapped around by a monkey, and I was thinking, what the hell just happened. I straightened up, wiped my forehead and walked out the bathroom door as if nothing had happened. I carried on and continued to dance with my friends. I thought that was that. But no! That was not that. Later when I was leaving the club and stepped out into the parking lot, I heard someone scream, "there she is." I just threw up my arms and said, "Here I am!" It was the spur of the moment comment. I was standing there like 'We are Sparta.' And boy, I must have grown some cojones. Stop!

Question? Someone asked this on Facebook and it made me rethink my cojones. (Why do "balls" equate to toughness and "pussy" equates to weakness, when even the slightest flick to the nuts, sends a guy to his knees and vaginas can push out an entire human being?) So, did I grow cojones or not? I'm thinking I grew an extra set of ovaries. But anyway, I had no idea what was about to happen next. She came charging at me like a starving hyena, as if I had a pound of bologna in my pants. I braced myself. The impact was violent, as we slid across the pavement and a speed bump. But once again, I was Nala. She ended up on the bottom. It was a little different this time, because she had one finger in my eye and I had the front of her hair, right above her forehead. The crowd gathered around and all I remember screaming is, "can someone please break this damn fight up?" They all watched for a moment as we both struggled. Someone finally got the bouncer after I screamed like bloody murder. "Someone break this damn fight up! Please!" Then that's what the bouncers did. Broke it up. The end. Nope! I was at the Club 68 one night and I was three sheets to the wind, when the same cast of characters came strolling in. The pregnant one came up to me and I had no idea what was going to go down next. She had already had her baby by this time. She was apologizing to me about how stupid all this was. This was a good bizarre twist. The band was loud like always and I was listening to her the best I could, even though I was struggling. Last thing I wanted to be doing in a club was having this talk. Although I did want it to all be over. So as she was talking to me, the other sister had her head over her shoulder doing and saying some smartass blah, blah, blah. She was screaming stupid shit like, "Why are you looking at my lips?"

"What? Do you want me to look at your boobs?"

Her sister kept telling her to shut up, but she kept on with her blah, blah, blah. She obviously was a spook (disagreeable person) I remember having to close one eye just to try and keep up with what either one of them were saying. Obviously the sister said one last remark that didn't set well with me and the last thing I remember is swinging straight for her face, but it was a swing and a miss. I must have folded like a lawn chair, because I woke up on maw-maws couch. End of story. Everybody wants to have the last word. Don't do it!

Some things are so unnecessary. People do things that make no sense. Guess that's why I used to drink, hoping that it all would make sense soon. My brain couldn't be stopped. Stuff seemed to stick in my head like fly shit does to a window. Sometimes it's hard to get out. It was drink, drink, drink, till I woke up. Sometimes remembering nothing. All I was left with was a hangover. SMMHHH

Real time:

Amy (employee) came blazing in the Café, looking as if she had been dragged through a prickly hedge bush backwards. I was thinking, what on earth, when I asked her, "what the hell is up, maniac?" She replied with fire in her breath, "Some bitch down Raywick done gone and bit me on the leg. That bitch is a fried green tomato, chicken eaten, mother fucker." I mean she was irate as she continued to speak. "That bitch is pushing the limitations of my medication." I thought I was never gonna calm her down before customers started to arrive. But I did. The next night she came into work and her hair was all did, and her makeup was to her perfection. I asked her. "What are you doing all dressed up?"

"I wanted to drive past that bitch's house and show her I was prettier than her."

I look out the window embarrassed for her and said, "Hey! There goes Daddy on his tractor." The point of my comment? Obviously, I didn't have a comment, because there was no Daddy on the tractor. And there was no nice way to say, you've gone cray-cray girl. She kept on and on with what else she was gonna do. I was dying to tell her to take a shit

58

like a dog, cover it up, and move the hell on. Grown women don't fight!

Just like I was about to tell the lady in town the other day. I was behind some ole angry bitch and she was blowing her horn uncontrollably. "Really lady! Blowing your horn that long? That is highly unnecessary! Eat a fucking avocado already."

But back to Amy. She should know by now, there is more than one way to skin a cat. I'm thinking, if she wanted to make a real impression, she should have had someone to drive her around the block, riding in the back of a truck, waving like the prom queen. Now that would be some proof of her beauty. "Th-Th-The, Th-Th-The, Th-Th…That's all, folks!"

I'm wondering if you readers wonder if I have a few regrets. Maybe! I'm not sure. We will find out together as I write, but I stay away from them at all cost. I'm not the smartest person on the planet, but I know life shouldn't be miserable, and that loneliness is not the plan our creator had for us. Don't create regrets. It's easy to do if you're not paying attention. We only get one time around, just make it special and be passionate. If you lose your passion, work hard to get it back. That's the only advice I can give at the moment.

Just a text:

I asked Ann about the Saint Francis Picnic. The time when we went and drank Brass Monkey and everyone thought she was *Farrah Faucet.* She said, "I have to think on that one. Don't remember much, except it was hotter than a hooker at a tent revival and I got sick the first night and you got sick the second night. I really don't know what else to say on that one."

Regret? Maybe! Nah!

That's my cuz…

WRECKED US ALL

So I was sitting here thinking about all the wrecks I've been in. One in particular crossed my mind, but I couldn't remember who was with me, not for the life of me. I remember the guy driving and the guy who grabbed the wheel and that was it. Ha!Ha! You thought I was the one that wrecked us all. Nope! It was a guy friend. But there were nine of us in there, that I'm sure of.. We happened to be in some orangish car, headed to the picnic. I watched from the backseat when for some stupid reason, the guy grabbed the steering wheel. I thought holy smokes dude, what is your reasoning?

We flew off the road and straight into a culvert, as I was hanging on by a wing and a prayer. When the car came to a stop, we all began straggling out one by one, untangling our bodies from each other.. I was screaming, "is everyone Okay?" as I was still helping friends from the car, a lady came running out of her house. It was our teacher and her mother owned the local clothing shop. It was called the Top Shop. They had the most popular ad on the radio at the time. It said, "come on down to the Top Shop, where Miss Ella has her bras and panties half off." Get it? Wink, wink. But it was a for real ad. I believe who ever created that ad, had a little sauce dripping down their chin or had a keen sense of humor.

But anyway, the guy panicked and started screaming, "Did you see that car? Did you see it? It was blue. That son bitch ran us off the road."

"How many people are in that car?" The teacher asked.

"Nine, there is nine."

Shannon, Marybeth and I, back in the day

Marybeth and I, later in life.

I just recently asked Mary Beth about this event. She replied. "Sadly, I don't remember. I had a half pint of the cheapest whisky in me. How do you remember things? You were always drunk, too."

"Well, I misremember all the time. Some of the time I don't remember who all was there. I guess it's cause I wasn't drinking the cheap stuff.

Marybeth said. "One of the things I do remember, is going to the cemetery going out towards school. We would always go look at that creepy tombstone with that man's picture on it. It read (Remember friends as you pass by, as you are now so once was I. As I am now, so you shall be, prepare for death and follow me.) that always creeped me out. Oh, and I remember a dog falling out of a pickup truck and being dragged in front of us because he was chained to the truck. I about had a heart attack and I remember you running over baby bunnies with a mower and I almost cried. You were slightly tougher than me."

"Slightly!"

"Oh! I remember something about the guy that wrecked us. He always played that song, *Hot Rod Lincoln*."

"Oh shit! He did. Like every time we got in the car. 'Breaks are good and the tires are fair."

"You remember at Buddy's? I saw my first porn with you. It was shocking!"

"To say the least. I remember all that. I hate porn."

"Yep! And pretty much if you've seen one, you've seen them all."

"I dated a girl that was into porn. Couldn't stick around. I'm not judging, I'm just not staying. If that's your thing, cool."

"Everybody has their own thing. I try not to judge either. Because hell! I know, I am messed up in my own special way."

"Everybody is. The Cleavers from *Leave it to Beaver,* mostly."

"That's too funny."

QUOTE: *"They say if you're always trying to be normal. You will never know how amazing you can be."*

As you all know by now, Beverly helps me read through these stories. She is always in my hair about my use of words. She wants me to let you know that she tries her damnedest to make me change 'seen to saw' and 'her to she.' We find ourselves bickering about it constantly. So the bad English is my fault for not changing it. I told Beverly, to just let me speak the way I speak, which isn't always correct, and when I'm in the zone and writing, my brain and my hands do not always connect. She agreed to let it slide, as long as I informed you, the readers, that it's not her fault. Then she started in on me again, about how she would never ride in a car with me. I said, "Beverly, shut your face. I may have had a lot of wrecks, but I have never wrecked another soul."

But we all know that's an alternative fact.

BTW Beverly, I got 100% on my grammar test. Guess writing this book has been teaching me something. Beverly said she needs proof!

THREE WHEELS

Rosemarie,,,,,,,,,,, Marybeth, Mindy, Chickie and Shannon.

Chickie seemed to like sitting on cars. That's where you could always find her. Hey! Where is Chickie? I don't know. Did you check the top of the car? Oh, there she is.

On another note, let me tell you guys this. We were all at the Club 68 parking lot hanging out and drinking like usual. I already had a few drinks in me, maybe more than a few, when Chickie yells. "Hey! Look at that car driving up the road with three tires and sparks coming out from under it. What a moron!" I just glanced, didn't have the view Chickie had and I didn't give much mind to who or what it was, anyway. I was good at doing that when I drank. If you weren't right in my vicinity and at close proximity, I didn't much know what was going on with you. Basically didn't care. I was always in my own little world. One of my cousins has a small perimeter like that also, won't name any names, Kristen. Oops! We will get to your close proximity situations in the near future. So anyway, I continued on with my drinking and socializing. I'm sure I eventually ended up in the club along with everyone else or maybe on one of our back road adventures.

The next morning, I got woken up by a call from my dad yelling at me. Well, he wasn't yelling, cause he don't yell, but his tone was frightful. "Why in the hell, is your car sitting down on main street with three tires? I drove by and the door was wide open and I had to run some kids out of it." Although my mind was still groggy I said, "Dad! Mom had my car yesterday." I heard him puff, "well, holy shit! That explains it all. Why in the hell did you give your mom your car?" Well, Dad, she always admits she isn't too bright, but she says she is cute." He laughs and said. "I knew I should have married a different Bickett girl."

Updated thought: In this day and time and after watching Dateline episodes, I would become completely unsettled if I found my kid's car in the street. Just saying.

DRIVE IN

Of course we had a drive-in back then. And of course we would sneak people into the theater in our trunks. Our friends would roll out like Mexicans in a mini van after crossing the border. We would mostly go there on Sunday nights. *Freddy Krueger* was very popular back then. Shannon and I would come to school and go up to people, throw out our hands and say, "You wanna get high?" Sometimes you do stupid things and you don't know why. Kind of like this next event.

Ann (my cuz) used to come visit all the time and stay at Maw-maws with me. We were driving around and I told Ann she couldn't leave Marion County, till she learned how to do a doughnut. She sounded like a cry baby when she said, "I don't even have my license." She really didn't want to, but we took her to the Drive-in parking lot anyway. I stepped out of the car and went to her side and said move over. I told her ass to put it in gear and spin. Just do it. Before I knew it, we were slinging rocks and they were pinging off the drive-in speakers. She did a figure eight and about slung us out the door. She threw it in park and said, "Is that good enough? Did I pass?"

"You sure did cuz."

She called me the other day and she was asking me if I remember making her pick peppers while she was hung over. All I could say is, that's the way we always picked them. Back then there was no other way to do it, except hung over. She said, it was so hot that it felt like the devil farted in her face. Then she giggled, it was the first time she had heard of, the hair of the dog. She said, I pitched her one of Daddy's Little Millers and said drink up and start picking. We will head to the river afterwards. She said we took her to Green River after we picked the peppers, drank beer all day and had a blast. Then we snuck down into your Grandma's house and stole some food. I think we ate the dinner she had planned for the people in the backyard. But we didn't stick around to see.

BLIND LEADING THE BLIND

When I was young, Dad use to drive me to ballgames. I remember him always talking about this one particular teacher. It's gonna be hard to explain why this story is so funny to me, because the story is completely in the voice of the character. This teacher talked in the longest, most monotone, country, drag along voice, I have ever heard. Well, I hadn't heard him yet, but the way Daddy was mocking him. Dad said, he had him in typewriting. So one day when they were in class, one of Dad's friends threw up his hands after the teacher said something. He mocked him in the same voice. "Mr. - George, - what - did –you - say?" It really pissed the teacher off and he sent him out of class. My dad raised his hand and talked in the same voice. "George, - why- did – you - kick - my - friend - out - of - class?" Dad said, the teacher said, to go follow his friend to the office. So that was just a story I had remembered. So when I got to the high school, it wasn't soon till I realized I had this same teacher my dad had talked about years ago. Shannon and I were sitting in class one day and we were helping each other do something. George looked over and asked, what us two girls were doing. Shannon told him she was helping me, and his reply was in that same ass voice. "Well--- If - it - isn't - the - blind - leading - the - blind."

My friend Dana was sitting in study hall, when he took his shoe off and threw his foot up on his desk. He had a hole in his sock and he said in that long ass voice. "D-A-N-A----I- need - a - needle - and - thread - to –darn – the – hole - in - my – sock." R.I.P. Mr. George.

Shannon and I were also on the year book staff. That teacher didn't like us much. We had that class around lunch time, and we would go to

67

all three lunch blocks at least twice a week. Shannon said, yes, we weren't his favorites, but he understood we were social and took great photos! He liked us, he said we was a very likable kind of sorry. We passed the class, but he gave us a bad grade the last 6 weeks, because we took advantage of him.

There was also no love lost between me and my English teacher either. She seen me coming down the hall as the bell rang. She smirked at me as she slowly closed the door. Rules were, once the door was shut after the bell, you go to the office. Biatch.

Me and Shannon. (Jamie Lee)

Figure it out.

So, one evening, we all headed out for the big warehouse party. It was a big event that took place about once a month. It is truly one of those things I don't know how we got away with, but in the eighties, we did. They were the most awesome parties I can remember. We were still mixing up our coolers of Hooch. I had kinda gotten a taste for Crown by this point, because it tasted like ice cream to me, but the big jugs of juice were just more fun for these kinds of parties. I experimented with lots of alcohol. Kandy and I, went thru a phase of drinking *Bartels & James*, but then again, I went through a phase of drinking everything. I had all the different cans of liquor stacked up in my room. Empty of course. When Maw-maw would ask about them, I would say, I'm collecting them from the side of the road for a project. I can't believe she bought that theory. But anyway, back to the warehouse. Everybody from high school and beyond went. I'm not sure who I rode with that night. All I remember is that at some point in the night things got weird. What kind of weird? Well, the kind of weird you feel after returning from the unknown. When I finally became coherent and walked back into the warehouse, I noticed the band packing and the warehouse was empty. I mean it was empty! I looked back outside and the parking lot was empty. How did all these cars slip past me without my knowledge? There were hundreds upon hundreds of people there. How the hell I didn't notice this on the way back in, I haven't a clue. Where the hell did I even come from and where had I been? Had I been in the Twilight Zone? I was straight up freaked out after finding myself lost. All I could think was, what the hell am I gonna do? I was in the next town over, and you have to remember we didn't have cell phones. Not a freakin soul to call. It was the weirdest fucking feeling ever. Did this place get raided or what? What happened? As I turned back around, I happened to look way across the warehouse and saw three guys standing there. I hesitated for a moment, but then I started walking toward them. As I was approaching, I recognized one of them. I was like, "Hallelujah, thank God." I ran over to him, grabbed him and said, "where is everyone?"

"Home in bed I'm sure! Party has been over for a minute. I will give you a ride."

What happened next? I have no idea, except sleep. I went into a deep, deep sleep. When I was awakening from my coma, I had a crazy dream and I was in the Land of OZ. Shannon was one the munchkins, with a referee outfit. Maw-maw was Oz and I somehow was the good witch Glenda. I was in a ring with the sister whom tried to whip me several times, but she was a toad. I told her very politely. "Don't make me drop a house on you, Biatch." She leaped at me and I dropped a house on that bitch. Dreams, oh boy!

New years Eve.

MISSY DID IT

Boy! This night was a doozy. A guy named David threw our New Year's Eve party for us. He lived out on a big farm. Not sure what my drink of choice was that night. Probably whisky, because it was colder than a witches titties in a brass bra. We were all standing around the camp fire when the song *Maniac* from *Flash Dance* came on. Joanie decided she was gonna do the dance, running in place as hard as she could, swinging her coal black hair all around. Then it started to rain and her legs moved forward, as she disappeared into the cornfield. I ran after her and some friends proceeded to follow. We ended up at a barn. We flung open the door and went inside. I seem to like to climb things when I'm drinking. So up the side of the barn I went and into the rafter, just like a monkey. That is my Chinese Almanac, maybe there is a connection.

My friend Lisa, who never does anything out of the ordinary, followed me right up the wall. I jumped down and yelled back up. Girl you are gonna get hurt up there, climb on back down. She was frozen in time and really didn't know what to do with herself. She found herself in a pickle when she realized she was stuck up there like a cat in a tree. We all tried to coax her down, when omeone yelled up to her and said. "I have to say, Missy has been a bad influence on you." When she finally jumped and hit the ground, she grabbed her ankle and started to cry. When her boyfriend finally found all of us, he started to fuss. "Why in the hell did you do that?" Her reply. "Missy did it!"

P.S. I still like to climb things.

A bunch of us stayed out all night that night. I had basketball practice the next morning. Why in the hell the coach would have practice the next morning, I haven't a clue. But I could not miss. When I arrived, I came strolling in with my muddy boots and all, from the night before. I was hung over as hell and headed straight toward the locker room, hoping to bypass the coach. I did not succeed. She stood there in her stretchy tight shorts and short sleeve shirt as usual, whistle around her neck, looked at me, rolled her eyes and said. "Well, at least you're here and I won't ask."

I thought to myself, self, you better perform outstandingly today or your ass is grass. So during practice, she decided to make us run suicides. Guess she thought it was a good day for it. What is a suicide? Well it's when you have to start at the end of the court, run to the first line and run back, then the mid court line and run back, then the next, then one more. And! You have to do it in a certain amount of time or you have to do it again. I used every ounce of energy in my body, just to stay out ahead and that I did, even though I was dying on the inside. It actually got all my teammates yelled at. Why? You ask? Well I'm not sure, but the coach yelled out. "What is wrong with you girls? Missy Luckett comes rolling in here after being out all night, hung over with her muddy shit kickers on and is still out running all you ladies. Give me another round." I was thinking, I don't want one.

What's funny, is that I still get reminded of this day from time to time. Like when the assistant coach came into the cafe and was telling everyone about it. Haven't been able to live that story down. But it's a fun one to tell. No regrets there.

BOOTS ARE MADE FOR WALKING

Well, here is another wreck for you. I'm thinking *Dr. Phil* would have a field day with me, if I was doing all this shit in this era. I had taken my friend Chrissy home one night after a little partying. She lived over in Loretto and down some curvy ass one lane road. After I dropped her off, I pulled out and headed in the wrong direction. Not sure why I headed in the direction I did. It definitely wasn't in the direction of Maw-maws. But anyway, I'm driving along and I come to an unexpected curve and a bridge, when I realized I was going way too fast to make the turn. My butt cheeks tightened as I took my boots and stomped the brakes, but I just skidded and shot right off the side and headed toward the creek. I was preparing myself for a polar bear swim. Luckily I stopped short of it. I took a deep breath, evaluated the situation and put it in reverse. I spun and spun, as mud begun to fly into my windows. Then I spun some more, but to no avail. I could not break free from the grips of the creek mud. Guess what? No cell phone. So, I get out and step into mud up to my calves and I slid to the back of the car. I kicked it, as in thinking that would do some good, but it only put me on my ass. I get up and start walking back toward Chrissy's house. The air was icy and it was pitch black, not a star to be found in the sky. I look around and realize I'm literally in the middle of nowhere. After walking about a mile, I saw headlights coming my way. Instead of stopping them and asking for help, I got scared and ran and jumped in the ditch. I laid there as they passed slowly as loud music was streaming out their window. Hell, who knew who it could have been, but I wasn't taking any chances for anyone to try and get in these sugar britches. After they passed, I stood back up, started back on my journey again. I had on cowboy boots. They're not really made for walking too far, despite what *Loretto Lynn* said. Well, *Nancy Sinatra* said it first. Maybe that's why Tammy Wynette stood by her man. But I kept walking. My built in GPS obviously wasn't working, because I thought I was closer to Chrissy's house, but don't guess I was. I finally came to a house, but I didn't stop. I thought I would just keep walking to her house. I didn't want to knock on anyone's door this late at night. So I kept walking and walking. Another house went by, it wasn't Chrissy's. Walked a little further, still not Chrissy's house. I was thinking you just don't give up, then all of a sudden, I heard a pack of dogs barking like I was gonna be their midnight snack. I was straight up scared out of my boots. At that point, I didn't care that it wasn't Chrissy's house. I went running to the next house, I was afraid either way. I didn't have much choice. The house seemed safer than the pack of wild dogs. Even though I was in a panic, I calmed myself down, as I stood on the porch and knocked lightly. I didn't want to startle anyone that may have a shotgun in their home. My guts would be splattered all over the front porch, then how would Maw-maw feel? Sad and alone. It took a minute for someone to answer and thank God they were gun less. They were nice enough to let me come in and use the phone and call Chrissy. I asked her to please call Maw-maw and to make up a suitable story and then please come get me. Moral to the story? There isn't one! But I do know what *Dr. Phil* would say.

Sharen in front. Carol, Karen, Shannon, Shannon, Kandy and me.

WHOLE POTATO

So one night, Kandy and Karen, (Karen who is a twin) were staying all night with me at Maw-maws. We had all three gone out somewhere, who knows where. I'm sure just riding around the county roads and I'm sure I was probably driving. I didn't like for Karen to drive, because I couldn't listen to music when she did. She would always say, turn the music down, I can't see. Which of course never made any sense to me, until I got older.

I don't even think I told Maw-maw they were staying, which ended up working to my advantage. Why you ask? Because all three of us were out and Kandy got sick and literally threw up a whole potato in my car. Seriously, a whole potato. It just laid there in the floor un-chewed, not even a tooth mark. We were quite amazed and confused at the same time. Who throws up a whole potato? Kandy did. She had that nickname the rest of the year. WHOLE POTATO.

Although today, my friends and I have a dispute on the size of the potato. I'm sticking to my guns that is was the size of a golf ball. Because if it wasn't, why the hell would I have been amazed? I'm just sayin.

My friend Joanie had an incident also. She threw up one night and when she pulled her head back up, she had something hanging from her cheek. It was disgusting! It looked like she had a raw slimy oyster stuck to her face. It wasn't small by no means either. Which dubbed her the name, Oyster Face, for the rest of the year. And Mary Beth, let's not talk about that one. Well let's. I was driving her around one night and of course when I drive, I only drive with one arm. Had to look cool you know. So that leaves my right arm sitting on the console. Her head starts wobbling like a bobble-head, when I hear her mumble, "I think I'm gonna get sick." Which was nothing unusual with my group of friends, but what happened next was an unusual circumstance. She didn't choose to puke out the window, or even in the floor board. No! She chose to turn toward me and puked all down my arm and in between my seats. I looked at her in disgust, "what the hell?" She was still bobbing and mumbling. "Sorry Missy! Sorry!"

"Why in the hell didn't you turn your head to the right? That's all it took." When I turned to look at her, she was out like a light. This was no puke and rally event. Jeff is the only one I knew who could puke and then resume with even more gusto than before.

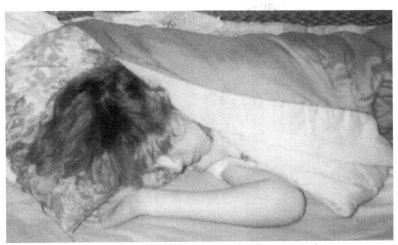
Don't worry Kandy, I got one worse of me coming up soon.
Sleep pretty girl, sleep.

But anyway, back to what I was saying. Karen and I took Kandy back
to Maw-maw's. Why was it a good thing? Because now we could stick
her in the bed and cover her head and if Maw-maw walked in, she would
think I was home. Then Karen and I snuck back out. It worked perfectly.
Only problem was, that everybody else went on home early. So we
eventually got bored and headed back in ourselves.

So since that worked so well, this other time I tried another approach
on sneaking out. I didn't have Kandy to stick in my bed, but I had
another plan to sneak out the basement door. I had to make sure Maw-
maw was sound asleep and I would be certain when she started to snore
zzzzzzZZZZZZZ. Down the hallway I went, straight to the door leading
to the basement that I lived in as a baby. Aunt Peggy and Travis also
lived in it and other people lived in it throughout the years. Not sure who
was living in it at the time. I know it wasn't T-rex, AKA Peggy, because
she would have caught me and we would have had one of our

confrontations. We had some goods ones, let me tell ya! We would be fussing and I would literally go from the playful dog sized critters on *Jurassic Park* into the aggressive poison spitting, neck-fluttering (Dilophosaurus) and she would turn into T-rex....... Gotta go!!!

Dad and Peggy. Yes Mom made fun of your hat.

But anyway, it had a chain lock on it and Maw-maw always locked it before she went to bed. I quietly wiggled off the chain and out the door I went.

When the night was over and everyone had gone their separate ways, I got dropped off and I headed straight to that door. When I went to open it, it only opened an inch. Have you ever gone to open a door, but something abruptly stopped it? Like your dumbass foot. I thought I was headed straight on in, but nope, bout knock myself completely out. The knot on my head was the least of my worries at this point, I was in the red. OMG! Does Maw-maw know I snuck out? Did she lock me out intentionally? Either way what was I gonna do? I rubbed my head and headed to the front porch. The street lamp was shining in my face, as I sat and worried, till I fell asleep. As soon as daybreak hit, a Semi gearing down woke me up abruptly. I was startled, and immediately began wondering, how was I gonna get out of this? Instantly, I got it! I got up and ran straight to Mary Beth's house. I knocked on the door and Aunt Louise answered. As I stood there with last night's clothes on, and matted hair, I said with a smile. "Hi, Aunt Louise. You look awful pretty today. How are you this morning?" I was trying to sweet talk her like Eddie Haskell did Mrs. Cleaver. She kind of looked at me with a tilt. "Why are you here this early?" I'm sure in her head she was thinking, you nappy headed looking little thing.

"Aunt Louise, I have a favor to ask. I know you might not want to do this, but I need a huge, huge, favor from you and Marybeth."

"What is it Hun? Is something wrong?"

"Well, Aunt Louise! Nothing is really wrong, except I might get my butt whooped. I decided to sneak out last night and I went out the basement door. While I was gone, I guess Maw-maw woke up and noticed the chain wasn't on. I don't know if she did it on purpose or what. She is gonna kill me either way, if she finds out. I didn't even have any fun when I went out and I pretty much came right back home. Can you do me this one big favor and not tell her? I still may be caught, I'm not sure. I don't know if she locked it on purpose or not."

"That would be pretty mean of her if she did. But come on in, Marybeth is back there in bed." She kind of looked at unease with the situation, but said she wouldn't tell this one time and hoped I had learned my lesson.

So I went and grabbed Mary Beth from her bed and told her the situation and that I needed her help. As we were walking back to the house, she said with glee, "Awww! Maw-maw is gonna beat your ass."

"Stop it, Marybeth! Listen." I was explaining to her what we needed to do. "Listen! We are gonna try this. You knock on the door and I will hide around the corner. You let Maw-maw think you need to see me."

"I hope this works." So Mary Beth knocks on the door. Maw-maw answered and I heard her say. "What are you doing down here this early?"

"Good morning Mrs. Luckett! Can I see Missy?"

Maw-maw opens the door wide open, and I hear her say. "She should be back there asleep. Is something wrong?"

Mary Beth is looking at me and I'm looking at her whispering, "Pst! Pst! Where is she?"

Mary Beth waves me back. "Get back! Hold on." Then all of a sudden she starts waving me in. "Go! Go!"

So I darted through the front door and back to the bedroom. Then Mary Beth starts walking down the hallway. "Missy! Missy! Are you awake?"

I look back at her and start to grin. I open and shut my door so Maw-maw would think I've come out of it. "Yes, Mary Beth! What's up? Why are you here this early?" I winked as I walked out into the kitchen yawning.

Short story: *Speaking of Mary Beth. I asked her one day. "Do you want to go out and eat tomorrow night?" Her reply. "I'm not hungry." I looked at her dumbfounded. "But I'm sure you will be by tomorrow."*

TRAVIS, ME AND MAW-MAW. I was younger and more innocent in this picture.

BOOGER SUGAR---

I know you might not like this story, and you may think less of me. If so, please look away, I mean... Please skip this story. I will tell you when you can look. Just look for the 'you can look now page.' I haven't told many people this story. I'm gonna break the silence, even though it may be opening up a can of worms. It's about my experience with cocaine. Yes, I said it and yes, I did it. It wasn't that big of a deal in the 80s for some reason. The coke heads were as thick as the fur on a squirrels back. It was cool up until the point, when a basketball star overdosed on it. Then the ads with "Just say no" began. Frying an egg. This is your brain on drugs. Any questions? It had a positive impact. And it wasn't cool to be a fool any longer. Actually the best commercial was the one where it had a nose on the screen, and when a radio went by it sniffed it up, then a car, then a house, then a plane. Bye-bye! That holds true for so many people doing that stuff. You put your whole life savings up your nose. But luckily that wasn't the case for me. I only purchased it once and I definitely didn't do anything else for it. Ever!

After telling these stories, I'm truly wondering how we made it out of high school alive. Luckily for me, it wasn't a very long experience, but it was an experience, none the less.... Didn't take me long to learn, to get out of that kitchen and into a real one. In this situation, I finally chose to walk down the road alone, instead of the wrong direction with the wrong people. Not that they were bad people, I just wouldn't have been able to keep up and complete my dreams if I had stayed on the same path for too long. Luckily I never touch the base pipe, actually never seen one of those. Never ever laid my eyes on smokable forms of cocaine. Like Whitney would say "Crack is Wack." And I agree.

The first time it crossed my path, was at my senior prom. Someone offered it and I tried it. Just took one bump. Seemed like fun, right? Well, it was! I had a blast! I'm sure I would have had a blast either way, because the company I kept, was just fun like that. But the coke came from a guy who had slid into the group.

Then I did it again with some friends, still seemed like some fun. We were at a *Shirly Muldowney* race. Well, it wasn't her race, but she was racing at the track. She was one of the first women in drag racing. She was also known as *Cha Cha*. She was an American pioneer and the first woman to receive a license from the *National Hot Rod Association,* to drive a top fuel dragster. I was impressed, totally. It was the first and only drag race I had ever been to. The noise was something horrible, and the smell of tires burning wasn't too impressive to my little smeller. But anyway, after the race, I was drunk in the back seat wobbling my head around like Marybeth. I didn't feel sick. It's just that my communication was disabled. Someone, (not gonna mention a name here) stuck some of that white powder under my nose. "Here do this. It will wake you up." I bent my head down and sssssssssss, one big sniff. Pulled my head back up, wiped my nose and bam! Holy hole in a donut! I was awake. Boy! Was I awake. I was as awake as a Bullfrog. Wow!!!! That shit sobers you up, this isn't so bad. That was just my thoughts at the time.

So one other night, a friend of mine and I drove to Lexington. Someone had given us some booger sugar for the trip. There was road work going on at the time. There were all these bump signs, like for real. Big yellow signs, that just said, BUMP. Of course we had to obey the road signs. We couldn't be breaking no traffic laws, now could we? So each time we passed one, we had to bump. It was actually funny at the time, but we were not very smart and ended up wired before we ever arrived to our destination. I don't remember where we ended up. Even though today, I chuckle every time I see the bump signs.

We had some guy friends who every now and then supplied us with some. Mostly on the weekend, when we road around in the van. "The meat wagon." We thought we were cool and just doing the cool stuff.

When graduation night finally came, I thought to myself, "Self" I will buy some just for me. Some friends and I were heading to Florida the morning after the graduation party. Some of my friends said they didn't have the money to go. I called bullshit on them and I said get your asses up here and I will show you how to get the money to go. Where there is a will, there is a way. So we washed cars till we had enough money to pay gas and hotel. So the trip was planned.

Back then most of our parties were outside, which were called field parties. They don't have many of them these days, due to the crack down on drinking and driving. Graduation parties today are now called Project Graduation. They lock you in the gym for the night and let you win prizes. Pretty good I guess, maybe that's what we needed. But I loved the eighties and what we were allowed to do.

So anyway, it's graduation night. We have walked the walk in our gowns. We are proud! We are educated and we are grown up. So now it's party time. I got my stuff, booger sugar that is....

So at the party, the field party once again, don't believe we believed in the indoors at that time unless it was in a warehouse. But, I had two sets of guy friends that kept offering me the shit.. So every time they went to bump, I went too. Then I would go do my own. Now you might not know what that means, but it means I was bumping three times more than anyone else, and before the party was over, I couldn't speak. Literally I could not speak! It was horrible, I mean horrible. I just stared at every one with my big bug eyes. They probably looked as big as a colossal squid and I'm sure, the sheer size of them made it obvious to everyone what I was doing. When people would speak to me, I had no response, I wanted to, but I couldn't. I was like a puppet without its Master. I felt as if my tongue was as big as Cher's, all swelled up and dry like a piece of cotton. No, let's say a bushel of cotton. Only thing that was coming out of my mouth was, Mmmm, Mmmm, Mmmm, Mmmm. I was sounding a bit like the song sang by the *Crash Test Dummies*. Never knew it would become such a popular song. If I had a recorded myself back then, guess I could sue them for plagiarizing today. No, I wouldn't do that. I don't sue people.

Even though this night wasn't a good experience, it didn't end there. I could have stopped, but I didn't.

Quote: *"Cocaine is like really evil coffee."* --- *Courtney Love*

Cigarette?

We were heading to Florida, the next day in Kandy's Dad's big ass van. So I had to stay awake, because we were driving through the night. So I took what I had left with me... not a good idea either. Nope! Not at all. Only one of my friends knew what I was doing, and she told me I shouldn't be doing it... When we arrived to our vacation spot, I had been up 36 hours. I thought, what's a few more. So I partied another full night without any sleep. This situation was getting out of control. Some of our guy friends that we graduated with went down too in a separate car. That night we played quarters all night long, but with a twist. Every time you made it, not only did you get to make someone drink but you got to pick a letter out of the alphabet, that we could no longer use at the beginning of our words. It was hilarious, if you can imagine. We were sounding a bit like *Sean Spicer* or maybe a hillbilly without his teeth. If you accidentally used the letter you had to drink another shot. One problem though, I kept sneaking off to the bathroom to do my thing. Now, looking back, spending your time in the bathroom isn't that much of a good time. Now is it? When it came the next day, I felt that I could be pronounced legally dead. I couldn't even leave the bed. When I tried, and walked out onto the balcony, I felt as if the sun had the same effect on me as it would a vampire. It burned, and it burned bad! I had to retreat back to the bed. It was the closest to feeling dead at that point in my life. I was stuck in the room for the next two days. It was bad! Oh! So bad!

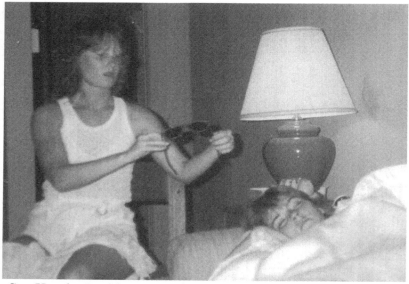

See Kandy, I told you my time was coming. I keep promises.

If I thought that would wise me up and do the trick, on, no booger sugar ever again, it didn't. It took me several more tries before I realized, Missy! What the F word are you doing? It should have been the time we stayed on the river, when my cousin had left her boyfriend on the beach that night. We didn't arrive back until dawn the next morning. Why? Because we had to finish all the shit we had...Keep in mind, I'm no quitter and let me tell you, it was a lot. Or maybe it should have been the time when I had moved in with my dad. I had been out all night and when I came rolling in at dawn his parole officer was there. All I could do was bow my head and head straight to the bedroom. I jumped on the waterbed all sprawled out. I laid there and prayed to go to sleep and not be caught. Please God, don't let him come in here. I was so wired up and was nauseous, twitchy and unable to focus. All I could do was stare at the ceiling for hours, as my body ached for sleep. I wanted to go climb on the roof and jump off. Maybe that would have been the turning point. Nope! Even though it was the last time I did it for awhile. Even had one of my buddies try and give it to me. He put it in the cap and I said, no thanks. He poured it in the floor board and filled the cap again, I said, no thanks again. He repeated and I said no, he finally got the hint after he realized he was wasting his time and his stuff.

It was years later and I happened to be drinking at the Club 68. I ran into this girl that I kinda knew. Who mind you, is deceased now. Ran into her in the bathroom. Oh no! Here we go again. The bathroom! That's where people who do coke spend most of their time. Sounds like fun huh? Not! She offered me some, and of course I accepted. She wasn't quite as threatening as Cow Patty and maybe not even at all. I was drinking and I willingly accepted. Before the night was over, I found myself somewhere lost in the hills of Marion County. Some strange house and no way home. There was some hurt looking people there. I was so paranoid and slightly frightened as I snuck into the back bedroom to call one of my cousins to come get me. I sat on the bed biting the inside of my cheek, when I realized at that point, I didn't even know where I was. I will never ever do this again, I swear I will never do it again. If I can just get out of here. And I meant it, at the time. I did, I swear...

It's amazing how we survived the times without GPS, google and cell phones. I miss the days of yellow pages, big dictionaries, and encyclopedias. Not! I do miss calling up my friends for information. It gave us time to talk. And GPS, they keep you from getting lost, but in my mind, I was never lost. I was always on an adventure. Except that one night, I was lost!

So moving on, I had told people around me, don't ever bring that shit around me! Ever! I don't want it around me. Cause I'm not one to say, I may not do it, if I happen to have a few too many drinks. My smart-o-meter gets dysfunctional sometimes.

Well, it was years later, many years later. So much later, that I had already had Summer and opened my café, when I had a set back one night. I was dating a girl who liked it. I fussed at her all the time for doing it. We had a huge fight about it and broke up. So I threw a small party without her. In my mind, I thought, I would show her. I have realized, every time I have said, "I will show you," it has backfired right in my face. Don't do it! Just don't.

I told one of my acquaintances to bring the stuff... and let me tell you what! When I do booger sugar, I do booger sugar. The only night that I limited myself to one bump, was my prom night. After that, if you stick that stuff in front of me, I'm gonna run you out. Follow you around like a lost puppy, and be up your ass like a colonoscopy. At least till I know you're empty, because I'm not a wasteful person. You immediately become my best friend, but just for the night, sorry to say. I mean you was still my friend, just not my best.

Sometimes it's easy to forget the bitter taste something left in your mouth. And with this situation, one more was never enough and one more always left you with just too many. So many that you thought you would never go to sleep. I thought this would be a good payback for her. Boy, am I an idiot! Yes, I said it, I'm an idiot. At least in this situation I was. You can't pay someone back like that, it's degrading only to yourself.

I was doing it out of dollar bills, from one end to the other. I felt my jaws tighten with every idiotic line I did. I was so jacked up. I was worse than that poor kid being all jack up on Mountain Dew and coming at people like spider monkeys. And I didn't stop till the sun came up. How was this paying her back? WTF... What was I thinking? Well, I wasn't. The problem with this was, well not the only problem, but the one staring me in the face. I had to open the cafe the next day. I was dying. You could see the hurt all over my face. I was pacing back and fourth as I was biting the inside of my cheek from nervousness, trying to figure out how to handle this situation I had put myself in. I had a friend, who tried to give me some advice on how to rectify this situation. She advised me to do some more, "Yep Miss! That's what you need to do. Only way you're gonna get through it." I was thinking... "are you kidding me? Isn't that how you actually become a coke head and begin your downward spiral to being a broke ass and six feet under." So I decided, I would just suffer it out. As you can see, it never was the frequency of my use, but the intensity.

My mom knew what I had done, but my dad didn't. I was at the grill cooking. People just kept coming through the doors. I was sweating and about to pass out. I was determined that I was gonna tough this out. Cause that's what I do, seriously that is what I do. But... Somewhere during the night, the doors quit opening. I was confused. I was looking around like, what the hell. Why is it dying down so early and abruptly? Then someone approached me and said, "Your mom is on the front porch telling people that they can't come in."

My dad was sitting at the bar with an unhappy gaze upon his face. "What is wrong with you? Why is your mom stopping people at the door?"

I was getting ready to reply when Mom walked up and said. "Buddy,

I think she has the flu. She needs to go to the house and rest." I nod, appreciating she thought to protect me like that. Although, Dr. Phil would ride her ass out and say. "What the hell are you doing by enabling this behavior?" She was covering for me and it was sweet, even though at the time I was upset that she had turned people away. I was gonna make it, I swear I was. But I was never so relieved to hit my bed. I felt terrible, physically and mentally. I can't be ruining myself like this, I can't do this ever again, and I didn't and I haven't and I won't. Well! Maybe, Haha, just kidding. Apply the lesson Missy, apply the lesson.

YOU CAN LOOK NOW ...We all make mistakes and I feel like this was my biggest one. It was an eye opener, no pun intended. I usually only make the same mistake once. Not to say I haven't made many. But for the most part, yes, I said for the most part, it's usually only once. So why was this over and over? I guess cause it didn't seem too bad at first, and it wasn't, but it could have been. It could have taken control of my life in a heart beat. I've seen many people's lives stolen by this drug. Now a days, there are many other kinds of drugs that can steal your glory and your life in a blink of an eye. All I can do is pray that Summer never touches a thing. She better keep her nose clean. No pun intended, once more. I personally will never touch it again, or will I? I'm hoping not, that would be pretty stupid! Now wouldn't it?

So yes, I've done many stupid things and I was learning day by day. I learned so much that it would hold the key to my success as a business woman, in the not so near future. I don't really regret my behavior, but sometimes I do regret someone wasn't filming it. The way I see it, if you did it, own it. I may not be perfect, but at least I'm not fake and that, I can be proud of. What you see is what you get. Even though some would think I need to be forgiven. Maybe I do need to be forgiven. But not for that, but for this! I'm the one who told my cousin there was no Santa Claus and he sat there on the stoop and cried. I ruined his holidays, and for that,,,,,,,, I do need to be forgiven.

Hold on, I left out one other coke story. You can look the other way if you want. It's short and back when I was still young, thinking maybe in college. I think the bump sign story was in college too. But I had been out all night with some friends and after they all went home except one guy, I stayed out with him. When morning was about to hit, he informed me he had to milk cows and asked if I wanted to join. Of course I joined, and I tried to milk a tit or two. Sliding those milk suckers on them tits wasn't an easy task and before it was all over, I had done been kicked by a cow. It was an awakening, to say the least.

This same guy, years later, shot a black man down in the streets of Raywick. That's why my little town can't get away from the stigma. I looked up the article, but I'm not gonna waste my time with it here. I don't wanna use his picture or the article and end up in court. No sir-e-bob.

What I've survived, might kill most of you. What other people have done would probably have killed me. In due time. We are all gonna die, no way around that scenario. Scientist, can you please get on that? Well, at least build me a flying car before I go. I really, really want one. It's about the only thing left on my bucket list, besides Africa and Australia. Then I could just fly my own little happy ass over there. I would probably need a refill from the sky though. Oh the future!

Just realized today that my bug man hung with all these people growing up too. Small world. Only one or two of the guys turned into rotten apples. It's amazing how normal all my high school girlfriends turned out to be after all this. But I do know a few acquaintances from a distance, that kept up the game, didn't fair so well. They should have known to quit doing it when they quit putting it in those cool little bottles. Just saying.

After Beverly read this last story, she turned to me and said. "Sorry I blamed your teachers for everything. I see now, how you burned up your brain cells," as she started to laugh and sing. "Cocaine Sally……"

Me and Mom

Of course that is my graduation picture and you already know the story. I decided to text Summer and ask her what she did on her graduation night and if anything crazy happen to her. She replied. "Um, I don't think so. Not that I remember."

"Boring." I said as I started to laugh.

"Why do you ask?"

"Well, I'm writing about yours, mine and Mom's graduation all at once. Just curious as to what you did that night."

I really don't remember!"

"Really! Nothing?"

"Really!"

"Well, I guess you're gonna find this out sooner or later. So here goes. I did coke at my graduation party."

"Tisk! Tisk!" she replied.

"Not a good experience though."

"Oh! Probably had too much."

"That's exactly what it was. Glad yours was boring. Good girl."

Summer's Graduation.

So that concludes Summer's and my high school graduation story. Let's ask mom what she has to say.

Kathleen and Marceline

MOMS STORY: It's short just like her bangs were that day. She said Grandpa cut them up to the top of her forehead that day. Then when she tried to go to the graduation party at the Horseshoe, Grandpa showed up and she ran and wrapped herself up in a curtain to hide.

All three of us today. I'm sure you know who is who by now.

HEADIN OUT ON MY OWN

Picking out a college was upon me and I was wondering how I was gonna pay for it. I was so broke I couldn't afford to pay attention, or as Grandma would say, I was a pauper. Although the 80s was a time of easy money, fast living and self indulgence and it was a "I want, what I want, when I want it," kind of time. That wasn't the life I was living. My dad was still in prison and only made 11 cents an hour, which we all know didn't add up to a hill of beans. I don't know what Mom was making, not even sure if she was working. Maw-maw was living off her social security check, and I was wondering where to turn. I didn't have enough dosh to be posh. So what was I to do, while on my pursuit of pesos. I ended up signing up for financial aid and that gave me enough money to go to JCC in Louisville.

I would love to see the rest of our society be able to attend college. I think we will devastate our nation if we don't decide to continue to help our young people get educated. Who knows what I would be doing now if I hadn't gotten the chance to broaden my horizons. Same thing. I would be doing the same thing. Once a foodie always a foodie.

When I packed up to leave for this challenge and headed to my first apartment, I was very excited. I left with some clothes, a 12 inch black and white TV and a lawn chair. I was living large.

Just a quick story:

Soon after moving, some friends and I decided to head over to visit a friend who moved to Lexington, to check out her place and to go party. When it was time to head back the next morning, we all just grabbed our stuff, no brushing our hair or teeth, because we knew we were going right back to bed. But no! Not that fast. We had to sit and wait for one of our friends to do the whole get ready thing. We were like, where do you have to go and why can't you do that when you get home? She said, "Hun, I'm not going anywhere when I get home but back to bed, but you will never catch me leaving any house, unless I'm in complete makeup. We were all like, what the hell ever! Come on just get in the car, we are not stopping anywhere. "No way! No day!" Is all she could say. So we waited patiently, hung over and hungering for our beds. I mean that was taking the saying, don't leave home in dirty underwear, to the extreme.

Let it be known: I'm sitting here at the computer and I keep hearing a piano note. Anyone? Anyone? Wish I could time warp to the far, far past and see who is lingering in my home.

BUT INSTEAD, I'M ABOUT TO TIME WARP YOU INTO THE FUTURE.

But wait! Since I was just talking about the eighties, I will give you a quick preview of my eighties party that was thrown just a few months before my house burnt to the ground. It was the last pictures taken in and around Summer's and my lost home. It was what I called a 40th of July party. Why 40th of July? Because I had just turned forty and I wanted to have a party and make everyone dress up from the 80s. Everyone was warned to come in costume or reap the consequences. I was dressed as *Robert Palmer* and a few of my workers came as the girls who played the guitars. They were quite sexy.

Mary as Tina Turner. Ann, Miles and Cecil as the Palmer girls.

Before the night was over I transitioned into *Tom Cruise* from the movie *Risky Business*. I was wearing nothing but my white button down, socks and 1986 underwear. Not underwear from 1986, but boy's underwear that said 1986.

We had a wide variety of characters to show up, ranging from: *Rubiks Cube, Rambo, Paula Abdul, Linda Evans from Dynasty, and Mary Lou Retton* and plenty more. And of course I'm the only one that came as a cast of two. Hell, I even tried to pull off Tina with Mary's wig.

One couple that showed up came as themselves and I immediately slapped a name tag on them that read, Jackass and Mrs. Jackass. They should have known I keep my word.

You will never guess who Kandy came as. Crocket! Miami Vice

Preview. LOL

Summer fell in love with the eighties and actually got this outfit from her closet. She is actually dressing the same in 2016 with her mom jeans and crop pants and side braid like her momma. Like her mom, she also has interest in arts and all things alternative. She also fell in love with the *Rocky Horror Picture Show.* She would stop right in the middle of the floor and break out in song and dance. "I'm just a sweet transvestite, from Transsexual, Transylvania, ha-ha-ha. Then continues on with "Let's do the time warp again. Let's do the time warp again." Let's!

SPITTEN PENNYS

It was May 30, 1996, when I got the call that my maw-maw was in the hospital. I was 28 and living in my little key hole house in Raywick at the time. I grabbed Summer and rushed to town to see what was going on. When I arrived, Dad was standing outside smoking, as the smoke rings surrounded his head. I ran up to him, to see what was going on.

"Hey Dad! What is wrong with Maw-maw?" I franticly asked.

"The doctors don't really know yet," he said.

"Can I go in and see her?"

Dad replied with his head down. "They won't let Summer go back there. She is too young."

She was only four at the time. Plus, they were only letting two at a time go in. The whole family was inside, and it was gonna be a while, before it was my turn. So I waited around for a bit. It was getting late and I really wanted to see her, but the doctors told us to go home and that we could come back to see her tomorrow. My aunt Peggy was going to stay with her, but she couldn't stay in the room. I remember thinking how stupid that was. Why fucking not? I thought to myself. Don't you think Maw-maw would want someone in there with her, with all those strange doctors and nurses. So I called Mom and asked her if she would keep Summer for the night. I wanted to drive back up to see Maw-maw first thing in the morning. Of course she said that would be fine. Don't know why I even bothered to ask. So I drove back to Raywick, to Mom and Gates. Mom and I talked for awhile, while Summer entertained us as usual. "That kid is the best," Mom would say. "The best!"

To Mom, Summer was everything. She asked how Maw-maw was doing. But, I had no answers for her, except for the fact, she was in the hospital. So I went back to the house. I decided to sleep on the couch, which I did most of the time anyway... I had nursing school the next day, but I had already planned on not going... It was going to be tough missing classes again. Because I remember how tough it was when Trish and Rick got killed, and I had to miss a bunch of classes and clinicals. I almost quit. Think I told you that before, but my teacher talked me out of it. That was a very, very hard semester. On top of Trish and Rick's death, one of my good friend's mother had died right before that. My friend had been very, very sad for months and wouldn't even leave the house, which leads me into this story before I fall asleep.

So, one night, I finally got my friend to go out. I had asked Mom to watch Summer for me. We headed to Connections (which is a gay dance bar) in Louisville. She was drinking pretty heavily, drowning her sorrows, but trying to have fun at the same time. I was out on the dance floor when, someone came up to me and said, "your friend is really drunk." When she walked up to me, she was stumbling. Then she proceeded to puke all down my leg. Mind you, I had on khaki pants, and she was drinking cranberry and vodka. My pants looked like I had murdered someone. "You may need to drive her and her car home." someone said.

And I tried! Boy, did I try. Made it about two blocks, before I drove down a one-way street, when the blue lights started blinking. I pulled straight into White Castles parking lot. I remember that someone had told me that pennies would make the drunken-meter read wrong. So I started to stick pennies in my mouth, by the handful. Then I spit them into the floor. They were coming out of my mouth like the bullets in an Uzi. When the officer walked up, the last one had just hit the floor.

Did it work? Nope! Didn't work. Still got put in the back of the car. Obviously it was some stupid advice or folklore I had been told by someone years before. They put her in a cab and let her go home. I guess I was taking one for the team. They handcuffed me and took me straight to Jefferson County Jail. When I arrived, they took all my belonging and threw me in a holding cell. I would have rather been in a pit of rattle snakes or buzzards picking at my ass, than to have been in there. There

I sat with two other drunks and a prostitute.

One of the female officers came up and peeked through the little cell hole and yelled my name. She needed me to answer some questions. She asked me my name. "Melissa Carol Luckett" I replied. Then she asked me what my maiden name was. I replied, "it's the same."

"What do you mean it's the same?" as she looked at me with aggravation.

"It's the same as my name," as I pointed to the paper.

"Don't you be getting smart with me!" She said aggressively.

"It's the same and I'm not getting smart. What part of that do you not get!!! My maiden name is the same as my birth name. Don't you have to get or be married for that to change?"

She looked as if she could have rung my neck. All I could picture was how Grandma used to tell me how she killed the chickens in the back yard. Pick em up by their heads and give a good jerk. My neck was next. The officer just stared at me with fury in her eyes like she hadn't been laid in months. I swallowed hard and shut the hell up. There was no reason she should be this angry with me. I was thinking, if I'm gonna be stuck in here with this crazy women, I sure wish I had downed a few more drinks. Maybe even be passed the plum f**k out, because this is some bullshit.

Just want you to know. I barely blew the limit. I was not wasted by no means, but at that time, I sure wish I was, and it got worse. "Someone please give me a drink." After her harsh stupid interrogation, of my maiden name, I sat back down with my cell mates. They blabbed on and on, how and why, they were there.

Then the another guard came by to give us a sandwich. He pushed it through the little hole on the door. When I pulled the bread off, there sit a horrible piece of purple looking bologna. I looked over at the prostitute. I shrug, unsure, "Are we really suppose to eat this?"

The prostitute replied. "For real, girl. What's up with this shit?"

Then, one girl, just started to eat hers. We stared at her like, really! You're gonna eat that rotted shit. Like I said, wish I was that drunk. I looked over at the prostitute. "Hum! What am I suppose to do with this?" She just kinda looked at me puzzled. So, at that very moment, I decided, I would pitch it back where it came from. Back out the square hole it came through. She laughed and I smiled, loving the fact that I'm making her laugh.

When the guard came back around, he spotted the sandwich in the hallway and then he looked in the hole. "Who threw the bologna in the hallway?" We all just stared at his eyes, with I will never tell. Lucky for me, no one told on me. No snitches in this holding cell, that's one positive for me.

It was a little while later when they came and called my name again. I was like, "Thank God! Carol called someone and I'm outta here!" NOPE! They pulled me out of the holding cell and put me right back in handcuffs. They had another girl in cuffs and shackled me to her. Then they walked us down this long hallway as our chains rattled. I felt like a dead man walking. Then an elevator opened. The doorway to hell! I was going to hell!

As they were trying to put us in, the one girl hesitated and resisted. She was full of some piss and vinegar. The lady cop, took her and shoved her into the elevator and up against the wall, as my little ass got dragged along. I was like. "Oh shit! Is this for real happening." My heart was about to beat out of my chest as we bounced around on the walls for a minute. I was literally about to shit my pants. The shuffle went on for a few more minutes, as I got innocently jerked around. When the cop finally pinned her down against the wall, with her arm up under the girl's chin, she calmed down. The elevator doors shut and away we went into the abyss.

When the elevator doors opened to what I guess, was the, for real, big girl quarters, they were taking girls into a private room. They were coming back out with orange jumpsuits on. I cringed a bit as my thoughts sunk. "Oh shit! They are gonna take my clothes off and search me." Just the thought, that maybe she was gonna insert her pinky, into thy butt hole, made me wanna try and escape. I was petrified and there was no escaping. I couldn't even believe it was happening to me. The lady officer took me to the room. The changing room. Then she put her hand on my shoulder as I jumped. I was probably pale in the face with fear, just thinking about what she was gonna do. She looked at me and said, "honey, don't worry. You can keep your regular clothes on. Those jump suits are for the real criminals. I just have to search you again. I'm just gonna pat you down." Shewl. To my relief. I gave her my best smile and said, thank you.

When she brought me out, she walked me over to a set of bars, as I stared in with discomfort. It was this huge holding cell that consisted of one big room. One huge ass holding cell. It had two picnic tables, a telephone and four individual holding cells that were open. There were women sleeping on the floors, out in the open. The guard opened the door and un-cuffed me and nudged me in. Me and the other woman, the one I was handcuffed to prior, was sitting on the picnic table. I took a seat on the other side. Then the guard handed us some sheets. The girl looked at me and asked. "What do we do with these?"

Tears pop into my eyes as I put my face in them and said, "Cry in them," and that I did. After I wiped my tears away and gathered myself, I went to the phone. I had to call collect of course. I called my mom. "Please answer! Please answer! Please accept." She answered alright, but the conversation went south. I begged and pleaded with her to come get me. She said, "That's a negative. Figure it out on your own." Wouldn't Dr. Phil be proud of her. As I was begging and pleading, one of the inmates kept screaming at me to get off the phone. "You little bitch! I'm trying to sleep. Get off the fucking phone." Mind you, this wasn't just some small girl yelling at me. She was one big rough, tough and ragged looking bitch. She had her sleeves rolled up with a pack of smokes stuck in there. She seemed quite at home, in her little open cell, with a cot. Which made me believe she had been there for awhile. So in my mind, she must have been a true criminal, and a loud scary one at that. So my mom wasn't happy with me, nor was this orange suited lady. I had to remain cautiously optimistic with the hope that I wouldn't be murdered through the night. I laid there at that picnic table with one eye open at all times, just like a dolphin. I was trying to sleep and protect myself from a predator at the same time. Let's just say, I didn't sleep a wink. Doesn't quite work for humans.

Morning was upon me, as this one girl awoke from her room and noticed me outside her cell. She started walking toward me, my thoughts went south. Was she gonna shank me? My butt cheeks grew tight. But I was over analyzing. She ended up being very friendly and only wanted to talk. She had her own cell, with a small window, and asked me in an ever so sweet voice, if I wanted to see it.

"Sure!" I said. You could tell she had been there awhile, she had pictures posted on the wall, and was showing this cell to me, like it was her home. As I was checking out her pictures, I heard the guard yell, "Melissa Carol Luckett!" Thank God! I'm finally outta' here. So I ran over to the big cell door. The guard unlocked it and I was excited as a dog who just spotted a bag of trash. They took me in some kind of office. I peeked over the counter to speak to the lady at the desk. I asked "Who is here to pick me up?"

She replied, "No one."

"What do you mean, no one?"

"We're just releasing you on your own recognizance." they replied.

In my stunned and frustrated voice, "Well! Can I make a call?"

"You will have to go back in the cell to use the phone, and there won't be anyone here to let you back out for a couple hours."

"Are you fucking kidding me?" I thought to myself. "Guess you better stick me back in then." So back in I went, with my head hanging down like Squidward's nose. I called my mom again and when she answered. I nonchalantly said, "What's up?"

"What do you mean. what's up?" she said.

"Who is coming to get me?"

"No one that I know of. I'm certainly not driving up there to get you."

I felt like I might cry. "Well, I figured you would already be here. What the hell?"

"Missy, I haven't planned nothing. I went right back to sleep after you called me. This isn't my problem." She said sternly.

"How is Summer?" I asked.

"She's fine! You better worry about yourself."

I started to get defensive. "I am worried about myself. I don't even know for sure where my car is."

"Guess you better be figuring it out."

So we argued back and fourth a bit and I finally realized, she wasn't coming to get me. So I hung up the phone and just sat there, staring at the clock till they came back and released me. They took me back down to the first floor to retrieve my stuff. It was where people pick up people. Or let's say it's where people picked up criminals. I had committed a crime! I was now a criminal, but with no one to pick me up.

As I sat there with bated breath, I started some small talk with the man sitting beside me who was there to pick up his friend. I was telling him about my night and that I was still in shock that my friend hadn't sent someone to get me, or that my mom wasn't coming to get me. I told him I had no money for a cab to get to my car, which was across town, parked at my friend's sister's house.

At that point he offered to give me a ride once they released his friend. Although I found myself standing between two stools, I accepted his offer. It's known to every one, do not get in the car with strange men. That's how desperate I was to get outta' there. I didn't know this man

106

from Adam. I had sleep deprivation and as I continued to sit there, I was wondering if they were trustworthy people, or had I set myself up for something worse.

One hour later I was walking to a stranger's car. Stranger danger was on my mind. Criminal was on my mind. *Boston Strangler* was on my mind. My body was quivering, and a growing nervousness was growing inside me. Thinking to myself, am I really gonna do this? Yes, I guess I was. What a Catch 22, my options sucked. I found myself in the car with four strange men, driving across town. One, whom had just got outta' jail, for Lord knows what. I had no idea and didn't bother to ask. As we began to drive down the highway, my hands were gripped tightly in my lap. My eyes were moving from man to man, watching their every move. I didn't really know how to get where I wanted to go. But the men ended up being very helpful, after I gave them some landmarks. Yes, they got me there. They turned out to be well-mannered southern gentlemen. Maybe I shouldn't have been judging. Shit, I just gotta outta' jail too. Maybe they thought I was a con, or a serial killer like Aileen Wuornos.. I got outta the car, and shut the door. I peeked back in the window and told them, thanks. I jumped in my car and drove home as fast as I could. Yes, I was breaking another law, because I was speeding like a fool. All I wanted to do was get home, back to my baby girl and hug her and kiss her.

Where was Summer during all this time? In a safe place as always.

Sorry, for that major story inside a story. So, back to the couch. Wondering about nursing school and how Maw-maw was doing. My eyes began to get heavy and I fell asleep.

RING, RING, RING. The phone startled me awake. I jumped and grabbed it, you know, the ones with cords. It was early morning and the sun was coming up. Shit, I don't even remember falling asleep! "Hello!" It was my Dad on the other end and there was an underlining sadness in his voice. "Hey Missy, you better get to town quick!"

"What is it Dad? What's wrong?"

"Just meet me at the hospital." His voice was clearly different than I had ever heard it. I jumped in my car and put the pedal to the metal. It seemed like it took me an eternity to get there, even though it was only about seven minutes away. I pulled up to the hospital once more and ran toward dad.

"What is it Dad?"

The feeling was different as he sighed and blew out smoke in a thin stream, pitched his cig to the ground and then hugged me. "Momma passed away last night. Everyone is really upset. They told everyone she would be fine. Your aunt Peggy is the most upset and she is back there cussing out the doctors. She wanted to stay in the room with her and they didn't let her. Everyone is pissed that she has passed away, alone in her room."

"That's some bullshit! They told us she would be fine. You mean to tell me, when she took her last breath, no one was there for her. I mean some one could have been in there. What's up with those rules? That's so fucking stupid. She needed to see a familiar face when she took her last breath. They can't understand that?"

I pushed open the doors and I ran on inside. I took off down the hallway, and through the swinging doors. I could see all the family gathered at the other end. They had all been called to come together and grieve our loss.

A bright light had just been extinguished from our lives.

It was the first loss I had experienced on my dad's side of the family. I had never seen him cry. I had only seen my Maw-maw cry once, at her best friend's funeral and it about broke my heart. Her heartbreak, made my heart break and now, my heart was breaking. I also had to watch my dad's heart break and of course the whole family. But... to see my dad cry. This was unfamiliar and painful.

The Luckett Fam Dam.

We buried her in Lebanon National Cemetery, where my grandfather was put to rest back in 1967. She already had her plot picked out. When we arrived and was walking to the plot, my dad looked at me and said "Don't expect me to pick my plot out before I'm dead. You can take care of that."

"I will Dad. I don't wanna pick mine out either. Guess I will leave that up to Summer, like you're leaving it up to me. But, I totally understand. Hope she does too."

Joking aside, it was a very sad day for the family. I don't think anyone understood the pain I was going through. To those who weren't close to me, it was just a grandma. Most people only visit their grandma at Christmas. But she was my Maw-maw and she had raised me. My close friends knew the pain. They knew how close I was to her. She had taught me all my values. That was to respect people, don't steal, don't lie, but have fun while you can. She always told me when you reach the end of your rope, tie a knot and hang on. She always told me not to wear my wishbone, where my backbone should be. Yes, they are quotes, but she told me first. Na-na na-na boo boo.

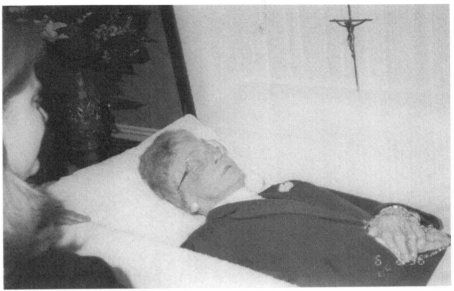
Me saying my last goodbye to Maw-maw.

One of the last few memories I have of her, was with Summer. She loved that kid. I don't know what it is about Summer, but she has put a spell on a lot of people. To Maw-maw, she was the only great grand child that she had, even though she had 11 kids, 46 grand-kids and no telling how many great- grand kids. Summer was the only one she talked about or wanted to see. I guess you could say she was obsessed with Summer. It could be that I was the last one she raised too. Summer, you don't get all the credit.

Right before she passed, she was getting a little senile. Somehow, Summer was still always on her mind. When I would stop there on my way home from nursing school, she would always ask, "where is

Summer?"

"Maw-maw, I just brought her up here yesterday."

"You did not!"

"Yes I did!" I replied.

"No you didn't! Don't be lying to me. I taught you better than that," she said with aggravation. So I drove to Mom's, picked up Summer, drove her back and watched her smile fill her face.

So I figured out really quick how to please her and when not to argue with her. Her mind was gone a little bit, well, maybe a lot. Yes! Maybe her bag had a hole in it and she had lost a few marbles. It comes with age, but she was still funny as always.

One day she looked at me with disappointment and pointed at the walls and said. "I don't like the wallpaper Darlene put up." As I looked around at the walls, I observed that they were painted.

"Yes, that is hideous. We are gonna have to change that shit immediately." It made me sad. It made me miss the days I used to make a pallet on her floor and sleep and watch Johnny Carson. Even though once Maw-maw would fall asleep, she would start to snore. I mean loudly and deeply enough to raise the roof. I would beat the floor and she would grunt and roll over and start right back again. As much as I hate snoring, till this day, I have to say, I do miss hers.

When she was at Summer's 2rd birthday party, I was filming her. The lights from the camera were shining in her face. She kept looking behind me, and saying, "who is back there?" As she wiggled around in her chair she said "What is going on? Missy, who is behind you?"

"It's just me Maw-maw. I'm filming you."

"Well, get that damn thing away from here. Who is behind you?"

No one was behind me. I was unsure what to think. Now that I think about it, someone or something could have been behind me. Maybe she was sensing the spirit, since she herself was about to become an angel.

I loved her all the way till the end. She was a fabulous, funny and caring woman. She always made me and my friends laugh, always.... Even when she was fussing at me, she never seemed very mean. She brought so much joy to all of us.

Maw-maw and Summer

HOOPTY-VILLE

I went to Louisville today to shop for houses. I was wanting to make an investment and to give Summer and Logan a place to live. Summer is in her final years of college and Logan just landed a nursing job. Shannon who is my childhood friend is now a real estate agent. She is married now and has three kids. Just a reminder. (Jamie Lee)

We were just riding around talking and looking at houses. We had been laughing about all the dysfunctional homes we had looked at prior to that day. One of them had farm animals raised on it. I could smell the stank from the front porch. I did not want to go in but Shannon convinced me to. I stayed in there a total of a minute. When I came back out the lady on the porch said, an ostrich, a goat, some bunnies and some chickens were found in there. She even tried to lock me in the basement of one that looked like the place Freddy Krueger would burn his victims. She laughed, as I screamed, "I'm gonna kill you if you don't open this door."

"You wanna get high?" I heard her snort with laughter though the door.

"I will show you high. Let me out."

But anyway, she got talking about Maw-maw. Tears were at the edge of her eyes. "I loved that woman. How long has she been dead now?"

"About 18 years. In my head it was years ago, but it my heart it seems like yesterday."

"Shewl! It does seem like just yesterday I heard her voice."

"She use to always say, I wasn't born yes-ti-dy."

"She was so funny. Do you remember that time we were coming from Calvary and there was a line of traffic as long as a train?"

"Not really." I said.

"You don't remember that? Come on Missy! You remember."

"No, I don't, Shannon."

"Well, when you sped past everyone to get out in front, we looked over and it was your maw-maw holding up the traffic. Guess she was coming home from bingo. We about shit."

"Was she driving that brown four door car?"

"Yep! It was her hoopty-ville." Shannon snorted as we cracked up at her comment.. "Don't you remember saying, leave it up to my maw-maw to be holding up traffic. We all ducked down in the seat, even you

Missy. Your car was passing her with no one driving."

"I'm sure it looked like that scene in the movie *Bridesmaids* when she is driving by the officer. Obviously it worked, she never said a word. Guess she was afraid to tell me had she seen a car with no one driving. That would have been a ticket straight to the nut house."

Ever since she passed away, I cry when I here the '*Toby Keith*' song, '*Cryin' For Me.*

I didn't seem to be crying for her, I was crying for me.

When someone dies, you miss what they bring to you. She brought me a tremendous amount of happiness and respect. I hope to see her again in whatever form she is offered to me. You can only have hope of seeing the ones you love in the way you remember them. But how do other people who died before them, see them? Will we remember them how we want? Everyone dies at different times. So we can't all remember everyone the same. I'm confused on how this works. I wish someone would tell me. Oh that's right, they can't. No one has ever really died and come back long enough to tell me. EVER!!!!! And when someone does try to tell me they know, I just throw up my hand like, Stop! In the name of love and say, my logical brain won't let me listen to your bullshit any longer. As Maw-maw might say, go boil your head. She you someday Maw-maw. Not sure if it will be sooner or later. Although I miss you, I must hope later. Summer needs me you know.

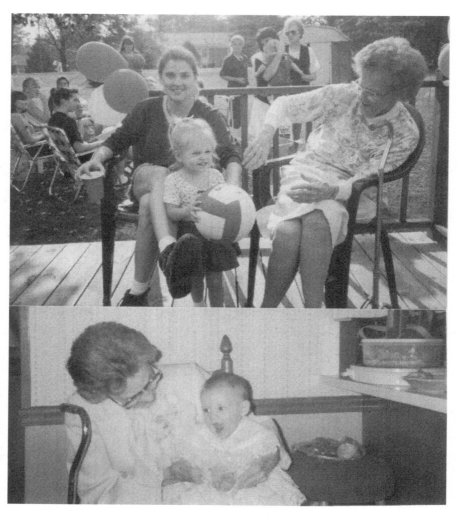

Maw-maw and Summer

Sometimes its very hard to Comatize a story like this. You can't comatize death, but you can comatize the experiences you shared. Remember that always. Also remember, we all die, but we don't all live. She lived and I'm gonna live too.

I don't know where this conversation came from. It was in my notes. First time I'm gonna put something in my book, having not a clue, who or where it came from. Here goes.

(What about your funeral plot? I don't want the traditional funeral, is what most people would say. But too bad you're going to get it anyway. Only get three days to figure out where to put your ass and most likely it's going to be in the ground. We're all going to die, we cannot dilute the situation. Unless we die first, we're all going to see the people around us that we love die. Which do you want?) Readers, we have talked about this. Same time! We should all go at the same time, to save the heartache. If not, at the same time, I want to be buried with a tree seed. Pin Oak to be exact. Even though I know I may get taken down by the wind or lightning, I wanna be part of nature and not in a man made casket.

Speaking of Pin Oaks:

Some people are just like them. It takes them forever to grow up. I fell like I'm more like a Bradford pear. I grew up quick and I get split all the time, but I keep growing out the sides. As long as no one comes and completely cuts me down, I'm fine. Even if they cut me to the ground, I will try hard to re sprout. If I don't, I must be dead. Then plant me with a Pin Oak seed. Please! I wanna take my time next time around.

My unknown future. Some may call that bleak. I see much much potential.

Quote: Continuous effort – not strength or intelligence – is the key to unlocking our potential. ------ Winston Churchill

You know what matters? Food matters!

You know the good thing about science? It's true whether you believe it or not!

COMING OUT

So how did I come out you ask? I know you did. Let's not pretend you didn't. You had to be a little curious on how that shit went down. Well, it took me till I was twenty-five years old before I came out. It was the year of 1995. Let's just say it took awhile, before I came to complete terms with my sexuality. I wasn't confused in my head about who I was, I was just confused in my environment. I knew I was gay, but I did not care at the time. I was in a different state of mind.

When I finally came out, I found out that four more girls in my class were just like me. We all rolled out of the closet like a can of soda when you open the box wrong. One being Julie. Wow! That's crazy. We were besties. How did I not know?

Julie and Me. Holy Shit! We're gay!

I was also friends with the other three. One in grade school, one in high school and played basketball with the other. None of us knew about each other. We were all in the closet. Thanks society, for making us lie all those years.

Please don't say I chose to be gay, because, that is just messed up. It's not a life style choice, I didn't choose to be gay, nor did I choose to stay in the closet. It was horrible! My daughter even told me the other day she felt sorry for me and almost came unhitched. "Mom, women are bitches and so is society."

I would love to be married to a guy with a family and be accepted to the social norm. It doesn't work like that. I was shamed and frightened into the closet, just like the government scares you, to pay your taxes. There were consequences, big consequences for some. Losing their life because someone thinks they have the nerve to judge and punish. Some people have been fired from their jobs because of it. I was afraid, to lose my family, my friends, and most importantly, my one and only daughter. That was my fear twenty years ago, and now due to this fucked up election in 2016, we are about to head back in time. It's unbelievable after all the progress that has been made on equality for all. Pence and his beliefs has got me scared to death for the young ones. I myself am not afraid of him, because I feel he can't touch me and as far as gay marriage I could give two shits about that, because its looking like I'm not getting married anyway. But am I concerned about my fellow people? Yes! Yes, I am. Completely worried. I have no regrets in raising my child with an open mind and a nonjudgmental soul.

Short story: When Summer was around 12 or so, I had the channel on *HBO*. Yes, she was too young to be watching, but nothing inappropriate was on. But then, they had a preview for a show called *Queer as Folk*. It showed a guy push another guy up against the wall and kiss him passionately. Summer blurts out. "That's hot!" My mouth dropped and

I just looked at her and didn't say anything. But what I realized at that very moment, is that people teach people what's appropriate. Love and passion is never inappropriate. Teach your kids to be accepting. Love is love and hate is hate.

So the first time I ventured to Connections (Gay nightclub) it was with Carol. Neither of us knew about each other's gayness. Hell, we both wore lipstick. So how were we to know? All of our friends had gathered a few weeks before and Carol had mentioned this place to me. I said to her, "Hum! I would like to go sometime."

"Yeah let's get together and do that." she said.

So were in the car headed to the gay club and you can tell she is nervous. She looks at me and says. "Missy, this place is a little different."

I look over at her and say. "I know Carol."

Then she looks at me again. "Missy, I really don't think you understand." She really seemed worried.

"Carol, I'm telling you! I know."

"Well Missy, they're not like you. They're a little different. Very different, as a matter of fact."

"Carol! I'm different too." She looked at me puzzled. She already knew I was different, but not in the way she was trying to tell me. "Missy it's a gay bar."

"That's cool, Carol. I'm just like them."

"What do you mean?"

"I'm just like them. I'm gay too."

She was shocked, yet relieved at the same time. How did we not know about each other? She gave me a big pearly white smile. "Missy I never even gave any thought to you being gay. You wear lipstick."

"So do you Carol."

During high school I didn't really care to date anyone, didn't much pay attention to my sexual orientation. I liked hanging with my friends and just living life. Even though I did have a couple of crushes on girls through high school, it didn't matter. It didn't matter, till I found myself really, really in love with someone. I had to stay in the closet, keep it on the down low. When that relationship ended, I went into a backlash and tried to act straight. I truly didn't know what to do with myself. Then after I had Summer and everyone was still chasing boys, I was lost. It was finally time for a real relationship. Not a fake one, not one to please anyone and definitely not one in the closet. A REAL ONE.

(DOMA IS DEAD) only in certain states, sad to say. INEQUALITY: Like the lady said. Ain't nobody got time for that....

Me, Kandy, Jackie, Lisa and Carol. Carol is now happily married to her long time partner, Kitty. They have a wonderful son named, Silas.

Even though Carol already knew, no one else did. It was still our secret. My mom is the one who dragged me completely out of that smelly old closet. I was at her house one day. She just looked at me and asked. "Missy, are you?"

Well, we all have heard this question before, back when she interrogated me when I was pregnant. I acted dumb, both times.

"What are you talking about Mom?" "Missy, I just want to know. Are you?"

I thought to myself, is she for real doing this again. Is she calling me out, once more? I don't want to talk about this. She kept persisting with, "Missy are you?"

"Am I what, Mom???

"Well, Missy, I keep hearing you cry through the baby monitor when you come in at night, and I know nothing else is wrong. I had my suspicions when Smiley was around."

"So are you talking about me crying the night I dressed as the scarecrow and Shannon had to throw me in the door."

"Yes Missy, you cried that night, along with a lot of other nights."

"Damn, I had fun that night too. We were all down Bickett's and I had a blast being the scarecrow. I walk and fall just like him when I'm drinking. It was perfect."

"Yeah, and when your friends dropped you off, they pushed you through the door. I bet you really was walking like him then. Then you scattered hay from here to Kalamazoo. So why was you crying that night if you had so much fun? Why are you crying every night? I wanna know if you are?"

Homemade outfit. It was the shit

"So you're asking me if I'm gay? Right?"

"Yes, Missy! Are you?"

I was feeling defensive. "Omg Mom! If you must know, then yes! Yes, I am!"

She replies with excitement, "Let's go tell Kathleen!"

I shockingly responded with, "are you absolutely crazy? You done lost some marbles, I swear."

"Why do you think that Missy?"

I laughed and sweated and the same time, feeling as Mom had put me behind the eight ball. "Well Mom you seem very excited about this situation you have just uncovered, but you know she says gay people are going to hell. She says it all the time. She says the bible says it. She will ostracize me!!"

"Mom replies, "Well Missy! She loves you and maybe she will understand. I understand. Look! I'm gay up here and straight down here." As she pointed to her upper half, then her lower half.

I put my hands on my hips. "Well! I'm not sure about that. Not sure about either one of you."

Mom grabbed my hand and started to drag me out the door. I resisted with great strength.

"Come on Missy!"

"No Mom!"

"Get your butt out this door. I promise she won't ban you from the family."

"We'll see about that."

So I walked out the door with great hesitation and got in the car. I was feeling quite vulnerable. We drove straight to Kathleen's, and walked in and sat at the kitchen table. I told her the news as sweat poured from my head. I was thinking is she gonna tell me I'm going to hell. At that time, I was feeling like a cat on a hot tin roof. Is she gonna tell me to repent, or that I need help. But no! No, she didn't. She looked at me, and said. "Missy, I'm just uneducated on that stuff, but you can enlighten me." I enlightened her and that's about all I remember her saying during that conversation. Thanks for the rain, this cat needed that. We have been very close all these years afterwards.

Quote: "We can learn a lot from crayons. Some are sharp, some are pretty and some are dull... Some have weird names and all are different colors, but they all have to live in the same box."--Facebook.com

Just a note: *I just wish we had an island we could send the really dumb people to. Not talking about someone who gets a 'F' in algebra, but the dumb ones, you know the haters. Deplorables.*

You would think with all the resources at hand, people would have learned something by now, instead of sticking with their narrow minds. That's why it makes me mad when people say. "Well, Hillary was against it. She is wishy-washy." Well, I would like to say, there is a difference between becoming educated and being wishy-washy.

I remember when I was pregnant with Summer and watching for the first time, the *Blind Melon* video, '*No Rain*'. It made me sad at first when the little bumble bee girl kept getting shoved away from everyone, because she was different. Then she found her people and danced and danced. Then I was happy. That's how I felt when I finally got to come out. I wanted to dance and dance, yell and scream. But in the back of my mind, I thought, be careful Missy, people will shun you with their judgments and fears. Oh what the hell! Who cares? I can't change and they're just gonna have to deal with it. I can't change, even if I tried. Just like *Mary Lambert* sang in her song. She keeps me warm.

I can't change, even if I tried
Even if I wanted to
And I can't change, even if I tried
Even if I wanted to
My love, my love, my love, my love
She keeps me warm, she keeps me warm

Back years ago: I was sitting in church with Robbie. I was looking around and noticing that a few of the people there were wearing sheep's clothing. You know, the few, who think they can show up in church and think they can hide themselves. Then spew hatred and lies and gossip outside the walls. Obviously I was already in deep thought when the priest started talking about homosexuality. I started feeling very uneasy. Robbie elbowed me, leaned over and whispered. "I knew he would get you at some point. He gets everybody eventually." I stood up and slowly walked out. I haven't been back, unless it was for a funeral or wedding. Seems like more funerals than anything. But I wasn't going to church to be belittled. I was going to church to build my faith, in which it was not doing. I felt angry and no one should feel that way after leaving church.

126

No one! I was almost as mad as Ann Coulter. What does she have to be mad about anyway? We will speak about her hatred later.

Quote- *"Life is to short to stress yourself with people who don't even deserve to be an issue in your life"-Anon.*

FYI: I'm sure my life is like a lot of peoples. On course, off course, back on again, off, back on, off. Then on again. It's the small things that can turn you on again, after being off again. Something simple as a lady calling me up with guilt. She said, "I'm reading your book instead of saying my prayers. Just thought you should know." Life's light just turned green again. Let's plow!

My coming out to the world experience ended up being very easy for me. Even though I feared the worst. Trying to figure out how to come out was the most fearful time in my life. Deep seeded fears that had been taught to me for two and a half generations.

I want to thank my mom! Seriously, thank you for your understanding and acceptance. Thanks for yanking me out of the closet like a band-aide. Quick and almost painless.

Kandy and I were close friends, but we became even closer, after I upchucked the truth. So the story goes, I was drinking a lot at that, time. Haha, bet you're really surprised. But anyway, every time I would go out with Kandy, I would tell her I had something to tell her. Through the night she would be like, what are you going to tell me? Can you just tell me already? You do this every time you come up. Quit hiding whatever you're hiding. I would tell her, just let me have another drink, then I will. I kept feeling a growing nervousness every time I went to tell her, then I would chicken out and down another one. I had totally succumbed to the social pressure. This went on for a long long time. Never could bring myself to tell her. Then after Mom yanked me out, I thought I had better

127

tell her myself. And so I did. She laughed and said, "really, is that all you have been trying to tell me? I thought maybe your mom had killed someone or something and you was covering it up. I thought the worst, as bad as you were making it seem." I was relieved and she was relieved. I asked her politely, "Did I ever hit on you at all during all those times I was drinking?"

"No Missy. Actually you didn't."

"Well, you know you was my first crush and I can't believe I behaved so well during all this time."

"Well you did!"

So one night soon after that, we had gone out again. We headed on down to the Butcher Town Pub and had a few drinks. There was this girl in a band that I had a crush on, fourth crush to be exact. She was the cat's meow. She had coal black hair, thick black eyeliner and would always wear black army boots and when she would sing the Cranberries, I would stare in awe, with hopes of going back stage with her. Never happened. Dream crushed.

So when we got back to Kandy's house, I went to walk into her room. Keep in mind she can read my mind sometimes. Remember the Gnome pot nights. I was going in there to hit on her. I had nerves of steel at that moment.. She said nicely, "Missy go back to your room." And that I did. She shut me down nicely and quickly and I knew my boundaries in an instant. We have respected each other ever since and became even closer after I let the cat out of the bag. I wasn't carrying around a secret to which she had no idea what it was. She said it always stressed her out. And all I could think was, tell me about it.

What happens to us makes us who we are. You have to deal with your demons as you go. This demon was eating me alive. But it really wasn't a demon, it was a secret and they will eat you up too.

Everyone else just kinda found out on their own. I didn't even tell my dad, he heard it through the grape vine. We have never really talked about it. He isn't much of a talker anyway. If I would have tried to sit him down and explain, he would have jumped right up and said, I gotta go check the cows. But I know he loves me and accepts all that I am. After hiding in the closet all those years, I have now become, what you see is what you get. No more lies. One lie, always leads to another and my maw-maw taught me better. I've always been out spoken, but now, even more, since I don't have a secret. I have no secrets and it feels awesome. Now I'm free.... free I say!!!! I would like to think, now, after all these years, I can keep calm. Because now, I have lesbian swag. So I thought.

Quote: *a different world cannot be built by indifferent people."---Dr. Peter Marshall.*

Thank you, Obama for helping with marriage equality and thanks for giving Ellen DeGeneres the medal of freedom. Thank you! Thank you! Yes, I voted for you. Yes, I would do it again. But no, I can't. Thank you Ellen for taking an even bigger gamble than me. She could have lost everything. Well, she did for a minute when they cancelled her show back in 1997 after she came out. She has proven what a strong woman she is and has fought her way back to the top.

So haters, be gone! Well, sad to say, haters will never be gone. Somehow my mom thought they were until the Orlando shooting. She was really in the dark. She looked at me and said, "Missy, people don't hate gay people."

"Mom, where have you been? In a closet?"

"Missy, I really don't think they do."

Then I showed her a video of some preacher down in the far south. He was up there acting all high and mighty, praising to the Lord that the shooting happened. He was literally glad the people were dead. Mom looked at me distraught and in shock and blurted out, "I will kill a mother fucker!"

Pardon her French, but that got way under her skin.

Don't be afraid to be different!!!

Just a thought: You remember the song *Don't you forget about me.* It played at the end of the movie, *Breakfast Club*, when he is walking across the football field. Well, if you don't, he is expressing how they are all different. We are all different and maybe, just maybe, I'm all of them rolled up like sushi. I am the mild rice, the wild salmon, the hot Sriracha, the smooth avocado, etc.. The cold beer to quench your thirst. The wine to soothe your soul and the Saki that heats you up. That's a hard maybe. But a thought! Some people could think, I'm shit on a stick. lol

Thank you Ellen, for your support, and out-ness and your statement:

Quote: *"I stand for honesty, equality, kindness, and compassion. Treating people the way you would want to be treated and helping those in need. To, me, those are traditional values. That's what I stand for. I also believe in dance"-Ellen.*

Summer and I agree with all you say and stand for. Especially when you made the comment...."Asking who is the "man" and who is the "women" in a same sex relationship, is like asking which chopstick is the fork." SMMHHH....... to people who would even ask.

Summers Smhhhh face

You know what else gets my goat? When a guy tells me I haven't had the right blank yet. Smh... Sir! I've had a few and I'm sure they were bigger and better than yours.

Shannon, Mindy, Rose Marie, Me, Marybeth Stacy and Dana.

December 23, 2016, I was having lunch with some of my high school friends. The three ladies on the left didn't join us this day. Actually I haven't seen Rose Marie in a coon's age. I need to get in touch with her. Shannon, (Jamie Lee) Shannon, came rolling in late like usual, but she always shows up for anything and everything. I'm starting to figure out her lateness. It's a good plan, she never has to wait on anyone, like ever. When she sat down, she said she hadn't even slept the night before, but she wanted to join us since Marybeth was home. She is that loyal and the glue that holds the group together.

When the conversation begun to get serious and I don't mean serious as in serious, but serious as in we weren't meeting and greeting any longer with the boring stuff, like the hellos and how are you? I began with giving them tidbits of my sexual escapades. First I was telling them about my coming out story. They were looking at me with sad eyes, when I told them I cried for months. I was like don't be looking at me that way, as I smacked across the table. Then Marybeth blurted out. "Sam said they use to picture us together. It was a fantasy."

"You know what's funny? When I hang around any girl, people assume I have a crush or I have been with that girl."

"Which one of us did you have a crush on?" Marybeth asked with curiosity.

"Sorry girls! I didn't have a crush on any of you."

They looked slightly disappointed when Marybeth said. "You're hilarious. Why not?"

"Well, I've only had a crush on one of my friends, and that was Kandy 30 years ago." Then I changed the subject and said, "I had sex for 8 hours." You should have seen the look on Marybeth's face. It was priceless. (I told you to remember her face. Refer to page 33) The whole table stopped in shock. Dana dropped her fork, Stacy's eyes grew and Shannon swallowed hard. 30 seconds later, Marybeth's face was still in shock mode, when she looked at her watch and checked it. "Listen girls, when it hits 30 minutes, I tell him to get off! I'm done! We're finished! That's impressive Missy!"

I looked at Dana and Stacy and said "I don't have any stories about you. You guys were always out on a date."

"The hell you don't!" Dana said. "I was with you guys on Fridays. And I skipped Saturday school with you Missy."

"We had Saturday school?"

"Yes, don't you remember driving me to Louisville?"

"Nope. I can't believe you girls are trying to convince me we had Saturday school."

"We had to go because we had missed so many days for snow. You picked me up and I thought we were going to school. Because I was kinda one of those goodies. You came through town and you took a left and I said Missy! Where are we going? We went to Louisville and spent the day with one of your cousins. You don't remember that? You don't remember, because you never went to Saturday school."

"It had to be Ann." I blurted out.

"Yeah, Yeah, it was Ann."

"How come I wasn't invited?" Marybeth pouted.

"It was just me and Missy and I was distraught." Dana said as she started to laugh.

"She didn't ask me because she knew I would start freaking out in Louisville." As Marybeth owned up to the truth.

"Missy we were suppose to go to school and you just kept driving. I said, my momma was gonna kill me."

Shannon snorts with laughter, "Eugene said, Missy likes what I like! Isn't that weird that he said, Missy and I really like, we really,,,,, really, like the same thing."

Marybeth looked over at me and said. "At the reunion, when your girl was out there grinding up on Dana a little bit, Eugene said. I could lie a little bit and say I don't like it. But I do."

Dana started waving her hands. "Listen you guys! Listen! When I got home, Eugene said. Remind me to always go with you to your class reunions."

"Eugene told us this one guy was getting a little handsy and we're like that's just him. He has always been handsy."

Dana turned up her nose. "That's just him. He's always been that way. He is always gonna be that way. I went out on one date with him and I tell you what. He was nothing but hands. Nothing but an octopus. I said, never again, sorry dude."

Speaking of dude, I got a good story for ya.

Summer, Haley and Evelyn

This night started out innocently enough. Summer was having an art show. I closed the café just to go. We took wine and snacks and celebrated her awesomeness. When we opened the wine, she said, "this wine tastes drunk." Not sure how that works, but I guess she was right. I left the Three Amigos behind to go meet up with my cousin and some friends. Ann and I sat at the bar at Dragons Daughter, and ordered a couple beers after I had already drank the drunk wine. The couple next to me ordered some Saki. I had only had Saki a couple times before, but not very much. Somehow I let these strangers convince me that Saki only gets you drunk for a minute, then it wears off. So I looked at the bartender and said bring us some. Either I was a fool or pretending to be a fool, I haven't really figured it out yet. Then some other friends arrived and we headed to the bar next door. Someone bought me a whisky and seven. Then they decided they wanted to go to this new bar I had never been to. It was called 'Play' and it had drag shows and dance floors. I was game. I let them drive my car. I remember walking in and one of the girls went charging for her ex, when she seen her standing there with another woman. I've done a lot of stupid things, but I'm not into messy drama. So I grabbed Ann's arm and said let's hit the dance floor. Well guess what? It was the last thing I remembered that evening. The next morning I woke up at Summer's house and my mind was as murky as the New Orleans swamps. I rolled over, seen Ann lying beside me and I grabbed her. "Dude! Where is my car?" In all my years. I had never lost my car. This is when I knew I had done something really, really stupid. You learn from situations like this. Like, when someone tells you wine taste drunk, believe them or when someone says Saki won't get you drunk, don't believe them.

Quote: *They didn't know why these things were funny. Sometimes you laugh because you've got no more room for crying. Sometimes you laugh because table manners on a beach are funny. And sometimes you laugh because you're alive, when you really shouldn't be." ---Terry Pratchett*

One day I told Charlie that I thought fire was out to get me. As he tugged his beard, he asked me if I would rather die drowning or burning up in fire. I said, I would prefer to get eaten' by a bear. The guy who was helping him write his book, giggled behind me. "That would be a good story."

"Yeah, it might take a few years to be funny or to comatize it. But I think it would eventually be funny. Someday when Summer and her friends are sitting around a campfire and getting stoned, it should be hilarious. It's the least I could do for her and it will be a way better story than telling people I died from cancer or something. Don't cha think? I think she will be able to make it funny someday, after it all marinates and as she is passing the blunt and someone asks her. 'So how did your mom die?" She will choke it out with laughter. "By a bear!!!!""

Charlie laughed in a deep laugh and grabbed me by the shoulders. "And I'm sure you hope it's a female bear."

"You better believe it."

"Do you think you will taste like chicken or tuna?"

"Chicken! Maybe a little fatty, but I'm sure we all taste the same to a bear. You might taste a little bit like sardines."

Moment in time:

Be careful what you wish for..
I keep getting calls saying my bear has been spotted in Raywick!
Yikes! It is coming to get me.

I'M NOT READY!
But please don't shoot the bear.

RANT:

People think it's a choice to be gay. This makes me wanna yell. So here goes.

QUESTION: HOW COME I WASNT AROUND GAY PEOPLE? BUT I STILL TURNED OUT GAY.

WHY?

BECAUSE SEXUALITY ISN'T A CHOICE.

JUST KNOW THAT IGNORNANCE IS A CHOICE AND SEXUALITY ISN'T AND IF YOU BELIEVE IT IS, IM SORRY BUT YOU'RE A FUCKTARD.

Calm down, Missy! Just calm down! Calm, Calm.......

Oh! Let me say one more thing. Our new vice president elect is a fucktard or a screwbie as my Aunt Beverly would say. Does he really think he can shock me back straight? Conversion therapy... SMHHHH!!!!

Mr. P! You resemble every villain that I can pull from my childhood memory. Like for real, your face is fake and it's scary. Obviously I'm not the only one that has noticed. You actually scare me more than Trump. Can't believe you are also trying to end Planned Parenthood. As far as abortion, I'm not going down that road. I can't say I'm for it or against and I have many reasons for that. And I know, I know, by saying that, I just pissed both sides off.

Guess this is one time, being gay might work to my advantage, because, we lesbians have 99 problems, but at least getting pregnant isn't one of them.

You know what is a problem? When I talk to Siri unnecessarily. I just asked her how to spell unnecessarily, because I was having a brain fart. She said, "I'm not sure I quite understand."

I replied. "Of course you don't. You never do."

I know! I know! Headed to the shrink tomorrow.

140

THANK YOU!!!!!

Quote: Every single American – Gay, straight, lesbian, bisexual, transgender. Every single American deserves to be treated equally in the eyes of the law and in the eyes of our society. –President Obama

FAITH

So as I write, I have quotes, metaphors, philosophies, illustration and many lessons learned. Trying to change what can be changed and leaving alone what can't. Acceptance of what is. Understanding that you can't understand everything, and it's ok. Knowing there is a greater power, and still be confused on who is right, if anyone is. I try to never see things black or white. So many lines are blurred. Although I would probably find it easier to see things black and white. Like they say, you better stand for something or you will fall for anything. Maybe! Maybe not. Just like karma. You know I wanna believe in it. But think about it! Karma doesn't always happen, now does it? I would love to see some instantaneous karma. Wouldn't that be a hoot, to toot your horn at? That's the God I'm talking about.

So after I experienced three deaths in a row, and watched people I love departing from my life, I struggled. I mean, I really struggled. Not in the way I did with dealing with losing my home, but with faith alone. It was back to back almost, all within a year. Lost Maw-maw, Aunt Trish and Paw-paw. I live in a community where I'm probably gonna get nailed to the cross for saying any of this.

Not believing much in prayer already, the greater plan is hard to understand. I'm finding it very hard to convey this belief, to the people around me. Being raised in a Catholic home and town, my religious conditioning tried to limit my beliefs. I was taught from an early age to go to confession, believe in Jesus and prayers. My grandma used to make me say the rosary in the car, coming home every time we went to visit someone. I never got the point in that. What good is this doing? Praying doesn't cause miracles, getting off your ass and doing something does. To me, prayer is movement. I believe in the power of the people, God's children.

Make no bones about it, I know prayer is meant for good, and we all know movement can be good or bad, and I believe in good movement to stop the bad movement. But saying the rosary in the back seat was no movement at all for me as a child. All I'm saying, is that I didn't enjoy it or believe in it. It wasn't doing anything for anybody, except my grandma, who thought it was doing something when it wasn't.

It's the month of December 2016. I decided I would do some pay it forwards through out the month. It was making me feel good. Then on a Saturday night during busy, busy service hours my electricity went black. I stood there in the dark. I said what the fuck, karma done got its address wrong again. And I heard someone say, maybe it's someone else's karma. I laughed, yeah was it someone's Karma not to eat here tonight? That's stupid.

142

I still don't believe in karma. I thought for a few minutes about my good deed and thought screw that, but later I had to rethink my position and continue. Because I know shit happens! It has nothing to do with karma or any other entity. So I go down Grandma's a couple days later. She is trying to give me a rosary. I'm like, "Grandma, I don't need another one, I got five and I would feel guilty if I had to throw it away. I don't say the rosary anyway."

"You better young lady."

I walked over to her and gave her a kiss on the forehead. "Listen Grandma! I just fed a homeless man today. Do you want me to go say the rosary or do you want me to go do another good deed?"

"Good deed."

Now, readers! I'm sorry, but here is where I may get a little to philosophical and anti-conformation. Stick with me. Sorry if I seem a bit anti-religious. I seem to have a love-hate relationship with it. Although when I'm alone, I feel God or what one would say, a greater being is with me. I believe in Mother Earth and humanity and I think any God would be proud if we take care of that. I feel that I'm an Ominist, just a person who does not really claim any religion, practice or belief, but I can find the truth in all of them.

I also refuse to fall for the televangelist bullshit that people throw their hard earned money to. Like in the eighties when they were masters of the universe on cable TV. Not gonna do it! Not gonna do it! I just can't relate to this phenomenon. It looks like after Tammy and Jim Baker duped everyone, we would wake up and notice that these people don't need our money. That's not how you get to heaven by sending money, so they can live in huge mansions, thanks to people's contributions. It breaks my heart to watch that when we could actually be doing some good and helping some poor helpless child. And you don't even want me to get on that subject at the moment. To watch people scream Trump!

Trump! Trump! Keep the refugees out and watch these children get blown to pieces, I don't even have any words to speak on that at the moment.

(RELIGION IS LIKE A PENIS--- It's okay to have one and its okay to be proud of it---HOWEVER--- don't pull it out in public, do not push it on children, do not write laws with it and don't think with it. Thanks face book friends...

This story is a few years back. I mean I wrote it a few years back. I love my grandma to death and she loves me just as much. Even though I don't conform to her ways and we rarely have a come to Jesus moment.

It's funny! She called the other morning, and asked me, if my plum tree was ready to be picked.

"Yes ma'am! I will pick you some."

She asked, "You remember when I use to visit Momma and give you a five-gallon bucket."

It took all I had, not to laugh out loud, because obviously she hasn't a clue about what I've wrote about it in the book.

So, rewinding back to a religious conversation I had with her. She said "Who doesn't believe in prayer? I pray everyday and you better start to, young lady."

I looked at her puzzled and with a little sarcasm, patted her on the hand and said. "Grandma, if prayer did the trick wouldn't your two sons be out of prison by now? Especially after all that praying we have done. Don't you think we should believe in the power of people, or maybe the judge, who could actually release them. Don't you pray every day for them to come home?"

"Of course I do!" as she paused and her thoughts went deep. "Hum! Maybe you're right, but you should still pray, or get your bottom spanked."

144

I laughed, "Don't you think I'm too old for that? So tell me Grandma, if that were enough, wouldn't it have already happened? I mean, I feel like prayer works, but only on mass quantities. I believe, when there is movement by many, then things begin to happen. I don't believe people should pray for self wishes either."

She takes a deep breath with frustration. "You know child, you're getting too big for your britches. Everything happens for a reason."

I'm sure I looked stunned to her, as I wondered where that comment came from. "Really! Grandma! No... No ... I don't believe that! Do you think God lets little kids starve for a reason? Or that Trish and Rick got shot for a reason? Or that he wants man to go to war, for land and greed? Here, let me read you a quote..

Dalai lama--States "If every 8-year-old in the world is taught meditation, we will eliminate violence from the world within one generation."

"So maybe meditation is the answer, or movement. Why do you only believe in prayer? When does prayer work? When do you know it works? How come it only works sometimes? I believe we create some of the things that happen, and some things just happen."

With her frustrated voice. "You better still believe in prayer, little young lady! God is all good."

I replied, "So if God is all good and he gives us our own will, do you think, our will, is to let kids starve? Because I don't believe it's God doing it. Is it us, as a society? Why would he create us to be that way? If he is all good! Is he a jokester?"

She yelps out. "Little Miss Priss! He isn't a jokester. You know what the bible says."

I quickly replied, "Well, yes I do Grandma, and I don't hardly believe a word of it. I believe it was written by some very controlling, greedy, men trying to control massive amounts of people and their surroundings. Men put fear in us years ago and fear is a great way to control people. And I don't believe God would really ask Abraham to kill his own son. Call it being obedient if you want. Sorry, but I'm throwing away all the trash I've been taught. I believe God is humanity. And by the way, how do you change the words of the Bible? What's up with the new testament? Who decided, now it's turn the other cheek, instead of an eye for an eye? Who did God tell this to?"

"You're getting a little sassy, young lady."

"No, Grandma, I'm just saying! I feel that nature is the core of our world and my God would want me to take care of it and its people. You need to watch AVATAR."

"What in the name of the Lord is Avatar?"

"Just a movie you need to watch. Maybe it will bring some light in your eyes. It did mine."

"You better be believing in something higher."

"I do believe there is something higher! Yes! of course. But could we survive without nature? No, no! We could not. Could we make things happen as a whole, if we were all to have the same thought at the same time? Of course we could. If we all wanted to end world hunger and we all thought about it at once, then definitely world hunger would end. Power of good thought by the people for the people, would be the answer, not prayer. I think we are just calling it two different things. When masses of people focus on peace together, it has been proven that crime rates go down, and peace is elevated. Here, you got to listen to this song by Jewel. Her songs and messages are my church and prayer and make way more sense than anything I've been taught."

JEWEL~ Life Uncommon. (Please buy her albums today!)

Don't worry Mother, it'll be alright
And don't worry Sister, say your prayers and sleep tight
It'll be fine lover of mine
It'll be just fine
Lend your voices only to sounds of freedom
No longer lend your strength to that which you wish
To be free from
Fill your life with love in bravery
And you shall lead a life uncommon
I heard your anguish
I have heard your hearts cry out
We are tired, we are weary, but we aren't worn out
Set down your chains, until only faith remains
Set down your chains
There are plenty of people who pray for peace
But if praying were enough it would have come to be
Let your words enslave no one and the heavens will
Hush themselves
To hear our voices ring out clear
With sounds of freedom, sounds of freedom
come on you unbelievers, move out of the way
there is a new Army coming and we are armed with faith
to live, we must give, to live
Fill your lives with love and bravery
And we shall lead a life uncommon

"Hum!" My grandma whispered, as she stared at the ceiling. "I tell you what, young lady. You might have a point, but I just wasn't raised that way. Marceline, can you walk me to my car?"

147

Mom winks at me as she helps Grandma from the bar stool. "Sure Momma!"

"Hey grandma, there is a few statements in the Bible I feel that hold true. One being the very first statement that God makes about human nature. It's not good for a human being, to be alone. -the giver of our God antidote, to our great human problem, so that we shall no longer be alone. Do you remember when I was younger? How you guys would try to scare me with the end of the world stuff. Quit trying to scare me with the world is coming to an end bullshit. Because if we all go at once, that would be fine by me. Because to me, the worst thing about death, is living without and missing the one you love. So, would it not be less painful to all go at once? Quit fearing the end of the world, every time some fool predicts it. We're all gonna die, so why are we fighting it? You know they say that the world is gonna end on December 21, 2012. Wonder if everyone is prepared? I think the Mayans probably just ran out of time and stone on their calendar."

My mom jumps in, "Missy, Mom is getting tired. Let me walk her on to her car. You know you shouldn't try to teach your grandma to suck eggs."

Then my grandma replied. "Child, I have to say! You do have a point. I'm just too old to do much movement or change my ways."

"Oh, Grandma! I beg to differ. It's never too late to change your ways. Old ways never open up new doors."

Quote: *"When the power of love overcomes the love of power, the world will know peace"-Jimi Hendrix*

Quote: *"In life, there are some things we might never really "get over." Sometimes the best we can do is just "get through." But that's okay-there's still a lot of beauty to find on the other side! ----Judith Belmont*

148

Quote: *"Our prime purpose in this life is to help others. and if you can't help them, at least don't hurt them."---Dalai Lama*

Religion and greed are the #1 and #2 killers in our society. A crazy girlfriend would be #3

Quote: *"Life is the jest of the Gods and there is no justice. You must learn to laugh... or else you'll weep yourself to death."---Bernard Cornwell*

JUST AN OPINION

I sit back and reflect and stare at the sky. Nature is amazing, the sky is so beautiful. I can't tell where it all starts and where heaven begins. Do I believe in heaven you may ask? Yes! I want to. We all want to. But I don't believe we should be scared shitless with the thought of hell, just so we can conform to only one belief. Heaven or hell, really... is that our only options? I need more choices than that. Just two? Really... really.. That's just like our presidential option, I need more than two and the green party don't count. They need to establish themselves first.

What about purgatory? Don't know much about that one. It sounds like maybe somewhere I would hang. If all the talk is true, wonder who's been there to know about this place? Plus, I bet my heaven isn't your heaven. I bet not even your own partner's heaven is the same as your own. My heaven would be backrubs and exotic foods. Some peoples' would be a fabulous golf course, or flowers or beaches and shit like that. We all have our own little vision of heaven and some of us create our own little heaven or hell. I wonder sometimes, was hell put in the stories to keep people straight and honest? Maybe! But thing is, most people are already good. Is God like our children's Santa Clause? You better be good, you better not pout, or he is not coming to see you this year. We put fear in our children before they even know what fear is. We instill their fears and prejudices. Actually if you think about it, we lie to our children for the first few years of their life. Like they say, it's your lie, tell it how you want to.

Here's my question about God,,, Do you test your kids with pain and hurt? Just let that marinate for a moment.

Let people think and create for themselves. Heaven sounds delightful... My heaven, not anyone else's. I want to take my memories with me, to that place, where all of those who get there before me and are waiting for my arrival. That's what I want to believe. Who wants the thought of nothing? It's terrifying. As long as we believe in something, there will always be hope. Don't judge other's hopes, just share yours with the ones you love. I don't know who is right or wrong. Maybe everyone is right, maybe everyone is wrong. Maybe just one is right, but I don't know who! Eeny-meeny-miney-moe! Maybe our own minds and souls will take us to the place we want to be. Maybe! Just maybe, we create our own heaven. Maybe, we are all just walking each other home. Carry the memories of people you love, in your hearts. Maybe they will travel with you to that place we will all go to some day. That place, that maybe, you, yourself created. Who are we really to know? I know who doesn't know. The people who carry and hold up their signs with names of stereotypes saying they are all going to hell. Please! I would rather be in what they call hell, than anywhere near them. Sorry! I would like to think I don't hate, but I hate haters!

JUST A THOUGHT. MAYBE WE ARE LITTLE BUGS OVER POPULATING SOMEONE ELSE'S EARTH. THEY KEEP FINDING, WHAT WE CALL "NATURAL WAYS" TO DESTROY AND ELIMINATE US.

Moral of the story usually comes at the end. I might just tell you this one first.

Quote: -*Men never do evil so completely and cheerfully as when they do it from a religious conviction---Blaise Pascal-*

In February of -------I took some of my workers/friends to Mardi Gras. I had already been there several times and seen these huge signs that said faggots are going to hell. They stand there all righteous with their children on their shoulders, in the middle of the street preaching and spewing out hatred. These are the type of people who would have written my daughter Summer off before she hit the ground. Gays can't raise children. We are the devil living in sin. Repent! Repent! They would scream in the streets. It just makes my blood boil!

Summer has survived and thrived, as I have myself. Her dad says, the more times we get kicked in the Roe Sham Bo, the harder we try. Now I know, Summer may have struggled at times, living in a community, that doesn't accept homosexuality. She had to get made fun of. I don't know for sure. She never had any complaints to me or she just kept it hidden. I even asked her a few times growing up, if people picked on her. She always said "No." Maybe she didn't, I guess I will never know. Maybe I wasn't hated, by most around here. For I had grown up here and maybe people could see, that I wasn't evil. Maybe a little wild, but who isn't around here. But I definitely didn't fit into their beliefs. We had defied the odds of what people think. Even you Ann Coulter.

151

Quote: *"A different world can not be built by indifferent people" Dr. Peter Marshall*

Quote: *"Before you speak to me about your religion, first show it to me on how you treat other people; before you tell me how much you love your God, show me how much you love all his children; before you preach to me of your passion for your faith, teach me about it through your compassion for your neighbors. In the end, I'm not as interested in what you have to tell or sell as I am in how you choose to live and give." Cory Booker*

Quote: *"I believe that the only true religion consists of having a good heart." Dalai Lama*

Quote: *"When I hear from people that religion doesn't hurt anything, I say. Really? Well, besides wars, the Crusades, the inquisitions, 911, the suppression of women, the suppression of homosexuals, fatwas, honor killings, suicide bombings, arranged marriages for minors, human sacrifice, burning witches, and systematic sex with children. I have a few quibbles." – Bill Maher*

We are all sliced from the same loaf of bread. We just happen to be toasted differently.

Quote: *"If this is going to be a Christian nation that doesn't help the poor people, either we got to pretend that Jesus wasn't as selfish as we are, always got to meet knowledge that he commanded us to love for and serve the needy without condition and then admit that we just don't want to do it." --- Steven Colbert*

Why do most churches focus on homosexuality? Especially when adultery made God's top ten list.

Please know that I'm not knocking anyone's religion during this spill. I know that before you speak you have to know your onions. Obviously this has all just been an opinion. I'm not rebelling against our creator, I'm rebelling against man's hateful teachings. Like the people in New Orleans. The extremists! They themselves become the biggest troublemakers, aside from the occasional drunk guy who wants to pull out his wienie, but he goes to jail. Why do these people feel they have the right to sit in the streets and preach hate and condemn all those around them? There are lots of good people in the world. There is no more evil in the world today than there was when the Romans were feeding people to the lions. Why does extreme religion always need someone to hate?

But anyway, Sarah, who is a friend of mine, (straight I mind you) began to wig out, just at the sight of these hateful signs. They had of course added some names to their list. It wasn't just homos anymore. They had upgraded to everyone but themselves. Democrats, sports fans, loudmouth women, name it and it was on there. Sarah screamed, "Hell no! Aw... hell no! That's some bullshit! Right there." She was getting so riled up. She had a few drinks and was actually hard to contain. She went up to one man and got in his face, "What is your problem, Dude? For real."

The man looked at her and said in a judgmental voice. "Hey lady! Go back home and fix your man some muffins. Cook for him and be home like a lady should be."

Sarah's nostrils began to flare instantly and shoots me and Cecil a look. "OMG! Did he just say what I thought he did?"

I made a deep whoo-whoo-whoo sound. "Damn!"

My friend Cecil chimed in as she did her swirly arm. "Hell yeah, he did!"

Sarah was completely wound up like a jack in the box. I thought something was about to go down. "I will show you some muffins," as she lifted her shirt. Then we all pulled up our shirts. We gave him some belly rolls. Which we all know are called muffin tops. If you didn't know, hum, sorry. That's what it's called, muffin tops and sometimes the Dunlap Disease. Belly dun lapped over her belt. Haha, but anyway, I bet you thought, Sarah was getting ready to show him her tits and call them muffins. Nope, no ta-tas. Just belly roll fat. Not every one that goes to Mardi Gras is there just to show their tits off. It's a diverse culture and you need a complete open mind to accept all the people around you in their individual ways. Acceptance would be the key.

Just remember, the most important thing. Well the thing I think is most important, Memories. Make happy memories, it's all we have. Forget about hate and judgment.

Joe Mack just told me the other day that he remembers me saying that when Summer was only days old. "Memories, good memories! That's what I will give my baby girl and that you have Missy. You have given her great ones. Sorry she doesn't have all those pictures you took, to help her always remember."

So I do believe it's the only thing, I mean the only thing, in this world that's really important. *"Remember when's"* they can't be replaced by a thing, except loss of memory. AND FIRE!!!!!

That's all I ask out of life, plus food and water and of course sex! Lots of sex.. Not random sex, but lots of sex with the one you love. But if you choose random, I can't judge you. I just don't prefer it. Definitely no sex if you're my child, under 25 and not married. Sound hypocritical? Of course! It's my baby girl! My world. So you think!!!! No sex for her. Think again.

Summer and Lauren

So one afternoon, I found myself sitting here in disbelief. Why? Because I found a love letter about her and her boyfriend's first time having sex at the age 16. My mouth dropped to the floor. What was I gonna do? You wanna call her out, but how embarrassing for the both of you. Especially since I didn't get caught till I wrote this book. My daughter has always been a good kid, a big hearted turd I would say.

Mind you, I don't think you're a bad kid just because you have sex. It is somewhat the natural thing to do. Just don't be my kid. Back in my grandma's days, they were already married off at that age. I'm sure they were having sex, even when they didn't want to. Hell even Maw-maw didn't want to even in her adult years. Don't know which is worse. It's kinda a catch twenty-two. Times are different now. But I was still struggling with the fact that my kid had done it and I didn't know. She had been a sword holder. Holy Shit!

I hadn't quite figured out how I was going to handle the situation. So when Summer, came home from school one day, I had to go ahead and call her out. Even though my plan of attack wasn't in order yet. I had to confront her on the letter, the sex letter. As her and her friend Lauren walked through the cafe side door, she casually said, "hey Mom, what's for supper?"

"I don't know, you tell me." I said in a smart ass tone."

"What do you mean? What's up with the tone?" She replied.

"You got something ya wanna tell me?" I kept my face even.

"HUUUUH?" She said with a totally confused look on her face. "You're making absolutely no sense right now. You been drinking?"

I was just taunting her and obviously beating around the bush. It was hard for me to even bring it up in a normal manner. "You got something you wanna tell me."

"MOM!!!! I have no idea what you're talking about." As she huffed and walked on over to the soda machine.

I looked at Lauren and winked, "Summer! Have you written any letters lately?" She knew, immediately, what I was referring to. She sat down at the bar as her head sunk.

"What are you talking about?" I'm sure her anxiety was soaring.

"I think you know. Have you done anything you haven't told me about?" They both already knew what I was talking about before I even said the words.

156

"Um, maybe!" as she squirms and replies in a very quiet voice.

"Oh really! Can you enlighten me?"

Lauren chimes in with a big shit eaten grin. "Missy, I never have. I wouldn't!"

"Is that right Lauren?" As I cleared my throat.

"Yes ma'am." As she looked at me again with her bleached smile.

"I call bullshit on both of you. So, Summer tell me."

Summer responded quickly in her rapid speech. "Mom! I only did it once for about five minutes."

"Five minutes! What do you mean five minute? Did he wrap it up?" I spurted out.

"Mom!!! It was only once. Stop it!"

"Summer, are you missing a couple colors out of your rainbow? Do I have to remind you? Do I? Your dad and I only did it once."

"Look and you got me!"

"Yeah yeah! Whatever! Don't play that card. Even though it ended up being the greatest thing that ever happened, because you came out of it. But I was 25. I once had a friend to ask how long I dated your dad, and I said, around 15 minutes. So how long do you think it takes you silly girl?"

"Mom! Please! I don't wanna hear about you and Dad." as she twisted her mouth with disgust.

"I mean really! Summer, that's all it takes. You know I told you about Ann. You still remember Ann don't you? She worked here."

"Yes Mom! I do."

"You remember her bragging one week about her pull out method and the next week we got the news she was pregnant. Now, I told you if you ever found yourself in that situation, you needed to be on the pill. He needed to wrap it and pull it, and you did none of those."

"Lauren chimes in raising her hand. "I will Missy, if I ever do." Sounding like the female version of Eddie Haskell.

157

"Summer, I would advise you to go to the house, workers will be showing up soon and we look like we obviously have a disagreement going on here. You should absolutely know better."

"Ok, bye Mom! Sorry." As she hung her head.

"See ya Missy!" Lauren says as she bounces out of the cafe waving like a beauty queen.

All I could think was, I've taught her better. To think better than that. But that's all we can do, is try to teach them. We can't control their environment or pressures. That would become smothering and things would maybe be even worse.

Life is also about understanding, and I was trying to understand why my daughter had sex. Oh!!!! I know why, she is a teenager. They're curious and horny and sometimes think they're in love. These parents who think we shouldn't try to teach our kids safe sex are fools. Especially when they got hormones pouring outta their skin. It's like keeping bees off honey. I mean, of course we should teach them not to, but let's be realistic already! We should at least, teach them safe sex, just in case. Don't cha think? But sad to say, kids don't always listen to our advice and this would be one of those cases. What's a parent to do?

QUOTE: Does sex education encourage sex? Many parents are afraid that talking about sex with their teenagers will be taken as permission for them to have sex. Nothing could be further from the truth. If anything, the more children learn about sexuality from talking with their parents and the teachers and reading accurate books, the less they feel compelled to find out for themselves. ---- Benjamin Spock, Dr. Spock's Baby and child care. --- Thank you Benjamin, my sentiments exactly.

RUBBER BAND BACK—

I was just in the chiropractor's office the other day. As I was leaving, the woman told me to take care. Then I fell straight out the door onto my face. Let's brush off and move along with a story. I keep having back spasm and all my muscles keep getting locked up. I had one of these things to happen before, but this time, damn! I was totally frozen in a position that wasn't very becoming.

Mary, thought this was funny and had to share.

Mary and I were in the cafe preparing to open, when she heard me scream. She looked over and I was stuck on the ground, doggy style. She had never seen me have one of these. So she came running over trying to pick me up. I screamed even louder.

She threw up her arms as if someone was shooting her, and said in a panic. "What is wrong?"

"I can't move. Do I have a boa constrictor around me?"

She was unsure what to think. "Do what? Are you fucking with me?"

"Actually I'm not. I was just trying to make a funny. But I really can't move and it's hard to breathe."

"What! So what do you want me to do?"

"Find me some muscle relaxers! Immediately! Like yesterday! I believe my back has locked up again."

She franticly called my mom and it seemed like she was on there for a dick year. "Why are you still on the phone?" I screamed.

"I don't know Missy! I don't know! What do you want me to do, Tiger? I'm trying to get someone over here to help."

"I need muscle relaxers! Call Amy!"

While we were waiting, Mary still was running around franticly. "How can I help you?"

"You can't! It's got to give on its own. My muscles are stuck!" I was kneeling there, as my hands began to shake. My body and arms were vibrating on the floor. So Mary got a bright idea and crawled under me to hold me up. This was a sad sight. We couldn't help but laugh.

"What are you doing?" I asked.

"Trying to hold you up."

Her body was under my body with her ass facing the door. I was laughing so hard, slobber was dripping from my mouth straight onto the floor. "This is gonna be so embarrassing. What if a customer walks in? This is gonna look really weird."

"I know right! We can say we're playing twister with an invisible board." she said.

About that time, here comes Mom and Joe Eddie flying through the door. When they spotted us, they stopped dead in their tracks. They stood there with concerned and confused faces. "I do believe you girls have found yourself in a pickle. What is going on here?"

We started to laugh. Mary crawled out from under me and there I was stuck in my position looking like I was ready for some more doggy style. Mom asked, "Missy, can you get up?" then she smacked Joe Eddie on the back, "Joe Eddie help her!"

"No! Don't touch me!" I screamed.

Then Amy came barging through the door and when she turned the corner she said. "What the hell are y'all doing to her?"

"Just give me the pills Amy! Stick one in my mouth. Hurry! Please!"

"Well Missy! We're gonna get you off of that floor, before someone walks in this cafe."

Joe Eddie begin to lift me. I swear, it felt like I was having a heart attack. My breath was taken away. My mom looked at me with concern. "You look awful. You are pale as a ghost! We are taking you to the hospital."

"I'm telling you guys, I don't need to go. It's just got to loosen up."

"What if you're having a stroke?" Amy said out of concern.

"I'm not having no damn stroke, you fool!"

"Maybe! You could be!" she said.

"But I'm not!"

They still made me go as they drug me to the car. It wasn't a stroke of course. I knew, what it was. Exactly what I thought it was. My muscles had constricted, just like a ball of rubber bands. Only this time they constricted around my lungs. When it does that, I'm done for, until I get the muscles to relax. Stress of the job, house burning, having a teenager. That's what the Dr. said. He asked me, "Do you smoke?"

"Yes sir, I do."

Then he replied. "Well, don't tell anyone this, but you may need to keep smoking for awhile with what you've been going through. Just try to stop as soon as possible."

Shit! I got sidetracked again. So the receptionist and my mom, somehow got on the subject of TV and sex when the woman said. "Omg, the stuff they have on TV these days. No wonder our kids are having so

161

much sex and having babies as teens."

I had to rudely jump in. "It's not TV that causes kids to have sex. I would rather my kid watch it, than be doing it. Now, I'm not talking about porn, okay! So chill." Lady in the back chuckled. "Take my mom for instance. She was 18 when *Leave it to Beaver* was on. So Mom! How many girls in your class left high school pregnant?"

She replied, "Oh about 18 of us. I think!"

"Wow!! That was in the 60s, right? No pregnant girls in my class and none in Summer's. So how would statistics add up to TV having a role in teen pregnancy? Especially if you wasn't watching any sex on TV."

Now I know, I said my kid had sex once, according to her. But most of the time, she was either watching TV, on computer or having friends over. I didn't put studying in that category, because I can't say I ever saw her do any. She is a pretty bright kid. She got a 24 on her S.A.T. score and made it into Bellarmine University. Which is a very classy school around here in Ky. KY jelly, haha! Brings me right back to the sex talk.

I guess by now you have all figured out I didn't care about sex during high school. I was different and didn't really think about it. All I knew at the time, is that, I didn't want to have sex. I was more into hanging out with friends, for the first 25 years of my life. But I did have sex. So I guess that's the reason I couldn't get mad at Summer if she had. Only because, that I found myself having sex at 16 on my maw-maws living room floor, drunk as hell. BTW, you remember Jake. I will never forget him asking me, "If we do it once, I won't ask again." 2 days later. "Can we have sex?" Two days later, I said. "Can we break up?"

Yes, over the next few years, I had sex again, but not till I was out of high school. When I would date a guy, I could never seem to hold them off from sex, more than nine months. If I decided to do it, or if the whiskey let me do it, of course we would break up. The thought of doing it again didn't please me much. So this continued till I was pregnant with Summer at age 25. Thanks Joe Mack, for ending my dilemma. It was the best unplanned journey I've ever encountered. I am thankful to have him as a baby daddy. I've known him forever and definitely forever, now. So if you do the math, yes I had sex with a few different guys. All my other friends dated, so it was a cover up I guess. I was trying to be normal. That in which, what normal was thought to be at the time. There is no such thing as normal, and everyone can't follow the *Leave it to Beaver* social norms. That's bull shit. Who gets to decide what's normal anyway? Normal has changed since the beginning of time. Live and let live until it intrudes on your own turf.

People should stop expecting normal from me anyway. We all know it's never gonna happen, or maybe I got that backwards. I keep expecting something normal, but everyone around me is aware, that's not gonna happen.

How about a blonde joke?

2 blondes are trying to unlock their car. The first blonde tries to unlock it with a coat hanger. The 2nd one says "hurry up it's starting to rain and the top is down!" **Mom didn't get it. Beverly said that Mom is a blonde at heart.**

LOUD MOUTH LIPSTICK LESBIAN LIBERAL

2016 has been a weird one Mr. Grinch. I mean weird in all sorts of ways. Let's start here at home with something simple and recent, like a life size talking Santa. Well it only talks when plugged in and something has to makes it talk. So it's Christmas Eve and the family is here. No one knew he was upstairs, except Joe Mack, because earlier that day he looked up and spotted him out of the corner of his eye, and about jumped out of his pants. We had been loud all night, so he should have been sounding off regularly, but he didn't. Then around 9o'clock Mr. Claus, sounded off with his loud, creepy, deep, Ho! Ho! Ho! Merry Christmas. Everyone jumped. Summer said, "that shit is creepy!" Then Mom chimed in, "How does he know we're Ho's?"

That was the last we heard of him that night. Then Christmas night, Summer and I are sitting here and he randomly starts to sing again. We about jumped off the couch. It actually made our hair stand on end. I thought about going up and unplugging him, but I didn't. Summer left soon after that. I ended up falling asleep on the couch. I awoke the next morning to the Santa singing abrasively. I thought that maybe Digger Bear walked past him or something. No biggie, I will just try to go back to sleep. I laid there unnerved as it sang three more times. Damn!

Instead of going and unplugging him, I headed to my bed. I thought there is no way he is gonna sing again. Damn, if that freaking didn't start to sing again. Just plain weird.

Yes, I know that is nothing compared to the madness of 2016, just wanted to start lightly and ease you in. Just an appetizer.

Well, what else? 2016 has stolen many of our Icons we grew up with from the 80s. It has stolen people like *Prince, David Bowie and George Michael, Muhammand Ali,* and many more. Like *Florence Henderson,* you know, we all loved her. Who doesn't know who the *Brady Bunch* is. Our first dysfunctional family.

Then 2016 went and took *Mr. Gene Wilder.* Everybody loves Willie Wonka, if you don't, there is something wrong with you. Just saying. Even during high school and my party days, we would all go to Maw-maws and watch it. We didn't have DVRs then, so we had to fit it into our schedule. We would stop and drop whatever we were doing, just to get our Wonka fix.

We lost *Allan Thicke* too, but I didn't much care about him growing up. But R.I.P. Allan. And of course we lost *Pat Summit.* Best woman basketball coach ever.

2016 please don't take *Betty White*. She is the sweetest thing ever. You've already taken all the good ones and left us with such a dishonor role, like *Trump, Locktne, Coulter and Weinner*. *Locktne* went on *Dancing with the Stars* to fix everything. Not sure why *Weinner* hasn't gotten on there yet? It fixes everything. Maybe he is planning on trying out for an Oscar Mayer hot dog commercial. Come on Trump and Ann, it's your turn, to dance your ignorance away.

Update: Holy shit 2016! Stop!!!!! You just took *Carrie Fisher*, AKA 'Princess Leia' from *Star Wars*. 2017 the Dishonor role is waiting for your call. Just saying. I'm wise enough to know it could be my turn too. I'm about to release a double HOLY SHIT. *Carrie Fisher's* mom, *Debbie Reynolds*, just passed away and it's only a day later. They are saying she actually died of a broken heart. Is that possible?

In conclusion your Honor. No matter who died in 2016, Trump is still the worse thing to happen. When is someone gonna have a come to Jesus talk with him. I feel so sad for America right now.

"Trump speaking his mind isn't refreshing. It's appalling. Coca-Cola is refreshing." ----*Carrie Fisher*

"Stay afraid, but do it anyway. What's important is in action. You don't have to be confident. JUST DO IT and eventually the confidence will follow."---*Carrie Fisher*

I would talk about some of my relationships, but too much shit going on in the world to talk about any of that. Like the lady said, "aint nobody got time for that." Plus, if Brangelina can't work it out. I guess no one can. But at least the Cubs finally won. Yay, for Cub fans. Just know that even a blind squirrel finds a nut every now and then.

165

ELECTION 2016

Watching the 2016 election should have made you feel uneasy if you have a conscience. When us girls (high school friends) were at my book signing, sitting at the bar watching the results, an overwhelming realization came over me. Houston we have a problem! Our country is still racist. Summer's eyes were swelling. "Mom! What's going on?"

"Well Hun! Emails. Trump does something racist. What about her emails? Trump does something treasonous. What about her emails? Trump makes fun of the handicap. What about her emails? Email, Email, Email! Marsha, Marsha, Marsha!"

SNL nailed it when they did that skit about the regular Joe watching the election. It was us to a T. Just watch the skit, so I don't have to tell you how we reacted.

I've got a few things to say about all this and I'm gonna say it, despite my daddy's advice to stay out of politics while running a public business. Screw that! It's time to throw my hat into the ring. I pretty much stayed quiet through this whole jacked up election. It was so controversial that people were scared to even put signs in their yard. This was a new one for me. I don't recall anyone having to be that scared before and worried about being assaulted by their neighbor. I mean come on! Come on people! I'm not trying to raise a red flag to a bull, but it's time to speak up for all humanity. At this point I'm not worried about selling books or feeding steaks to people who are hateful, racist and homophobic. Prior to this I used to be carefree and wasn't much into politics. But this election has changed my life, not sure if it's for the good or bad. We will see. I think it has made me worry about others well being a little more than usual.

Summer cried the whole next day after the election. Not because she is a millennium cry baby, but just for the mere fact, she is worried about humanity. She watches documentaries and is concerned about what our nation will become. This is not a Democratic or a Republican dispute I am having. It's a humanity thing. Maybe everyone should chill and go eat some ice cream.

I am a humanitarian. That's what I am. I've been quiet, but it's time to unleash the Loudmouth Liberal Lesbian inside of me. It's time to throw the ice cream out the window for a moment.

2016 is the year of people standing up for what they believe. I am here to join the fight. I can't do much from my location, stuck out here in the boonies, but I can speak up and speak loud and I can do that without hate.

I don't want Trump to fail, let me get that straight. He is gonna be leading our country. I don't want to see people fail, starve and fight. It's a catch 22, because we will get so many, "I told you so's" if he does succeed and I guess that will be an easy pill to swallow. But the message that he is sending out is hatred, and that, I can't take. I literally need an air horn for every time I have to listen to him speak. We should all respect people's different points of view and the right to speak out, as long as it doesn't spill out hate and violence.

Capernick, could have been a good example until he decided not to vote. Let's get one more thing straight also, before I go any further. I do not agree with anyone who burns the flag. I also believe our Veterans need taken care of way better than they have been. It is our government's responsibility to do that with our tax money.

Let's talk about social media for a moment and the fact that our President elect tweets in the middle of the night. The first lady says she wants to stop cyber bullying. Yeah! Right! When her husband, Mr. President elect, is the number one guilty bully. Take his twitter account from him. Start there, woman! And speaking of woman! What about women's rights? You know who should be in charge of women's rights? Some dudes. You know that's a joke, right. No man should ever be able to vote on anything when it comes to women's rights. The republican government wants to deregulate everything, then turn around and regulate a woman's vagina. WTF

And what about women shaming women on social media. Wow! I've never seen so many ugly people call people ugly in my life. If I was like you guys, I would have done posted your ugly asses. What's up with that? Especially when you're shaming an over weight lady for being in the gym. You are a complete fucktard.

Let's talk sexual harassment and rape shall we. What the hell is going on with that? How does someone only get two months for getting caught in the act of having sex with an unconscious girl. How is that possible? Especially after my uncles sat in prison for years for growing pot, a commodity that people want!

Joe Keith, Grandma and Jimmy

Thank God, *Megan Kelly*, finally called out *Roger Ailes*. But even he only got a smack on the hand. No wonder women don't speak up. Especially since someone who got accused by 12 different people still got elected as our president.

President elect, is allowing young boys to think it's okay to disrespect a woman. Locker room talk, my ass. "AIRHORN!!!!!!" Every thing he said was cringe worthy. I had to stop one of my young employees right in his tracks when he was messing with one of my young female workers. It's disgusting. But he is young and hasn't been taught better. Monkey see monkey do, and approval from our president elect. He got all defensive with me when I called him out and said he likes her. And I said, son! That's not what I stated. We all have lust for people. Realize the difference. You're too good to be ending up in jail for sexual assault, because you think it's okay to grab a woman by her pussy."

North Dakota pipeline. Water protectors for us all. Who are the idiots that think we can survive without water? Fucktards I say! Fucktards! I would like to see someone drink a coin, a dollar bill or how about some delicious tasting oil. Let's see how that works for your survival.

Temporary victory on December 7th. Let's see how this plays out in 2017.

Quote: *"It's been almost a month, will I ever get used to Trump? Hell no. It's like watching a toddler playing with a gun. You're always nervous." ~Bill Maher.*

Yes, I'm a dirty liberal. I will accept that to be all that I am. I will take it any day. And if someone wants to knock my liberal behavior when it is based on the willingness to respect or accept behavior or opinions of people other than my own and open to new ideas, yes that's me. You can try and shut me down for this. But that makes you a narrow minded ass hole, afraid of change. Yes, that makes you a fucktard too. And I'm also sorry that it would offend anyone, that I respect, individual rights, freedom and favoring individual liberties. The way I see it, that spells out. TRUE AMERICAN.

Quote: *Patriotism means stand by the country. It does not mean stand by the president. --- Theodore Roosevelt.*

I like traditions and all, started a few of my own. But when something has to change, something has to change! Fear not! Fear makes us weaker! We need unity! When you know your neighbor, you always feel safer. Let's do this on a national level. Except for Putin! I can't accept Putin! Putin stinks just like a poot. Reminds me of a rhyme we made up in school about a teacher and a student:

Sister Teresa Martin, came a fartin once along a day. Billy Newton came a pootin and blew her out of the way. Come on Billy, we need you to do some pootin on Putin.

And I can't accept Ann Coulter either. Wait a minute! Someone said I need a niche to be successful. I just found my niche. I HATE ANN COULTER. I will do everything I can to shut that raggedy ass hateful bitch down. She is a fucktard devil. Now let's move on. Changed my mind on the hate thing, I ain't got the time or energy for that. Hate literally wears you out, for real. Where do people find the energy for that?

Summer sends me a text:

"Btw. *Rob Kardashian* and *Chyna* had their baby and named it Dream. *Dream Kardashian*! We now live in a world where (reality star!) Donald Trump is president and there is a *Dream Kardashian*! What is life? Am I dead? Is this a dream? A joke? The twilight zone? What is happening?"

"Summer, honey, I hope that the name Dream stays the least of your worries."

"No Mom! This is the least of my worries."

"Well, baby, I hope that stays the least of your worries with tiny hands running the country now."

"Is it possible?"

"It's possible."

Bad Day

Who won????

Actual Trump statements:

"You have to come up, and we can come up with many different plans. In fact, plans you don't even know about will be devised because we're going to come up with plans. Healthcare plans! That will be so good."

"I actually don't have a bad hair line."

"People love me. And you know what, I have been very successful. Everybody loves me."

"If Ivanka weren't my daughter, perhaps I'd be dating her."

"It's freezing and snowing in New York – we need global warming!"

I got to hide. What's happening right now?

Trump's plan to fight ISIS

……………………………..

……………………………..

……………………………..

 ……………………………

……………………………..

……………………………..

This is intentionally left blank. But the plan is great. Let me tell you. So great. So great we don't even have the plan yet. So great!

How about a joke?

An airplane was about to crash. There were four passengers on board, but only three parachutes. The first passenger said, I am Steph Curry, the best NBA basketball player. The Warriors and my millions of fans need me, and I can't afford to die." So he took the first pack and left the plane.

The second passenger, Donald Trump, said, "I am the newly elected US president, and I am the smartest president in American history, so my people don't want me to die." He took the second pack and jumped out of the plane.

The third passenger, the Pope, said to the fourth passenger, a schoolboy, "my son, I am old and don't have many years left, you have more years ahead so I will sacrifice my life and let you have the last parachute."

The little boy said, "that's okay, your Holiness, there's a parachute left for you. America's smartest president took my school bag."

Come on you guys, he is smart. He is coming up with such new wonderful vocabulary. Like Big-ly and Brag-go-doc-ious. What a fucktard? Mom and I have just created a new word too. Maybe we will run for President in 2020. We were confused for a moment. When I said the house was jalapidated. She looked at me, "I think Momma has used that word before. What exactly does it mean?" So I googled it. Nothing! I told Mom to call Grandma, because I know I have heard her say this word. When I googled it, it came up dilapidated. Which means shaggy, battered, beat up, rickety, shaky and unsound.. It was kind of the definition we were looking for, but not the word. But I still knew that jalapidated had been said and I was wondering where we got it. Then the word jalopy came to mind, which is an old beat up car. So hence came the word, jalapidated. Which I, in return, think tiny hands, is

175

a Jalapidated man. How is that for a new word, Mr. Chop? I'm sorry readers, but I think Trump is all smoke and mirrors.

Which takes me back to Facebook. I feel proud that I come up with new words sometimes. I can never get my books published quick enough to get my new word out before someone else post it on Facebook. I don't know how this happens.

So the quote on Facebook is "I'm aware that I'm a bitch. Are you aware that you're a fucktard?"

Oh well! Moving along. Trump, won and I respect our voting system. But I don't respect him. I do not have to respect him! So forgive me, if I don't take my readings from his moral compass. He doesn't seem to have one. Obviously he doesn't understand as president, every word matters. Because believe me, I'm sure people are judging every word I say. I don't believe in complete political correctness, but from my president elect, I do. Comics keep it coming though. We know America is about to get butt hurt and we better be able to joke about it.

Did all you Trump supporters not catch the fact that Trump called you all NUTS. He literally made fun of you for coming up with the term, "drain the swamp." It wasn't a media spin, it came right out of his mouth, just like an egg shooting right out of a chicken's ass. It's true, not fake, that's where eggs come from.

I would love to feel the burn at this moment. This would be a time for prayer for me. Grandma would be proud to know I'm thinking about it. Please Lord, Please! May Trump not destroy us! May he do well.

Please! Please! Please! Dear Lord! I am begging you.

LITTLE BUTT

Hope she has better luck than me in that tree!

So here lately, I've been watching my little 8-year old cousin. We will call her Little Butt. She reminds me of my own little butt (Summer) when she was this age. I really miss her getting off the bus here. I guess this little butt is my replacement for the moment. She has more sense than most adults I know. Like for real. Even though she can be a hard headed little shit. I told her she was one and no sooner than the words came out of my mouth, I realized. I sounded just like my daddy.

Little Butt was up here educating herself, when she asked. "How do you get a fine if you touch the wire? You can't get a fine if you're dead. Look right here, it says. Touching wire causes instant death. $200 fine." Then throws up her hands, like is this shit for real. "Look at this one. It says garbage only. No trash. What's the difference Missy?" Then she goes on reading and starts to rattle. "You don't know if a Walrus is Gay.

Shut up world! Missy you're gonna have to suck on one of these Skittles. It's delicious."

This kid has a comment on everything. I put in a movie. When the FBI warning came up she said, "Say hello to your friend at the FBI. They're not your friends."

Then a movie trailer came on about a scary movie. If you say or even think the evil thing's name, it will get you. She looked at me with confusion and threw up her hands, "If they tell you not to think about it, you have to think about it, to not think about it. You know what I mean, Missy?"

"I sure do Little Butt."

Then she changes the subject. "I want to be an unattended child."

I was confused. "Why on earth would you want that?"

"Because, I wanna free puppy."

"Well, I can leave you outside by the dumpster tomorrow. I wonder if they will think you're trash or garbage?"

She falls back on the couch and starts to laugh. "You made me snort my laughter." Then jumps up and starts jumping up and down on the couch.

"Calm down there, Little Butt."

"I won't calm down till you give me a hug." So I hugged her and we started watching the Lion King. She notices the comparison of Scar and Trump. Her logical brain is activated. This kid is smart and has a heart. Then she got to telling me a story about a man beating a baby. Now, I don't know if that's something she should have ever seen, but she did. And I'm sure it was on social media. But she threw out her hands and said sadly. "Missy, I just don't understand why people are so mean! This dad was playing X-box and his little two-year old unplugged the game and he beat the baby. All he had to do was plug it back in. The world is so crazy!"

"I know baby, let's watch the movie."

178

OPINIONS AREN'T FACTS

So when people on social media just keep saying, I'm just voicing my opinion, that's good and all, if you know the difference between an opinion and a fact. "AIRHORN" When you go against a fact to voice an opinion, that's when it becomes stupidity. You are definitely a fucktard. So can we please stop justifying ignorance. Telling someone that you hate this book would be an opinion. Me struggling to write this book, would be a fact.

I'm all about unity and working together and opening my eyes and my ears to all ideas. But it doesn't mean that my beliefs and views just got wiped off the map. Not gonna happen! There are too many people on both sides spewing hatred and I'm not down with that. Nor will I conform like a robot. That's what they did when the Jews experienced Genocide. Were they good people? Yes, I'm sure they were, but to look away and pretend things are okay when your neighbor is being dragged from their home, for no other reason than they are different, you become part of the problem. I will not look the other way. When people see injustices, everyone should stand up. I'm not the type that is gonna sit back and watch someone being wronged. It's time to separate the sheep from the goat. Just like that bitch at Jefferson Mall! How sad! Spewing out racist rhetoric! That lady probably doesn't know the difference between coon poop and honey. Although I hate drama and involving myself in someone else's business. Lickety-split, I would have stepped up. Someone needed to punch that hateful bitch in the throat. Not that I agree with violence. I'm just saying! Now that's an opinion. Here's another opinion or let's say statement. Bitch! Before you run your mouth, look at yourself. Seriously, look in the mirror and tell me what you see. Mom said, you looked in the mirror and seen a big oversized vagina the size of Mammoth cave, and that's why you're so hateful.

I've seen a lot of denial in my time. It's very strange and hilarious but at the same time quite scary. I can't believe that people can't look back and see that we were all immigrants once upon a time. I thought hind sight was 20/20. So how is history about to repeat itself? Do I want terrorist in the country? No! Hell no! But come on! How can people set back and watch people being bombed and sent away to starve to death? It's easy for people to turn their heads until it happens to them. What are these people gonna do when they are wronged and there is no one to turn to?

We have so much more in common with people than we think. Just like a point Summer brought to my attention the other day. "Mom! Why do people around here call Islam people goat humpers? We've got goat humpers in Kentucky."

"Yes we do Hun! Yes, we do!"

Sorry! Thought that was funny. Hope that's not what we have in common.

Eight years of Obama. Does everyone still have their guns? I do! He better hurry up and get busy if he is gonna do all the crazy things people said he was going to do. Shit! Time is out. Guess it's time to turn back the clock.

HYPOCRISY! HYPOCRISY! HYPOCRISY! Why should we support Mr. Chop when Obama was blocked at every turn? I feel that America has messed up by voting in the fox to watch the hen house. But we will see. Fingers crossed.

Beverly and I are having a dispute again. She keeps trying to stick words together that don't belong together. She stuck air horn together and it turned red and she yelled out "shit! That makes me madder than hell." I just started grinning like a Cheshire cat. We are both about 50/50 on our rightness. She also kept capitalizing trumps name, but I don't think he deserves a capital y'all, or as Beverly would spell it, "ya'll." Another one of our disputes. Humor in the workshop again.

MOM'S POT STORY

Mom trying to look like daddy with that hat on.

One evening I was coming home from my book signing party, that my friend Erin had thrown for me. Heidi and I were sitting in the front seat and Mom and Kathleen were in the back. (They're twins! So we don't need a picture of both of them.) We were all just chatting away when Mom yells, "Y'all need to bring it on down a notch. You are talking too loud. I got to tell you about my pot story." So the conversation pretty much turns to the two ladies in the back, the very interesting duo. "Well, go ahead Mom." I said.

Mom paused. "Well, we kept on smoking and smoking, Kathleen and I. We smoked one together. It must have been really good pot."

Kathleen said, "It was. It was called…" Before she could tell us what it was called, Mom interrupted, "So anyway!"

Kathleen interrupted back and said, "It was Thai weed."

"Whatever kind of weed it was! It's not going well for me at all. These son of a bitches start saying, 'What are we gonna do with her? Talking about me, because I had gotten higher than a Georgia pine."

Kathleen said, "He said what?"

"The girl said, what are we gonna do with her? I knew she was talking about me. So that got me really leery."

Kathleen tried to speak, "listen to this….." But Mom continued to speak over her. I was curious and asked. "Who is high?"

Mom said, "I was! I knew something was wrong with me now, something is wrong! Wrong with me! So we go to her boyfriend's house. Grundy's house Missy. We're in Lebanon, at some ole big haunty looking house. I get up there and I'm just so high."

Kathleen is still trying to give her two cents worth, but momma ain't stopping or letting her get a word in edgewise, as Mom continues. "I'm just thinking of Missy. I'm never gonna get to see her again and I'm gonna stay like this forever."

Kathleen giggles. "It made me feel the same way."

I replied in confusion. "I thought Mom was high."

Kathleen said, "Well in this story she is."

"You two are confusing."

"Listen Missy! They were in the room, going "pst-pst pst-pst-pst" whispering about me."

Kathleen smacks her leg. "Tell them about the song. The one about them coming to take you away."

"No.... no!"

"Yes... yes!"

"No, no, no! That wasn't the song. I was really thinking they were gonna do something with me. So before I know it, they got a freakin fucking (loud) doctor in there. Just in there looking at me."

We all bust out laughing, as Heidi asked in disbelief. "A doctor?"

"Look, because they don't know what to do with me."

Kathleen laughed. "The doctor is coming to take you away?"

"It was Doctor Wilber.. Look! Look! And I was in a corner."

Kathleen says, "Listen......." As if she is gonna get a story in. Mom isn't gonna let that happen as she hits the back of the seat. "No! Wait! Look I was so high. But anyway, I know why they called the doctor! Because I'm in a corner, daring anyone to come close to me. Then I look up, and that's when Doctor Wilber....." She paused. "Back in those days, they wore their white coat and white jacket everywhere. He looked at them and said. "Get some coffee in this girl!" Then I said, you ain't coming neeeeeear me! All I knew is that they were coming to get me! They're really..... coming to get me. So anyway, he knew I was really high. I remember plain as day what he said, "If we get some coffee in you, you're gonna be fine." I was like no! No! I'm not! I'm not ever coming down!"

We all laughed again and I said, "Mom you must have been going off the deep end?"

"Bet I was cute doing it. Look y'all. I kept thinking about Missy. I can't never let anyone see me like this. Don't you understand. He kept trying his hardest to give me that coffee. So he would take his foot and slide it over to me, cause he didn't want to hand it to me. He was scared to get near me. Guess I was like some ole cornered crazy dog. He put that coffee on the hardwood floor and he would take his shoe and scoot it over to me. I started drinking it because I knew, I needed to do something. I think I might have even been licking it up like a dog, I'm not sure. When I finished, he said we're gonna go outside. I want you to get some air. But by that time, I'm thinking, I'm gonna knock the plum shit out of White Boy. That's what he called himself, White Boy. The doctor said, let White Boy walk you up the hill. It was a big ole hill. He said trust me. So we went up and down, up and down, and probably on my third round coming down that hill, I felt me coming down. I mean I r-e-a-l-l-y felt myself coming down. Said I would never smoke it again. And I've done a lot of heavy drugs and ain't nothing ever felt like that. That damn joint! I'm serious! I will never smoke pot again. It was the worst feeling in my life."

At this point I would have jumped in and told my experience like that, but I knew there wasn't gonna be a chance to do that with these two in the back seat. So I just sealed my lips and listened and waited. Then Kathleen goes for the field goal. "I had a bad feeling myself. It was in sixty-nine."

Mom said, "Tell Heidi about the bomb fire. Big monster's shadow."

Kathleen said, "that's normal."

Mom laughs, "That's normal? Why was it normal? That's not normal! Who smokes pot and wants to see big monsters? You think I wanna see big monsters?"

"I was paranoid, is what is was. It was Marceline!"

Mom said, "That's what happened to me. I got real paranoid on it. I really thought, oh man! Go ahead Kathleen."

"Well, we went to Green River."

As Mom interrupts again. "When you hear someone in the back room

184

whispering, what are we gonna do with her? That's scary. I was really messed up and them talking about me like that. I thought yeah! They will be coming to take me away. Coming to put me in the funny farm. Go ahead Kathleen, finish your story."

"Well you know Phyllis's husband was big on pot, okay. I got three stories, I smoked it three times back then. And that John, God bless his soul, he is dead now. He jumped out of a plane to parachute and it caught the tail of the plane and he landed on the ground. Hard! Poor thing. He really did. He wasn't smoking pot though."

"Then Mom says "Get to your story."

"Where was I?"

"You're at Green River, goony. The bomb fire!"

"Oh yeah, Green River bomb fire. My sister in law asked me to smoke a joint, and I said I'm scared to smoke a joint, because I heard things about it. Just take a couple hits she said. Then we're out by the tent and the tent next door...." Then Mom interrupts again. "Is that where you saw those monstery shadows?"

"Yes! They had a dog, and it was the size of the tent." as she laughed and repeated. "It was the size of the tent."

Mom started smacking her arm. "Don't get laughing. Tell the story."

Kathleen holds her side. "I can't help it. I was crying, and I saw that shadow on the tent. It was a dog, but I really did think it was something from outer space or something."

Mom gets all rowdy. "Your story doesn't compare to this one I'm about to tell. Go on and finish it."

Kathleen replies with frustration. "Well! If it doesn't compare to yours, I'm not gonna tell it. Really Marceline! Can I tell a story? Can I tell my story?"

Mom said, "I doubt it."

"Missy, listen to this. Phyllis's husband. He was a nice, good looking guy."

Mom jumps back in and says, "Tell your story. We don't need a description."

"Anyhow! He was into pot early in the 70's and I am not lying when I say this. He rocked the ole time Kroger bags. You know the big ones like this." As she stretches out her arms. "Y'all girls up front are to young to remember this, they were full of pot. He called it Thai weed. That's how I remember it. So anyhow, Lou Ann is pregnant. So it was in 1971, is when it was. You know what? She was pregnant, and when I smoked some of that, and I looked at her, and said you're going to have a mongoloid baby."

Mom raised her voice. "A mongoloid baby? Did you say that to her?"

"I did say that to her."

"You think that's funny, Kathleen?"

"I do!"

"Why you laughing, Kathleen?"

"Hold on I'm not through. Do you remember his uncle Bernie? Well, after he left, he was staying all night and he had that burnt hair coming down hanging over his eye, and I am not kidding you. I actually saw this. He scared me so bad Marcy."

Mom said, "Who? Bernie?"

"He was going up in the air hitting his head."

"You thought he was." Mom said sarcastically.

"He was! Well hell! I thought he had springs in his shoes. He scared me so bad. I get along with him good now, but he scared me so bad, that I ran and jumped in bed with Danny. I scared Danny so bad, he pushed me out of the bed. That's how that stuff affected us."

Mom says, "WOW!"

"That was the last time I smoked it. I couldn't do it anymore after that. He had one BIG ole eye showing. He has great BIG ole eyes any how." I heard mom puff. "What if you were dating a man like Richard? Look Missy, I can't stand him."

186

Kathleen replied with sincerity. "But you liked him in the beginning."

"Who? Richard! When I heard he had a heart attack, I couldn't stop laughing. I don't know what it was about it, just made me laugh."

"I can't hear that. That is not nice."

"I know it's not nice. But you Kathleen, you don't know how he was! Look, the last time I saw him, let me tell you what he did. We were doing some stuff, I won't say what kind of stuff, but stuff. He walks out of the room, then heads to the back bedroom. Then that crazy son-of-bitch walks out dressed as the KKK. I mean he had the whole uniform on."

Kathleen pecks me on the shoulder. "She told me this story."

Now readers, I'm just gonna warn you that the use of a certain word coming up does not fit in my vocabulary. But it will surely explain the disgust Mom had for this man.

So Mom repeated herself one more time just for good measure. "HE HAD THE WHOLE UNIFORM ON. He said, I'm going to go kill me a nigger. I thought, Oh! I really messed up now. If I ever get out of this house, I will praise the Lord. Then he takes my fucking purse. He won't give me my purse or my keys."

"He broke his leg and he had a leg off. Then you said you pushed him over the chair and grabbed your keys and left. You said that's what he needed. You said next time you will just punch him in the throat."

"You're damn right that's what he needed. He came to Raywick a year ago. He always called me M. he said "M. You want to see my leg off?" I was in my car and I said, No! I don't Richard! This was last year Kathleen. I was going to be nice, then he said, "Do you want to see my wheel chair?" I said no Richard. No! I don't wanna see no damn wheelchair. I got to go. Remember Missy how he use to call me all the time. You didn't like him at all. Well, I wouldn't date that son of a bitch again for nothing. And in the beginning who would of ever thought he would have turned out like that?"

"He seemed like a well acted man."

Mom's voice got louder, "Believe me, that man was crazy as a loon! He cut a snow suit off of me! He cut my new good snow suit off!"

"I believe that you have been in some situations."

"I thought. You, Son-of-a-bitch you! I will kill you!"

"Was he wanting to do something?"

Mom said in a LOUD voice, "YEAH!"

As I look in the rear view mirror, I see Kathleen twist her mouth in disgust. "OMG! He was sick."

Mom laughed and said, "Not in the beginning. I think I made him sick. You know women have that effect on some men. He was very possessive."

"You probably did. You have that effect on some men."

"And look here Kathleen. Momma wants to talk about Ken, like he is a saint. He was down at Momma's yesterday and he stayed down there for 2 hours, talking about how holy he was. He brought Momma some rosaries and I told Momma, don't forget to tell him to tell you about the first time I went to his house. I didn't tell Momma this, but listen. He lived on a big hill. He was coming down his yard, as I'm pulling in. He is on a fucking riding lawn mower, mowing naked! I mean buck naked! His penis was just bouncing around, and I didn't know what to do. God! What am I'm going to do? So, I go ahead and pull on in his driveway and thinking he is going to put some clothes on. But nope, that didn't happen. He gets him a beer, like he didn't even care. I was embarrassed to death. He said, "I always drive my lawn mower naked.""

Kathleen said quietly, "You were so embarrassed because we're so modest."

Mom said, "Yeah we are. We always have been. I don't like getting undressed in front of anyone. Hell, when I was with Gate, I had to get undressed and get under the covers first. But boy was I good under. But anyway, I thought Jesus! Can you put some clothes on? His thing was just hanging there staring at me. I wanted to cover it with a sock or something. Omg! Thank God I have Joe Eddie."

I see Kathleen turn up her nose. "I didn't like Ken any how."

"Well Ken was alright. He had plenty of money and stuff. He was a sneaky son of a buck. He had a girlfriend in every town. Then down there giving Momma the rosary like some saint."

I finally have a chance to ask a question. "So Mom. When I write this story what name do you wanna use for the naked man?"

"Call him Ken, because he was naked like a Ken doll and brushes his hair to the side like a Ken doll and he thinks he is a Ken doll. You know what they called your dad back in the day, don't you?"

"Sure don't Mom. What was it? What did they call him?"

"Bud the Stud. But he didn't act nothing like Ken, even though he was more endowed and probably could have. His momma taught him right."

I had another story in here. But after Mom read it, I had to take it out. "Please take the "blank" story out. He is a well known man in these parts. Wait till he is dead before you publish that."

"Let me know when he is dead Mom."

Real time:
When Beverly got through reading this section she looked at me and said with concern. "You better not put this story in your book. Richard's family will come over here and kill us all!"

When I repeated to Mom, what Beverly had said, she replied. "He ain't got no damn family! Thank God! He wasn't nothing but an old racist schnauzer."

CAFÉ CONVERSATIONS.

Beverly was just sitting there at the bar pretending to read my book and something I wrote about Logan. What she was saying was total Improv and complete bull shit. It went a little something like this. "Logan drinks all the time, smokes pot and catches raccoons and who cares. He has two nephews and one niece who never call him, because they think he is a punk. They leave him alone, because they say he is a pot head and is dumb as a rock. Logan loves spending time with his older sister, mom and dad. They try not to have anything to do with Logan. But he still hangs around like a piece of lint on my black sweater. But we love him, even though he gives us the heebie-jeebies. We wanna be proud to call Logan part of the family from low down Raywick, but we just can't."

As she puts the book down and says, "that's pretty sweet." Mom, Logan and I, are all laughing. Beverly says, "what more could a man ask for?"

Mom yelled out. "Beverly Bickett, you're a riot. How did you have all that in your brain? I know Missy didn't write that about Logan! Where did you learn to make shit up like that?"

She says, "Well... It's just in there."

Logan laughs. "Potatoes got to her."

Mom got up to go to the bathroom. Logan grabbed a fly swatter and wop! Smashed a fly right on the bar. He picked it up real quick and threw it in Mom's coffee. Beverly tried to take it out and looked at Logan and said. "Logan! Marceline is gonna hate you."

"Pay backs are hell!"

One other morning, Kathleen was telling Mom a story about her and her husband Danny. Kathleen looked at Mom with a serious face, "Well Marceline, you know I'm not suppose to smoke. But I was outside sneaking one and Danny came out and almost caught me. When he walked out, I pitched it and acted like I was praying and staring at the stars. He looks up and says, "I don't see any stars." then she starts to laugh.

Mom just stares at her. "Kathleen, if you think that's funny. I'm really worried about you."

Then Kathleen says real loud, "I said..... I was looking up at the stars. There wasn't any stars!"

Mom says, "I know, but I didn't think it was funny."

I jump in. "Mom! She was trying to lie and got caught."

Mom rolls her eyes. "I know this, but I still don't think it's funny. How boring could this be?"

Kathleen looks at her again, "Well Marceline, it was the first thing I could think of. I was praying and looking at the stars. And he still says, where are they? I said up there." as she starts to laugh again.

Mom put her head down, "that's still not funny."

So Kathleen changes the subject. I'm guessing she thinks this story is more interesting. "So, the other day I'm going to town and I see this family. I see them walking toward Walmart as I'm driving into town. When I come back from town, I see them in the parking lot. I'm driving, but I got to go through the green light to get to them. I'm gonna give them some money to eat on. It was a family of three little boys, big fat girl, skinny man, and a baby and a baby carriage and a stroller. I thought, you know what? I'm gonna give them 25 dollars to eat on. You know what I'm saying? Well I get up there, and I see 'em at the green light, but when I get to the parking lot they're gone. I drove back and forth looking for that family. I thought, well, they've gone in Walmart. They couldn't have got in there cause they got all them kids."

Mom jumps in impatiently. "Get to the point Kathleen!"

"I go to the dollar store. I'm thinking. I'm thinking, that's where they went. Not any of them in sight. They have vanished."

"Is that the end of the story?" Mom asked.

"Well yeah! That's the end of the story."

"Well, that was as exciting as the first one."

Kathleen looks at Mom seriously. "I think God sent them to me."

Moms looks at me and rolls her eyes. "God sent them to her."

"Yes, Marceline. For me to give them some money or something. He was testing me to see if I would do it. I didn't see 'em again, but I had my money ready."

Mom puts her head down. "That's not funny or interesting."

"No Marceline! That's a spiritual thing."

Moms looks up and says in a long voice. "It's a spiritual thing...... Whatever,,,,,,, Kathleen. This story is boring the shit out me."

"Mom, there is a fly on your head."

"Is it full of shit like Kathleen?"

Kathleen frowns, "That's not nice."

Mom jumps up from the bar stool. "I gotta go poop!"

Did Nana just say that?

Quick note: Mom use to be known as Marceline. Now she is known as Missy's Mom. This her pretending to rest.

Just a thought or maybe a brain teaser.

What got this thought started? Well! Amy asked. "Have you ever been attracted to your cousin?" My reply of course was, "hell no!" Then she asked, "Do you think, if your family tree looks like your Christmas wreath, you're inbred?"

"Most likely. Listen, my cousin Ann was telling me and Sara a story. She said she went to a funeral or a wedding or something and this man walked up to her and was talking to her. His wife had just passed away or something and he was telling her that they were kin folks. She was

193

like really? Which side? And he replied, "BOTH." Well Sara and I just about fell out. Then Sara said, well Dr. Oz or Dr. Phil, one of those doctor people on TV said, hey, if you're cousins, don't worry. You can breathe easy."

What's your thoughts? Lol.

How about this for a thought?

If Adam and Eve were the only two people on earth, then I would have to think incest is okay, right? One with a brain would think so. If not, the buck stops there. How do we exist?

Just a brain teaser.

Does this make Amy a lesbian? No! No, it doesn't!

They say, control your environment. Don't let it control you. But sometimes it does and that's just the way it is.

So on to a new topic and a discovery about oneself. My workers and my daughter tell me that I don't pay attention to anything they say. But then again why should I? I have selective hearing when they are talking to me about something off the subject, while I'm busting my hump. I'm usually in my zone and focused on my food and I can't seem to help it. My actions can be quite delayed. We Aquarians are just built that way. We can be a little aloft at times. It comes across as not giving a shit sometimes. But I swear, that's not what it is. Although sometimes I can come across as wound up as tight as a coo coo clock.

Summer complains about it all the time. "Mom, you never pay attention." She gets like totally butt hurt if I ignore her. She can't comprehend, that anything more important could be going on. She is like "Mom, pay attention! I'm your whole life." I don't know how she could think I ignore her on purpose. I pay attention to so much.

I sent her a picture of me at prom. Everyone else was staring straight ahead and watching something and I was in the background doing something other than what everyone else was doing. I told her, "look I didn't pay attention back then either. I don't get captivated very easily." She responded sarcastically, "You not paying attention? NO!"

"It's just selective attention disorder. I tend to ignore uninteresting data."

I try to pay more attention to it these days. Especially, every since my dad about choked to death. And that was some interesting data, that I somehow missed.

One evening before the power went out, I was at the grill, slinging steaks out left and right. I blurt out, "I'm gonna have everything on me before the night is over, except vagina juice." Kathleen covers her ears and says, "I can't hear that." Luckily my dad didn't hear it. He was sitting there at the end of the bar eating, like he always does. A few minutes passed when someone said. "Geeez Missy! Your dad was choking and you told us to hold on."

"Do what?"

I swear I didn't hear the first time. I must have been busier than a one legged man in an ass kicking contest to not have heard that. I don't know how I could have tuned something like that out. But I am guilty, I guess.

"He is turning blue." Someone yelled.

"Who is turning blue?"

"Your dad! We done told you he was choking and you said hold on."

"I couldn't have been saying hold on to that."

"Well you did!"

"Where is he?" I replied.

"We already took him to the bathroom."

So I ran to the door, I was yelling through the door. "Dad! Dad! You OK?" I could hear him still choking and gagging. He finally came out and was pale in the face.

"Dad! Are you OK?"

"Sure Missy, without any help from you!"

"I'm so sorry! I swear I didn't hear it was you."

"Choking should have been the key word, period." as he continued to clear his throat.

"You're right, but I swear! My mind does that some times. It takes a minute to fire."

He ended up being fine and the night moved along as usual. Until the power went out. But that's another story.

Maybe you can give me an answer to my delayed reaction, to certain things. Here is another time I am aware that it happened.

As I was walking toward the house, my mind was keyed in on what I was going to get. Then this lady comes speeding up my drive. She jumped out of her truck, looked at me and said. "I just hit your dog."

I replied, "Hold on! I got to get something from the house." And kept walking.

Can you believe it? I said hold on. As messed up as it sounds, I don't know what I was thinking either. BUT, as soon as I got in the house, my mind relayed it to me once more. "The lady just told you! She ran over your dog!" Yes, my mind was talking to my mind. I don't know if my right brain yells at my left, or the opposite way around, but one of them is the boss and sometimes one of them is aloft.

But I instantly went running back outside. "Oh my God! Which one? Where is he? Is it Snoz or Blue? How did you hit him?" I was full of questions.

"He just ran out in front of me, right down there at the end of your drive." So I darted out across the yard and ran out toward the road. There he lay, not moving, but breathing heavily. Mom came running out. "What happened? What happened?"

"Go grab my phone Mom! Now!" She turned around and sped back over to the Café and ran inside. She peeked back out the door and shouted. "Where is it?"

"Really? On the bar. Hurry!" I was getting highly irritated. I started to run toward the Cafe myself, when she came running out with it. She handed it to me and said, "I'm sorry honey, I couldn't find it."

"That's alright Mom. I just need to call Dad."

So I called my dad and told him Snoz had been hit and he was laying there dying. I told him that he needed to come down right away. He said, "I will be down after while."

As I was pacing back and fourth, I replied. "Are you kidding me? You got to get here now."

"I said, I would be down later."

So I hung up the phone. Maybe I got my delayed thought process from him. Was I just supposed to leave Snozberry laying there in pain, till he decided to come? No! I think not!

Since Dad didn't seem that he was gonna be in any hurry, I called Jimmy. Jimmy always comes to my rescue. He arrives quickly. When you're in need, he shows up like Superman. He is just built that way. Like I've said before, he is Mr. Favor. He has gotten possums and snapping turtles out of my pool and dead animals that Blue or Keyda has drug in. I'm gonna have to tell you the possum story later, not later later, but shortly in this book.

But it was too late for poor Snoz. Tears popped out of my eyes as he laid Snoz in the back of the truck. Jimmy said, he would go bury him on the Bickett farm. Now his poor brother Blue, is so, so sad. I mean really sad. Those two were conjoined at the hip, like Siamese twins. They didn't walk, sit or lay unless they were on around or near each other. I never seen two dogs as close as butt cheeks before. I heard Blue howling for the first time, the night it happened. It scared the shit out of me. I was lying on the couch when he began to howl. It was something like a wolf, but with a very eerie ghost like sound. It seemed quite unnatural. Just asked Logan if you don't believe me. He was house sitting one night when he called me and said he was about to leave, because Blue was unnerving him.

I don't know what's up with everything sounding ghostly around here, but it does. I truly believe I may have ghosts, but I tell myself to GET USE TO IT. We are sharing a space, and obviously, it was here first.

Blue and Snoz

I've also been told 'get use to it' when it comes to pets. Because when you have a country dog and he is free to roam, stuff like that happens. It's the chance you take when you let your dog run free. At least he was free to run and be a dog, a free dog. Not chained up, or cooped up in some ole apartment or house. They are meant to run free. Now chill out house dog owners. I'm not talking about your little hairless house dogs. I'm talking about dogs that thrive on freedom. Freedom dogs. That's what I'm naming my next one.

So, once again, get use to it! My delayed reaction that is. Because obviously, it's hereditary or something. I don't know why it happens in certain situations. Maybe since the fire, my brain reacts to stress differently. It doesn't affect my work at the Cafe, but it does happen in other stressful situations. Thanks Dad or whatever the reason.

Aw... I forgot to mention Keyda. He definitely deserves a spot in here. He was my Cafe and farm dog and long time companion. He was an Akita and he was big and white with a few designer brown spots. There goes that name thing again, pretty original don't ya think? I at least changed the spelling.

He looks dead up like a polar bear, minus the spots. He was an outside dog and got to travel anywhere he liked. He was a modern day Lassie. I don't keep animals in the house, maybe a little, just when they're little so they don't get eaten by something. Then they get booted to the outdoors, and they love it. I don't chain them up and they get free range of the land. They always stick around because they get to gobble up left over steak from the Cafe.

When it would storm, Keyda would head down the road for cover. I always wondered where he would go, because there was plenty cover here. I guess somewhere he felt more safe. Maybe he didn't trust Walter to keep him safe. He actually hightailed it outta here the day the house burnt down.

I always talked about getting Keyda stuffed when he passed away. Only because he was the Cafe dog and I thought it would be cool to set him on the porch to greet the customers. I know it sounds a little morbid. But everyone that came in the Cafe loved him. There would be people who put pictures of him on Facebook and little kids would ride him like a horse.

I walked out back one day and a little kid had his fist completely down his throat. Neither of them seemed to mind. One of my worker's kid, was determined that he was a polar bear. He would point at him and say, "Mom, look! It's the polar bear." There was no convincing him it wasn't.

Yes, I wanted to stuff him. It would be a tribute to him. I know it's a controversial subject, but, Joe Mack and I always jokingly talked about it. Even if we were serious, I guess it never could have happened.

Only because, one hot June day, I stepped out onto the deck barefooted to yell for him. The deck was so hot, I had to jump around like popcorn. I yelled one more time but he didn't come. He always comes, always.

Sometimes it takes him a minute longer than usual, since he had gotten older. I wondered where that shit could have gone? I thought to myself, if he doesn't get home soon, the coyotes will have him for dinner. They had gotten my dog Rainbow, years before. So I went back inside unsure what to think. Think positive! He will be home soon. Then I went on about my busy day as usual.

So the next day when I awoke, I went outside again to yell for him. Then I went to the back deck. But I had on shoes. Where could he be? Then I got a whiff of something horrific smelling. It was stomach-churning. Shit! Is there another dead possum in the yard! Keyda! I'm gonna kill you if you dragged another possum in this yard. He had done it many times before and it is disgusting, but it was also nice that he killed them. He was my pest patrol.

The very first time he caught one, I was watching him from my front window. He was out in the field, running circles around this possum. The possum was standing his ground, with his teeth protruding from his mouth. It looked like he had an acre of teeth, and it made me nervous to watch. So I called my aunt Beverly asking what I should do. She said the possum would eventually wobble away. Then she asked, he hasn't killed anything before has he? I told her, not that I know of. Then she said, okay then. It should be fine. You just don't want him to get bitten by that nasty thing.

So I went back to whatever I was doing. A couple hours later I was sitting in my back room, (house that burnt down) at my make up mirror. When I glanced up to look out the bay window, Keyda was trotting toward the barn with the possum hanging out of both sides of his mouth. He went behind the barn and within minutes, came strolling back down to the house without the possum. Now that is some serious pest control.

Possums are the only animal I despise. I mean despise, even more than snakes. It's the one animal I don't bother to dodge on the road. They come around here all the time, despite my hatred for them. I feel they are taunting me or maybe they are really attracted to this land. Oh shit! I'm about to go off the subject again. Here goes.

After work one night, Amy was singing, *I whip my hair back and fourth,* as she strutted out the door. We were sitting at the bar laughing at her. It wasn't two seconds later when she came running back into the Cafe screaming. "Oh My God y'all! Get out here!"

We all ran out to see what was up, when we spotted a nasty ass possum wobbling around the cars. Amy screams, "Do you know, I thought that damn nasty thing was a cat! I reached down to pet the possum. Then it snarled at me with those pointy teeth. I could have been kilt."

"Oh Geez Amy! Those things carry rabies. What if it would have bitten you?"

"I know. It's bad."

I was panicking. "How we gonna catch it and get rid of it?"

"Do what you did last time and throw a rock on it."

"Amy, I can't do that. The only reason I did that the last time is because it was messing with my puppies and I was scared it was gonna bite one of them. There happened to be a big rock beside it and I rolled it over on it. It was terrible. Its little babies came rolling out of its pouch, looking like rats on crack. I didn't know what to do. That momma possum laid there under the rock roasting in the sun, like a fat turkey on Thanksgiving day. The FN critters were crawling all around and they wobbled out into the parking lot. They were scattered from here to Kalamazoo."

"What did you do with the babies?"

"I didn't do anything with them. I wouldn't dare pick up a nasty critter like that. I had to call Jimmy."

Amy looked at me seriously. "What did he do with them?"

"I doubt Jimmy took them to the shelter. What did you have for dinner

203

that night?"

"Oh! Shut up, Missy! Jimmy wouldn't do that to me. Let's chase it in to the pool and let it drown" Amy said as she started to laugh.

"Haha... Yeah right!"

She recommended that because I had to call Jimmy after finding one in my pool while swimming with a friend. When we spotted that damn thing floating in the corner, we couldn't get out fast enough. Have you ever tried to run in water while trying to escape from something. It's not ever fast enough. Just ask Summer, after escaping the sting ray. Once we escaped, we couldn't hit the shower quick enough. Just plain disgusting I say. Yep! Swimming with possums. I don't think I want to get into all the methods of ridding of the possums or what we did with the one that night. Just know I didn't do anything to any of them. Well, the rock, but it was self defense for the puppies. But anyway, we will leave it there. I don't want PETA knocking at my door over some nasty ass possum.

Real Time Quick Story

Amy called me on the phone the other day. She was in distress. She was breathing hard when she said. "Missy, I am having a psychotic moment. I woke up and it was still dark outside. I went to use the bathroom and I felt shit under my feet. I turned on the light and there was mud every where. Missy, I just got down on my hands and knees and scrubbed this whole floor yesterday. Then I go into the bathroom and Scrappy has shit all over the floor. You know what Jimmy did? He wiped it and smeared it with toilet paper, then sat the dirty shitty ass paper on top of the trash can. I'm so mad, I could bite a screw in half! So you know what I did? I went and got a bucket and went to my garden and filled it with dirt. I was on my hands and knees, just shoveling it in there with my bare hands and saying, you will see! I was so mad Missy! I went straight into Jimmy's space in the garage and I started at the front door and poured dirt all the way through his building, on the rugs and all. Then I hid the sweeper."

"Girl! You're acting like a pressure cooker ready to blow. Just breathe and calm down."

"Okay! I will." Then we hung up. Then the phone rang back about five minutes later. It was Amy. "Missy! You wanna know the stupidest thing ever?"

"Sure! What?"

"Did you see that moron Kanye meet Trump at Trumps Towers?"

"I sure did. That's just a sight for poor eyes to see. Everybody is gonna have to draw in their horns for the next four years."

"Either that or take up arms."

"Oh, I will stand up! But my expectations are surely shot."

"Mine too. Okay! See ya in a bit for work."

"See ya."

So back to Keyda. Readers, I know you may be lost, but so was Keyda. So, I'm still waiting on him. I went back inside and got to thinking really hard. Where is Keyda? This is so unlike him. I got a weird knot in my stomach and a light bulb went off in my head. Oh shit! No! No way! No! No! Can't be! I rushed to called Mom. "Mom! I need you and Joe Eddie to ride over immediately."

"Why?"

"I just need you to. Please!"

"Okay, honey! We will be right there."

So when they arrived, I looked at her with sadness. "Mom! I think Keyda may be under the deck. Dead! I just can't bear to look."

"Missy, are you sure?"

205

I nod, "No! I'm not sure, I'm hoping it's a possum. But I haven't seen Keyda in a day or two and you know he is old and has been sick."

Joe Eddie sighs as he headed under the deck. He is a bigger man, so he struggles to get under there. Mom and I waited above pacing, with our fingers crossed. Then we hear him blatantly say. "It's Keyda!"

Now, I never thought I would cry this hard over an animal. I love them, but just never have really, really, cried. But when he said those words, just two words, "It's Keyda!" My heart sunk. Mom and I both busted into tears. My heart was truly breaking for him and I cried for hours. Everyone at the Café was so sad.

When Summer came home from school and I had to tell her, she was heart broken also. She really loves our animals, even though she doesn't help much when it comes to taking care of them. But she is always concerned for their well being and expects them to live and be around forever. That just doesn't happen with pets. We should know better, but we do it just the same.

Mom and I were sitting at the Cafe, having our morning coffee. Yes, once again. We got to talking about him. Mom looked at me all sad and said. "Bless his little heart. He was the best dog that ever was. I cried days after that."

"I know, wasn't he? Did I ever tell you about the time Kristen and I came home one night after being out drinking. Let me tell you this first. You know how Kristen's lack of need to pretend she is interested in anything you have to say, then she comes off with some crazy comment, that will have you in stiches. Anyway we fell asleep back in the back bedroom of the house."

"You ain't got no back bedroom."

"No, Mom! The old house."

"Oh!" she said.

"Anyway, we were both passed out and it was storming like crazy. Then I felt Kristen beating on me, trying to wake me up. I was like, what do you want? She said, quit snoring. Then I said, I'm not! Then she said, but I heard you snoring. At this time of course, we're both awake and we still hear something. It was also raining in the window. It had been knocked out. I was like, What the hell? As I was looking around, we could still hear a panting noise. We weren't frightened then, like we would be today, because we didn't have suspicions of ghost way back then. Keep in mind, that's back before I feared anything. So, I decided to look under the bed. It was Keyda. How the hell he slid under there, I will never know. He is a big feller. He had knocked the window out and was panting like crazy. Kristen thought it was me snoring. I guess if it was an intruder, Kristen and I, would both be dead."

Mom starts laughing. "You remember when I had to chase him out of the apartment with a vacuum. He was really afraid of storms. The vacuum is the only thing that would make him get out. Guess that scared him more than the storm."

"I know. What about when he would get in the Cafe? I would have customers in here and he would crawl up under their table and all I could do was look at them and say, sorry, but he ain't moving till the storm is over. Enjoy your dinner."

"He weighed a ton, when he didn't want to move. He was like black iron. I had to beat him harder than the storm, to get him out of here one day. No... not really, but you couldn't budge him. Then the poor thing went and died under the deck, so he wouldn't hurt our feelings."

"I loved that old dog."

"You remember when we went to the pound and got him? He already had a broken ear?"

"I do!" I replied.

"We gave him a good life, didn't we, Missy?"

207

"Yes, we did Mom."

Damn, I need a blonde joke: Two blondes fell down a hole. One said. "It's dark in here, isn't it?" The other replied, "I don't know, I can't see."

SHORT STORY

Kathleen once had a run in with the law. When I say run in, I literally mean run in. "911! What is your emergency?"

She was headed down toward Bickett's bar one evening, when up ahead the cops had someone pulled over. As she drove past, she clipped the officer's door, almost taking it and the officer with her.

Thus began the wild goose chase through Raywick. It was at high speeds, although Kathleen has never driven over forty. I was just kidding about the high speed. It never happened. But she did drive on toward the bar as if nothing serious had happened, like she was driving around Miss Daisy. She said she pulled in and waited on the cop and rode around the bar like she usually does just to check on it. That's her version anyway.

Obviously the cops drove on past at high speeds looking for her, having no knowledge that she was sitting there waiting on them. Well, that's what she says. Then she said, oh well if they're just gonna drive on past, I will head on home. I'm not chasing them down to see what happened, by no means. When the cops realized that maybe she had pulled over into the bar, they turned around. Kathleen had already nonchalantly started to head home at her high speed, not realizing she was still the main suspect of a CRIME. She thought, well, maybe I didn't hit them.

But as she pulled into her own driveway, the cops were hot on her trail. They surrounded her, ran up and got her out of her car and put her on the ground. They handcuffed her and arrested her.

She later got out of the situation, because the week that she hit the officer's car door, she had been to the doctor and diagnosed with vertigo. Which may have been an early sign to her aneurysm, not sure. I'm not a medical doctor.

She said that my dad put up the money to get her out. "$10,000 dollars. My favorite man. Who else am I gonna call on a Sunday morning to get me out, when Danny is in Louisville with his sick mom?" She took a deep breath. "Thank God, for your dad and thank God Danny didn't see them put me in handcuffs."

JUST SOME STUPID THINGS.

I really think I need to let you in on the bean thing. What bean thing? Well, one of my workers was telling me that one night she was laying in her bed downstairs, when her dad walked down and caught her flicking her bean... Whole new meaning of the word bean. Wouldn't you say?

This guy called the other day to see if we had opened back after the summer. He said, "I called, cuz we knows you be closed in July."

Common sense is not a gift. It's a punishment. Only because you have to deal with everyone who doesn't have it.

Things we do just to embarrass people. Sometimes when the phone rings, Amy will yell out loud for all to hear. "Hey Frankie, your gynecologist called and says your STD medicine worked." Sometimes when a new worker shows up, we will yell out to them. "Hey! Your parole officer is on the phone."

BRIANNA

So maybe you are still wondering what I meant when I said. "So I thought." Back when I was getting my license at the age of sixteen, short a day. Probably not, it's been a few chapters, I mean books, but just in case. Remember my parents thought I was born on Groundhog's Day. Well, I wasn't and when I got my license, I was pissed to find out I wasn't born that day. How could they not remember with only one kid? That's what I thought at the time. Only the future would tell me differently.

Oh, and before I forget, when I wrote Groundhog's Day in my first book, I wrote it as two words. Nicole had to call me out on it and write to the side. She said, "it's one word unless you mean ground up hogs day and that would be a pretty weird holiday."

Yes, it would be Nicole. Yes, it would.

So anyway, here goes. A couple of years had passed since I had lost my grandpa, my maw-maw and Aunt Trish and Uncle Rick. Things were getting back to normal, as normal as things could get after dealing with four deaths, the trial, the DUI and all sorts of things. Coming from a colorful family living in a world that seems as messed up as a soup sandwich, I seemed to be dealing. I was getting pretty good at getting bad news and was opening myself up to whatever forces ruled the world. I was still working at the car lot at the time, and running my place at Bickett's bar. I had previously bought Trish's little red station wagon so I could haul my DJ equipment around. It had been just sitting up at the farm collecting dust ever since her murder. I guess Summer was around six at the time. Mick (yes, my new girlfriend) was also living with me at this point.

So I was sitting at the car lot answering the phones while all the guys went to have lunch, when I received the.... call. When I answered, there was a woman on the other end. She asked quietly. "Does a Missy work there?"

I answered. "Yes ma'am.... This is she. May I help you with

211

something?"

"Well..... this isn't a business call or anything like that. I was really needing to talk to you about something important, and I don't know how you will feel about it or how to bring it up."

My suspicions were being raised. What is this about? For I've had a lot of bad phone calls in the past few years. Ones that turned out to be tragic and I was worried. So, we sat there in silence for a moment, as I heard her take a deep breath and say. "Here goes.... ready or not. I would like to know, if you would like to meet your sister?"

I was flabbergasted! My heart dropped and lifted at the same time. I was excited and shocked all at once. I was in a state of sudden, intense, and overpowering emotions. Good ones. I had remembered my mom asking me a question years ago. I was younger and remember sitting on Aunt Kathleen's bed. She asked if I wanted a brother or sister. Then I heard nothing else about it, I mean literally. It was never brought up again.. I remember I used to tell Kandy I had a brother or sister somewhere and that it saddened me, not knowing where or who... but now..... it's happening. That long awaited phone call. I answered with "Omg! Yes... I would love to!" I mean this call was totally out of the blue. I was so freaking thrilled to hear the news. I would say ecstatic. I get to meet my sister! I get to meet my sister! I threw the phone up in the air. Don't remember much more of what was said in the conversation, except that we made plans to meet at a town in between both of us. Just a few towns over. For years, my sister who was 15 now, had lived there all this time. That damn close and I had not a clue.

When we met for the first time it was a bit awkward. We hugged and I stepped back with awe. "You look just like my aunt Beverly." The resemblance was insane. I wish I could remember some of the things we talked about, but I don't. We took pictures at the mall in the photo booth. But you already know, I don't have them anymore. We met a couple more times and I had told my mom that she needed to meet her, but she

212

never would. She was way too nervous and worried about what her daughter would think, giving her up like that.. But she needed not to worry about her decision made back then. She made a couple very happy when she handed over her baby. I know that some people look down on someone who may do that. But what would people who wanted to adopt do, if that situation never arrived. It's a catch 22 kind of situation. Mom didn't have the stability at the time to raise a kid and this family was in desperate need and want of a baby. So she basically made someone else's dreams come true by doing this. No matter how people look at it. But here's the kicker. A fucked up kicker, a dramatic devastating kicker. Brianna's parents wouldn't be happy for much longer, nor would I. The events to follow are not easy for me to relate.

I was sitting on the couch one night when I received another phone call. It was my grandma. When I answered she starts talking without hesitation. "Missy, did you know that girl Brianna got killed today." Hearing what she just said, I was beside myself. I just sat there, frozen in time, stupefied and all choked up with no reply. I heard her voice through the phone once more. "Missy! Did you hear me?"

I was stunned and confused and thought how could you be so nonchalant with your news. It's my sister ... How dare you say... "That girl." But in her defense, my grandma didn't know her, and I guess she wasn't considering my attachment to this situation, but it hurt. It hurt like hell! It was one of the deepest cuts I had received up until that point, and I had received many. I was an emotional wreck and I don't think many people around me, understood the devastation. It was like, well..... you only knew her for a year. But I was thinking... Fuck you! So.... if your sister, who was only one, that wouldn't be so bad because she was only one and you only knew her for a year. Really! A sister is a sister. I had been waiting for years to know if she was out there. I had finally discovered her and got to know her. Then it was just ripped right back away from me. I just don't understand people's thoughts sometimes. I don't want to go on a tangent here, because it would be very easy to do. So we will move along with the day of the funeral.

Mom, Beverly and Grandma decided they would go.. Mick and I drove separately. On my way there I got pulled over. What's the odds? When the cop came to the window, he said. "Ma'am! Do you know you were speeding?"

"Not really sir. My mind isn't where it should be."

"Ma'am what do you mean by that?" Assuming the worst I'm sure, like pills or something of that nature.

"Well, I'm heading to my sister's funeral."

"Oh! I'm sorry. Which way you headed?"

"Vine Grove. She was the one that Sheriff hit. He hit her and her friend. They were only sixteen."

"Oh! I'm so sorry, ma'am, I know all about that...It was really big news around here. I'm so sorry for your loss. You can head on now. Do you need me to drive in front of you?"

"No sir! I can get there."

So readers, I guess I forgot to tell you how her death came to be.. She had just turned sixteen. Her and her friend, were pulling out of this road, onto the highway. A Sheriff who was on a call for a disturbance in a church parking lot, came flying down the road at a hundred miles per hour and sideswiped the car. It killed them both in an instant. The disturbance wasn't even life threatening. So why did he have to be going that fast? Brianna's mom Brenda, ended up suing the department and won. Not that, that makes things better, but there was a tragic wrong doing and no need for him to be going that fast. No need at all.

When we all arrived at the funeral, we all walked in together. My mom was nervous as hell. When we opened the door, the heads turned and all eyes were on us. Keep in mind, no one in that family, had ever met our family. Only Brenda (the mom) and her sister had met my mom years ago, when they did the adoption, and of course I had meet Brenda and

Brianna. We all started to introduce everyone to each other. As I stood there, I could see out of the corner of my eye, my sister laying there lifeless in her casket.

Some of Brenda's family came up to Beverly, not my mom. They started rubbing her face in amazement and awe. They were telling her how much their loved one, Brianna, looked like her. "Brianna is the spitting image of you." It was so heart breaking. I remember my throat started to tighten, as if I were being choked to death by the Boston strangler. We moved on into the crowd, as Brianna still laid there peacefully in her casket. What was going on around me and in my head was far from peaceful.

The last thing I remember was standing up by the coffin for prayers. I could feel myself choking up and trying to hold back my tears. My hands started to sweat and became clammy. I could literally feel the constriction in my throat and tingling across my skin. My heart started racing and beating loudly. It seemed as if the sound of my heart palpitations was gonna shatter the room. My chest began to tighten and I could barely breath. I was feeling a new level of pain, as my stomach knotted and my lips quivered. It was causing a significant amount of psychological distress. Then I broke out in an uncontrollable cry.

Here is where, it blows my mind... I remember nothing! Nothing else about that day. I mean absolutely nothing. It's totally fucked up and it kind of pisses me off, knowing I can't remember this shit. I mean really. What the hell is going on? I was just tempted to call Mick the other day and ask her, but then I thought, nah, why dig it up. Something that is very odd to me. When I've mentioned my sister to several friends here lately, they had no idea I even had a sister. Either the subject was never brought up, or we had lost some serious touch during that time in my life. Either way, it blows my mind.

The minute you start to love anyone or anything, you have to accept the risk, that someday, they or it, may not be there. I talk of memories often in this book, but I didn't get to have many with her. It's sad that I have no stories to tell. She was taken so young and quick. I would like to say that I keep in touch with her mom, but I haven't really. Basically the only contact we have had, was after my house burnt down and I lost what few pictures I had gathered of Brianna. So she photocopied me a few and sent them to me. That's it! That's all I have of her. I am gonna get back in touch with Brenda soon, I swear. Where does the time go?

So, earlier in the chapters or maybe my other book, I talked about destiny and how would we know when we were there (at our destiny) that is. I guess it would be when we meet the great creator of ourselves. No matter what religion you believe in, we all go back somewhere. To where? That I'm still not sure of. We all have different opinions on that.

I was telling someone the other day, as tragic as death is, we really do need to accept it. Our only destiny, from the time we are born, is to die. It's the only thing we can't change. No matter how desperately we want to.

REAL TIME

I just had a bible pusher to show up to my door the other day trying to push the bible on me. He asked, "do you have an opinion on the subject." I said, "Why... yes... I do! I have lots of opinions. But the thing is, I don't push them on anyone else." He slowly put his bible back in his case and slid back to his car. I hope that was appropriate for me to say. I don't want to judge him and I don't want him to judge me. Have your beliefs and I will have mine.

I know readers, you have read a lot of my beliefs. Just know that I am not pushing them on you, or think you should think the same. Just be open to everyone's thoughts and ways, especially when they harm or effect no one. If it makes them feel good to believe what they feel and it makes them comfortable in the world and what the after life will be like, then I say have at it. I think grey, even though black or white would be easier, I still think grey. Not that my thoughts are dull like the color, because they're not. They're as bright as the rainbow. Well sometimes. Lets just say open minded.

REAL TIME. Well, real time for now, till something else comes up and side tracks me and tries to throw me off my game. It's been like a delayed ballgame when it rains. You stop! Then you go back out to play.

217

It rains again. You wait, then you go back out. Just hoping you can finish the game. Sometimes the storm just won't let up. See, I already forgot what I was gonna write about.

EDGER ALLEN POLE-----"I remained so much inside my head and ended up losing my mind."

Drawing by Destiny Adkins

I DIDN'T REMEMBER A THING

I wanted to go visit Brianna's grave sight for the first time since we buried her. I know it's been way too long. So Brenda gave me an invite over. When I first arrived we hugged and she stared at me, like, oh my! You two so resemble each other so much with your beautiful blue eyes. Then we we sat down and had a nice talk. Then I just sat back and let her tell me the whole story. This is Brenda's story and words. She was telling me in the sweetest voice, how she and her husband were looking for a baby.....

"The priest, Father Mouser, said he would keep his eyes open. So soon after that, he called my sister Denise and said I have a baby for you. My sister told him, my sister already has a baby. He said it doesn't matter. Denise called me in Alaska. I lived in North Pole, Alaska. I had just gotten off the pipe line. I was working construction and I came off work to get baby #1. So when she called me, she said, I got a baby for you and I said, oh God! She said it was Father Mouser's cousin and the woman was a twin and from a large Catholic family. A thirty three year old divorcee and had a 13 year old daughter, which I'm assuming is you my dear. That's what I remember! I told Denise to do me a favor and go meet this mother. So she went to meet Marceline and Kathleen. She said they were two peas in a pod. She said, Oh Brenda, you got to have this baby. I said why? And Denise said omg, she is so beautiful. You just got to take this baby. I know you can do it! I told her let me talk to Paul, and Brandon was only two weeks old. We decided we would check it out. So I left Alaska and flew down to Kentucky. I went to meet the two girls at Kathleen's house in Louisville. Your mom came out in the cutest turquois outfit. Little one piece adorable thing. She was so freaking cute.

I about died! I never told your mom I had another baby. Not that it would have mattered, beings your mom was a twin. That's kinda how I looked at Brendon and Brianna, as twins. Two weeks difference, it was a balancing act, I have to say. Your mom said, I will call you when I go into labor and I was like are you kidding me and she said no. I want you there. I looked at Denise and I thought, is she kidding me? I was so ecstatic! I ended up missing the birth, but they called me soon as they could from Saint Anthony's. Mom had flown in from Alaska too. Denise said we are not going without the diaper bag and I was like, what are you talking about? We are bringing that baby home. Your mom told me to go get the baby and I was like are you kidding me, and she was like no, no it's your baby. Wow! I was so blown away about that. So I went into the nursery and they had Brianna in there by herself. She started to cry and they told me to feed her. When I went back to the room, I was telling Marceline she is beautiful. Marceline said, do you wanna take her home? The baby is okay and everything is finished and they know it's a private adoption. I had to call my attorney and he had to meet me and it was eleven o'clock at night. When they handed me the baby, Denise and I looked at each other like, Shock Ville! The baby was 27 hours old, I felt like I had stolen her. And what is so cool about the whole thing, about Brandon and Brianna's adoption is, that in Alaska you have a ten day waiting period, in which the mother can change her mind. I stayed ten more days in Prudo Bay and the men I worked with gave me a baby shower. I got drunker than a fart. I had such a good time. I was suppose to meet my husband at the airport and he was late with my baby boy. He brought him down from Alaska and I had Brianna. One born in Alaska and one born in Kentucky. Isn't that cool? Paul bent down to kiss me and he was drinking and I thought oohh! And after I had my babies, I decided, I wasn't gonna put up with this. I'm just not gonna do it. I can raise these babies on my own. I had lost so much weight after we split. I only weighed 80lbs. I had no idea how I was gonna make it.

But I knew I had to get out of Alaska to bring those babies back to green grass and civilization. They were two when I brought them back. Ten of us were living in the same house. It was a little old farm house and it was so teensy tinsy and my clothes were in Walmart bags hanging on nails going down to the basement. I slept in a room with my young niece. Brandon slept with his nephew and Brianna slept with the other two nieces. Denise did the cooking and I did the laundry. That's how I survived. That's how we did it. Yep, sure is. But when I finally got my own place I felt like the cream in an Oreo cookie, one on one side of me and one on the other. It was the best feeling in the world."

This story is being interrupted for an opinion.........

Ann Coulter, it's me, Missy. I have something to say to you. You are freaking crazy! I just seen you on an interview. You said, 'all' and I stress, that you said "All" single mothers should give their babies up for adoption. What the hell are you on? My mom did and it was a great thing. But what about Brenda, when she decided to leave her alcoholic husband? Give them away? Really! My Maw-maw was single, when she helped raise me. Was she to give me up for adoption? I'm a single mother also, and raised a perfectly good, educated, open minded child. You have not only lost the cheese off your crackers, you have lost your crackers too. This long slow handclap is just for you. Yes, you can leave the stage. But hold on, before you go.

Let me welcome *Jewel* and others to the stage of *Comedy Central Roast* of *Rob Lowe*. They roast everyone. That's what they do. It's okay. I like politically incorrect comedy, but that's where it belongs, on the comedy stage, not in the White House. *Ann Coulter* was a guest, but she obviously didn't really know what a roast was, which left her wiggling in her seat. Everything they said to her, left her face stuck in permanent rigor mortis. Lets just say she was way beyond uncomfortable. Why do I despise her so much? Well, she is a white nationalist puppet, that refuses to find any common ground between any of us. Everybody has the right to believe what they believe without persecution, but preaching hate is out of bounds. I don't think Jesus intended for his teachings to create hate.

Let's review a bit of the roast shall we. *Pete Davidson* said, and I quote, "last year we had *Martha Stewart* here, she sells sheets. Now we have *Ann Coulter*, who cuts eyeholes in them." *Jewel* stated ever so sweetly, "first of all, me being a feminist, I can't support everything being said up here tonight." Then she pauses. "But as somebody that hates *Ann Coulter*, I'm delighted." *Jeff Ross* chimes in, "*Ann Coulter* is against gay marriage." Then he stares her straight in the face. "What's your thinking on that? If I can't get a husband, they shouldn't either." *David Spade* looks over at the panel. "Is he black? Is he white? *Ann Coulter* needs to know, so she can decide if she hates him." Ann's eyes dropped to the floor. When she got up there to joke, that shit went over about as well as a screen door on a submarine. Poor Ann stated later that she had no idea why she was the target of most jokes. Take a close look at yourself honey. You are a hater, and most people don't like haters. Yes, there are a percentage of you out there, very small percentage I hope. I pray to God anyway. Once again it would make Grandma proud just to know I'm praying for something.

So back to mine and Brenda's conversation. I was telling Brenda I couldn't remember much about the funeral and she said with shock. "What?"

"Yeah! I don't remember a thing."

"Well, let me tell you this. I included your mom in the service. She was at one end of the casket and I was at the other end of the casket. For me, if it hadn't been for your mom, I wouldn't be a mom. So I did it out of love and respect for your mother. It might have been too much for her, but I didn't look at it like that. I just thought it was imperative to have her involved. She is the one who gave her life to breathe and I was the other one and I wanted her part of the funeral service. It was important that she be there. People just couldn't believe it. They were like, you did that?"

I asked. "Why does it matter?"

Brenda started to whisper. "See, adoptions are hush, hush. Brianna had the prettiest blue eyes I've ever seen."

"We all have blue eyes, baby!" Then I showed her a picture of Summer.

"Now, Brianna had a very small mouth."

"All the Bicketts have small mouths. Summer has her dad's lips. See how puffy they are? She looks a lot like me when she was younger. You remember mom's sister Trish. She got murdered when she was 38."

She gasped with air. "Oh! That's right. I remember that. Did anybody find out why?" And of course I told her the story. You guys already know. "It was a messy time."

Then Brenda started talking about the law suit. She had a folder in her hands and was wanting to show me pictures. I could tell she was still devastated from what happened to her daughter many, many years ago. When she said what they were, I felt myself stiffening and I changed the subject. "Can we go the the grave sight?"

So we took the drive there and we did what most people do when they go to the grave sight of a loved one. When we arrived back at her home, I could tell she was still itching to get the folder out. I could tell she needed to share this with me. But I knew it was gonna be a moment where I would feel the pain of seeing something that was gonna break my heart. I knew it before she opened the folder. But I still wasn't prepared for what I was about to see. As I flipped from page to page, my heart was sinking. A lump in my throat was growing as I continued. When I flipped to the most exposing picture of all, I was almost at a blank stare, while my head was telling me to flip the page. Brenda said quietly. "It's Brianna's body hanging out of the wreckage on the passenger side." Of course I knew this, but I was frozen. Brenda was explaining that the girl driving, was shoved into Brianna's side and hardly recognizable. It looked like half a car and I couldn't even imagine where the other girls body could have even been. I asked Brenda about the lawsuit and she looked at me and said. "I won. But there is no dollar sign on a peace of mind."

I have to repeat the stupidest comment that has ever rolled off anyone's lips and onto my ears. It wasn't funny stupid, it was hateful ignorant stupid. Six words! Just six! "You only knew her a year." I can't explain the heat that went through my body. I literally felt my blood change temperatures, and they hit scalding. But I had to change the channel in my mind, before I ended up on *Dateline.*

I'm not sure if I've ever known what it feels like to be whole. I've always felt a little broken. But I survive and not only do I survive, I feel I thrive. I will be happy today. What about you? *Tomi Lahren*, on *Louder with Crowder*. Sorry that I'm gonna throw a judgment in here again. But you're nothing but a little blonde 24-year-old bimbo, spewing out anger and hate. All you like to do is chew the cud for attention. What's happened to your white, spoiled, privileged ass, to make you so angry? You're just a mini-me of Ann Coulter with nothing to say. You target people from your tacky hateful show. The words you say are ghastly and vile. She's always saying she won't apologize for her whiteness. Bitch! No one asked you too. But you need to shut your racist, hateful mouth. Obviously she was born to be a bitch. Someone should stick your head in a toilet and flush and repeat. I don't know how *Noah Trevor*, from the *Daily Show*, even interviewed her obnoxious ass. He came from a harder place than anyone of us. He was born a crime. Did you hear what I said. A crime! How can a child be a crime. (unless it's rape, and its not the child that's the crime.) It was against the law in Africa to mix races. He came to America just so he could be black. You know, because a mixed person is automatically dubbed black in America. He felt the need to be one or the other.

I've got an unhappy face right now. I personally think no one should feel the need to be anything other than what they are, unless of course you're a murderer, child molester, rapist or hater. Those people will always be on my shit list.

Trevor, called her out about being angry about everything and I agree, she seems very angry and I don't know why. I need to send her a video of bunnies screwing so she can lighten up. She thinks it's time to make America great again, by spewing out hate. Whatever! I won't go any further, I really don't want to get started. Well, I already got started, I just don't want to continue. Waste of good paper to even talk about it.

DIGGER BEAR

I don't know if I have introduced Digger Bear to you yet, but he is my first indoor cat. I hate indoor cats because they stink up the house, meow during movies and leave hair in your popcorn. But when I get a new kitten, I always let them stay in the house for about a month, so they can get use to the surroundings and that my dog will know they aren't dinner. What I realized real soon about him, is that his shit didn't stink. I mean, it really didn't and it really doesn't. My cat's shit does not stink.

At first he didn't meow like all the other ones. So guess what? He got to stay inside. Until, he came up to me one night and had something to say. He is now an inside and outside cat. I like to think I'm the boss, but he kinda is, since he comes and goes as he pleases. He usually sits at the door when he wants out or on the flower stand when he wants in and sometimes he just stares mysteriously at nothing. Or at least what I think is nothing. Sometimes I even hear his pitter patter coming down the stairs, when actually he isn't coming down the stairs at all. Which leads me into this story.

One night I came home from work and he went to the door and I could have sworn I let him out. Then I hit the sack and got all snuggled in. Then I feel something crawl into bed with me and lay by my side. I'm thinking, and trust me, I'm thinking hard. Did I let Digger Bear out? I swear to you, I believe I was scared stiff. There was no movement from me the rest of the night, while I let myself believe he stayed in and was snuggled by my side. You may ask why didn't I check. I just told you. I was scared stiff. That's how that works. You can't move. When I awoke the next morning, I sat straight up in my bed, after remembering the event. I looked around. No Digger Bear. Moved the covers around, no Digger Bear. Jumped out of my bed. You're wondering how I jumped after being scared stiff aren't you? Wore off in my sleep. So, I went out to the living room, no Digger Bear. I said here kitty, kitty, kitty. No Digger Bear. I looked on the front porch and there he sat, perched on the stand. Yeah! You tell me!

Sometimes I just look at Digger Bear, with his childlike behavior and wonder. Is she in there?

WELCOME TO THE FAMILY

This message came in at 7:14 on July 23, 2016. "Hi, Missy, I just read your book and I absolutely loved it!! I literally laughed out loud at times and had tears in my eye as well and I'm a stranger. Lol. This is weird, but I do think, I may possibly be related to you. Could I give you a call or chat on here and ask a few questions?"

I hadn't seen the first message yet when at 8:21, another message came in. "Hi Missy, I'm extremely nervous writing this. I don't know what to say or how to begin. I'm beyond uncomfortable realizing I am actually sending this, as it could reveal something, never to be revealed.

Your book, its honesty. Things/quotes you wrote and what I felt is that it was written by a genuine good person. It gave me the courage to do this. So here I go! I'm Michelle and I was adopted in 1970. I believe yourself or Kristen could be my sister/cousin. I recently did the ancestry.com thingy basically to know my background, for fun. I get asked nonstop my nationality. I had no idea it comes back with DNA matches. As I'm writing, I realize this was going to be a very, very long, long message as I explain everything. I just decided I would wait. You may not even care. If you do, then I would love to share. But I'm 99% sure, either Kathleen or Marceline is my birth mother. That's the tricky part and yay! My birth mother would have been a twin. It's been interesting and I admit scary to read about the Bicketts. Well, here I go sending this. I'm scared. I hope this finds you in good health and spirits. Take care, Michelle."

My reply. "Wow! I'm lost for words. But yes, if you believe that, I would love to talk to you. Don't be scared of the Bicketts. lol. This kind of news would shock most people, but I have to say my life has been full of changes and out of the blue surprises. It's as if nothing shocks me anymore and I deal with it as it comes. So where do you live? And if I don't respond quickly, it's because I don't keep my notifications on, lol.

I was gonna send you a friend request on Facebook but it doesn't give me that option."

Michelle replied. "I will try and send you one. I am originally from Louisville, Ky. And thanks so much for your reply."

"You're welcome. How old are you? Just curious? How come you don't have any pictures on Facebook?" After I sent the question, I realized she had already told me she was born in 1970. I was hoping she didn't think I didn't know how to do the math.

She replied, "This is an old page I created years ago. It's not my real one. I chuckled in your book when you said that drama finds you via Facebook, Snapchat and Instagram. I didn't know at that time if I would even reach out to you."

"Didn't know you could have two accounts."

"I'm 46 and my birthday is July 3, 1970."

So she sent me a picture and said, "From the few pictures I saw, I don't think I look like either of the twins. But it was baby pics and maybe two others and one in your book. It made me doubtful of my birth family being a Bickett, but I'm pretty confident they are."

"Very pretty. You got me scratching my head because my Mom was married to my Dad at that time. So I'm thinking it's not possible, but who knows. I look more like my dad."

"Thank you. I match the description of your mom and Aunt as far as the hair and skin. What does your mom look like exactly? And when I read your book I thought it can't be Marceline and the divorce, was maybe a year or so after my birth. So I don't know. Was Kathleen single? As far as me having two pages and this may be too lol. But I was engaged two years ago and my fiancé was a major cheater. That's why we never got married and I created this page to reach out to one of his girls one time. I've never used it, that's why you don't see anything on it at all, but when I Google and it takes me to Facebook, it uses this page oddly sometimes. And I figured it was the safest page to use for this."

"Well, my mom looks like Mowgli from the *Jungle Book*. LOL. I'm pretty sure Kathleen was married at the time. Not 100 percent sure. So how does one go about getting the results that lead to this conclusion? Not sure how all that works. Did it just lead you to the family?"

"Well, if that's true and both of them were married and one is actually my birth mother, definitely makes sense as how an adoption would be a choice. One of the reasons, probably not the main, but in my head anyway."

"Well I have another idea in my head. But I need a little more info before spitting it out. Lol"

"It leads strongly there. It's easier to explain verbally probably. But I can type out how it lead me to you. Or you can call me if you like."

So I gave her my number and asked if it was too late to talk. It was going on midnight. I was kind of curious to know some things. Now I have to sleep on it.

So she called and of course I can't remember what all we said. I love talking in person more than texting. But now that I'm writing this story, I just wish she would have messaged me all the conversation. Would make my life easier at the moment. When she started talking about her DNA hit and that it was to Robbie's son Pat Pat. It reminded me that I had just went to dinner with Joe Mack, Summer's dad, that evening. He was talking about Robbie doing that DNA test and Summer wanted to get it done for her birthday, but he laughed and said she ended up wanting something else.

So we talked and talked. It felt like I had known her forever. I told her if she just mainly wanted to know for health reasons, I would meet up with her and have a DNA test done between just the two of us. She said she was living in Georgia with her ailing mother, but she would be bringing her daughter back to Kentucky for school in a few weeks. I told her we would do it then. So I slept on everything, but my head spun, but I had an idea. So I investigated the following morning. I just couldn't rest. Checked out Kathleen's pictures, no Beverly. That's about all the conformation I needed. I thought, screw the DNA test.

MRS. DANIEL OLDREN CECIL

So I decided to head on over to Beverly's. I was quite nervous, when I pulled in her drive, thinking how do I bring this up. I pulled up and blew my horn. She came strolling out to my car and leaned over into the passenger window and asked what's up. I really had no idea how to approach this situation or how she was gonna react. So I just asked. "Did you do anything in the seventies?"

"She replied, "I did a lot of things in the seventies. Why? Who is asking? Who is talking about me?"

"No one Beverly!"

"Well Missy, we will talk about it Monday. It's so hot out here my chickens are laying hard boiled eggs."

I just sat there. She said, "Missy, what is it? Quit beating around the bush."

"Beverly, I like beating around the bush."

"I bet you do."

"That's beside the point. Did you do anything in particular in the seventies?"

She opened the door and sat in the truck. "Well, I did have me a baby."

"I was thinking maybe you did. I just talked to her last night."

She went straight into tears. "Missy, I've always wondered if she was alive or not. It was just her birthday last week and I was thinking about her."

"Well, I have her number if you wanna call her."

"Well, of course I do! I never expected this to happen, not after 46 years. Never dreamed! Never dreamed!"

On my way home I called Michelle and said without hesitation. "I found your momma! Beverly is your momma!!!!!!"

"Wow!!!! How amazing! I didn't expect to find out so soon. Make sure she knows she has a granddaughter too! Her name is Logan!."

Then she sent me a picture of her daughter.

Welcome to the family, Doll.

She said she just sent a letter to the ladies who originally helped her and she told them, "I found my birth mother. They asked which twin and I said neither. And they said they had just finished reading Raywickians and said they are very scary people and for me to be careful. I asked why? (but I already told you I was apprehensive) They said they are criminals and proud of it. It's bad. (but all families have some not perfect-ish people.) and then they said, the book said, Charlie's bar had a melanin limit.

Most scientific way to call someone a racist. I already assumed that as well and was 100 % the reason for my adoption. Then I looked at Charlie's Facebook and could kinda tell. I told her you said to not believe it all, and then I recommended they buy your book and read it."

I had to do some damage control and told her. "They seem scary from the outside looking in, but I promise you, they're not. They're like ciabatta bread. Hard on the outside and and soft in the middle."

"Well' it's in my blood too. Even though I'm not remotely intimidating. Plus, I knew, before I reached out to you."

"And yes, the DEA arrested my uncles for growing marijuana back in the 80s and made an example out of them and put them in prison for 20 years or more which I deem insane. My uncle Jimmy wouldn't hurt a flea. He is the best man I know. My uncle Charlie is absolutely controversial. We were just talking about him today and said if he was a woman he would be the most dramatic woman we had ever seen. He is even acting like he is a Trump fan. I'm sure for shits and giggles. He can't be that stupid. Plus his father, Mr. J.E. Bickett, would beat his ass if he was still alive.

"I believe all families have someone who has done something and most of us are lucky we didn't get caught."

"Well, I believe our family may have found themselves in more predicaments than most. That's what my books are gonna be about. The real people, not the outsider and the media's take on it."

"Lol! Regarding Trump. I haven't read Raywickians yet, but that one really scared them ladies and they told me to be careful."

"People have been scared of Raywick in the past. Has a bad reputation for that. But my place is nothing like any of those bars back in the day. We welcome all creeds and color. Charlie has softened up a bit since he found out his own daughter is gay. My aunt Kathleen use to say people like me were going to hell. Then when I came out to her she just said she was uneducated and apologized. Keep in mind, Charlie writes his books for shock factor. I wrote my book to heal after my house burnt down. Now that I've healed, it's for fun and to document and tell all the stories that surround me. Well, it's not always fun."

"That is awesome that they turned their negative thoughts around. It's sad, but many people have bad thoughts. Racism is pretty deep in some places and I may be a hard pill to swallow for aunts, uncles and grandmas. I definitely look (multicultural) in my head. When I have gotten speeding tickets, it says Caucasian. But I think there is something else, which is what intrigued me about Ancestery.com, not the DNA matches but was a blessing I think."

"We shouldn't have to check mark or race on anything." "True! I always skip on the answer."

"And not to keep talking about Charlie, but he is going to make fun of people whether they're black/white fat/skinny grandma/kid straight hair/curly hair, straight teeth or crooked. That's just him. He is the most sarcastic person I have ever met. And I have to say, I find him quite funny sometimes. As long as you don't wear your feelings on your sleeves, because he hits everybody across the board, literally. He gets me all the time, but I just have to strike back and make fun of him. I make fun of his long ass, nasty beard with food stuck in it. I ask him if it's for dinner later. He will try and get smart back and say, "why ain't your lazy ass working?" I just have to reply, "Unlike your mouth, I occasionally close."

"Thank you; I will be ready, if I meet him." So then I sent her a picture of Summer. "Cute picture."

I got to tell you a real quick story about the boy in the middle. I came in late one night to find him asleep on the floor. I had never seen him before in my life. Summer was asleep on the couch. So I stepped over him quietly and nudged at Summer. When she awoke, I started pointing down at him, like who the hell? She looked at me and said in a very sleepy voice. "Mom, he is gay." I replied, "Okay, goodnight."

So anyway, back to Michelle. I sent her a picture of me being out on the lake.

"Beautiful! My Kentucky home. By the way I spoke with Beverly."

"She called me and she seems very happy. I hope you feel the same?"

"I do. I was thinking about coming out in a couple weeks and coming to your place. How was opening weekend?

"Crazy busy." I said.

"That's good. What's the most popular dish?"

"Steak Nicole and S.O.B. potatoes. My daughter's name is Summer

Nicole."

So Michelle finally came out to visit the family. She came to the Café first. She seemed comfortable enough, but Beverly wasn't gonna let that happen for long. She had to be her regular jokester. Pat Pat was hanging out by the bar with us, but then he disappeared. Then I noticed a black couple sitting over at the table. I looked at Michelle and said, "See black people come here." Then Beverly said, "yeah! And Pat Pat is outside cutting their tires."

Yes, we made a joke about race. Nothing hateful and with all good fun. Then she went with Beverly's to look at pictures and learn about her heritage. But somewhere through the night my grandma had a heart attack.

But before you worry. I will give you the update. Grandma is alive and kickin.

SUNDAY SESSION

I fixed Sunday breakfast as we all stood and sat around the kitchen bar. Byron and I were the only two standing up on the opposite side. Michelle started talking about the Mom that raised her. She was saying that they never had a friend-on-friend relationship, but of course they had a mother daughter relationship. I could tell Beverly felt a little weird with the conversation, as Michelle talked on. She said Logan and her had that kind of friendship connection and she wished she had that kind of relationship with her mother. She said her adoptive dad had to sleep in the back room because he snores and had no control of the house and she felt sorry for him. My mom ruled the house. Then I showed her a picture of my sister and was telling her the story.

Then Michelle said, "Wow! So, she knew who her real mom was? It was an open type of adoption? So your mom knew who was adopting her baby. Like she really knew who was getting her baby that day."

"Yes, they had met."

"Mine was totally closed. When I was typing you Missy, I was like, am I really typing this right now."

Byron started to laugh.

Michelle giggled, "You know like really. My name is Michelle, it felt so weird."

I raised my hand and said, "I was sitting here on a Saturday night all by myself. So she text me saying, I think your mom is my mother. My mind should have been blown, but it wasn't. You know, not much surprises me, coming from the family I come from."

Byron leans his head back like, oh my God, and everybody started to laugh. Then Michelle laughs and said. "Yeah! She really said nothing surprises her."

Then Byron asked. "So you put your DNA out there? Like wherever?"

"Yeah; but I have to be honest with you. I wasn't doing it to find her. I've always known I was adopted, always. My mom would always tell me about a little special girl and that they went to a place and specifically picked her out. Then they brought her home. Then, when I was in the first grade, they told me how I was the special girl, and they used the word adopted. My mom said, I went to school that day and told the whole school. I ran around blurting out. I'm adopted! I'm adopted!"

We all laughed again as Michelle continued her story. "I always knew the pregnancy was inner racial and in Kentucky. So I guess, in my head I was thinking that Beverly got pregnant and then she was like, well, I'll go stay with Uncle Byron. Then I'll come back and no one will know." She looked at Beverly and asked. "It was in 69 when you got pregnant right? So in rural Kentucky, I knew why she wasn't going to have this baby. I even told Beverly last night, if they would've kept me, I would've been the little Negro slave."

We all busted out. I mean I was clapping my hands out loud as I said, "I had to pull weeds for $.10. She would've had you out there for free."

Then Michelle put her hands over her face. "Lord, I would've been up in attic with the dolls."

Byron was laughing his ass off when he said, "There would've been a movie about it. Like *Flowers in the Attic* or something."

Michelle looks back up. "Then in your book, it says something about you having to pick walnuts. I thought Lord, I would have had to pick all the tomatoes."

Then Byron jumped in, "Some beans and corn, everything else."

I was still laughing when I said, "Damn! I wish you would've been here to take my place."

Michelle said, "I would've been outside all day just picking whatever we had to pick."

"You remember the story about me talking about me and Kristen, getting dropped off, with the bucket to fill it up with walnuts?"

Byron was standing over there looking up in the air saying, "blackberries, blueberries, strawberries." I got to talking about driving over to great grandma's house when Beverly chimed in, "I got to tell you guys this. Grandmother was mean."

Jimmy finally puts in his two cents to the conversation. "Grandmother was mean! She sure was. Momma always said, if you talked back to her she would come at you like a bull."

I straightened my back. "One of her sisters got mad because I wrote in the book about Grandmother. I tried to explain to Grandma that I was only a kid. And that I didn't like being dropped off with the bucket, then going to a house that I can't go in because she don't like kids."

Beverly said, "Yes, Mom would deny it."

Byron agreed, "She sure would."

I continued with my childhood story. "She gave me that nasty ass Wrigley's gum to chew and I would sit in the backseat praying, Hail

239

Mary full of Grace blessed are these. I was just a little kid."

Jimmy laughed and bowed his head. "She makes them kids work for an hour or two, for a piece of pie!"

I replied, "she gave that boy,,,,, let's see what's his name. He joined the army. Can't think of his name. She gave him a toboggan and a bologna sandwich for mowing the yard. He told me he was heartbroken."

Michelle's high pitch laugh echoes through the house.

Jimmy nodded his head. "Mama's Mom! Boy! I've never seen her grin in my life. You know these old pictures that you see at *Cracker Barrel?* There ain't never one of them grinning. You know why? They didn't have nothing to grin about. They had to work like hell to keep meat on the table."

Michelle jumps back in about the DNA test. She said, she didn't even know *ancestry.com* did that. "I just wanted to know medical stuff. But the older I get, I wake up curious."

Byron said, "Hell yeah! I understand."

Michelle said, "I always get asked. What nationality are you? It'll be my first day at work and by lunch, they say, I have a question for you. This has been my whole life. So I just wanted to know. So I just started making up stuff and said that I was exotic or that I am Latino. Every time I would tell people that I was black-and-white, they would say, I don't see the black. They kept saying, I don't see that. So finally I said okay, I'm just gonna make something up. I could have said, I got a little mutt in me. So this ancestry thing, I was trying to figure out if it was legit. Then I seen that's where people find people and I was like, hmm…. So I did *Amazon prime*. So I spit in my little cup and I sent it back the next day."

Byron asked with curiosity. "Is that how that works?"

Michelle said, "Yep! You just spit in it. This literally all happened within a month. The first thing I had was the first cousin match. Then it tells the percentage. My match was extremely high. Then it goes down to the fourth and fifth, then it was a big gap. There was a Facebook group called DNA detective. I told them there was a first cousin match and asked, so what do I do now? The flow of people that were responding back was amazing. I thought that was the lottery ticket of DNA."

I start explaining to Jimmy about how they do this experimental test with people on TV. They got about 20 different people, and got them to spit in a cup. They asked them to name one nationality that they like the least and to write it down. When the results came back, they were all surprised to have a percentage of that nationality that they disliked, to be part of them. All of a sudden the conversation got mumble jumble with everyone talking at once. Then I heard Michelle say clearly. "When you turn 21, you can go to the courthouse. But then I realized it was a sealed document and you have to pay to open it up."

I looked at Beverly. "You owe her some money for having to pay for that."

Jimmy started laughing. "Oh Beverly!" And we were all laughing, but laughed even harder when Beverly said. "I can pay you back in pears? We know she didn't contact us for money. We don't have any."

"After I looked you guys up I knew I wasn't going to be a congressman daughter. I could have been *Kris Kristofferson's* daughter. I might have been, I didn't know. Then I realize it was Raywick, Kentucky."

I said, "Raywick!" as I laughed. "You should have ran!"

Michelle said, "I knew the family was Catholic, because I was raised from a Catholic charity. I'm not Catholic anymore, but I was raised that way. It also said they were one of nine and had a set of twins. I thought wow! Then they sent me a census. It has all the siblings out there and Beverly's name was first. So I thought she was the eldest, and it didn't have a year for her birth."

Beverly blushed. "That's because I was born at home and I didn't have a birth certificate."

Michelle said, "You was completely off the radar when I was looking all this stuff up."

I chuckled, "Beverly has always been off the radar."

"Trish's age was on there and I knew she was too young. Then they sent me stuff about Charlie's book and they said, I was colorful. That was the word! You come from a colorful family!"

Bryon laughs really hard. "Ha ha! You got that right!"

"Then I get the Cornbread Mafia book and I'm just reading, thinking wow! Then an article says how two of the kids are doing long term time and one daughter has been murdered. So I'm just thinking everything! Then I started reading about Charlie. I went to his page. Initially I was like, I'm good! I don't need to look no further. I really was! Charlie was the first one they pulled up."

Byron said, "Oh Lord! Charlie!"

Jimmy said as he chuckled. "I bet she thought, what is this? There is Bigfoot. Lord! We're gonna have to cremate his old ass, because there isn't 6 people who would carry him."

Michelle continued on. "Let me tell you what I thought about doing. I was just gonna come to town one-day and look for the white house. Then I was gonna to go to Missy's Café. I was thinking, I'm going to eat and I'm gonna peep and see who I look like. Because, I was thinking I don't need all that shit. But then I was on Facebook, looking at people and I seen Marceline's daughter and I found Kathleen's daughter. But I don't know how I found Missy's book. But I was able to put Kindle on my phone. So I read it that day. I read it in one day! It was something about her book, because I'm being honest. Because I was really like, I'm going to let the good dog lie. I'm just going to let this lay, especially since I'm not the Governor's daughter. Like I said, I read about Raywick. You know what I'm saying!" She looked at me and repeated. "You know what I'm saying! So I thought maybe I should look up who the man was, you know, my biological father, because maybe this family doesn't want this brought out. Maybe his family would be more open. I was afraid your family might be like, don't be coming around here telling nobody nothing. But something about Missy's book." As she paused. "I don't know if it was her honesty or what? It was just something about it."

Byron said, "Yeah! Well that's good."

"So I thought, I'll reach out to her or say something, because I couldn't find any of you women on Facebook."

"Because they are all living in the ice ages." I said with laughter.

"I was so scared to reach out, but I decided to. Even though I didn't give you my real Facebook page."

"Why?"

"Because I was scared. If you look on my Facebook page, it is mostly black. I was afraid I might have a picture with one of my sisters, with a pick in her hair or something or something about Black Lives Matter. With all the stuff going on, I was scared. You know what I mean? I just wanted to make sure, before I would friend Missy."

"Yeah, that's a pretty hot button issue."

"Just because I'm anti-brutality doesn't mean I'm anti-police." "I concur."

"But anyway, another subject for another day. I reached out to Missy. Beverly is nowhere on the radar. Still wasn't adding up. So Missy was saying, I don't think it was my mama and she didn't think it was Kathleen either."

"Lets just say this, after Michelle Facebooked me Saturday night, I had it figured out by Sunday morning."

Bryon slapped me on the shoulder. "Good detective work, Missy."

"You know it! I went over Kathleen's and said I want to see your wedding pictures and low and behold there was no Beverly. Absent, nada. Right then and there I knew."

"Hum!" Beverly paused. "She wasn't pregnant was she Missy? I wasn't in them at all. Because I was about seven months pregnant."

243

Michelle said, "Missy said, I will tell you what I will do. I will do a DNA test for you, if you're just trying to figure out your heritage. So that night I'm thinking, I have a month or so if I still want to do this. But the very next day, she said, I know who your mom is, and I was like, this is crazy." Everybody laughs and Byron laughs and shakes his head and said, "Private investigator!"

I chuckled, "I always wanted to be an investigator."

Michelle said, "She said it's my aunt Beverly. It's a small town and I remember hearing whispering about Beverly going away for awhile. Then she said she looked at Kathleen's pictures. And the wedding was May 31 or something and my birthday is July 3. So you would've been good and pregnant." as she looked at Beverly. "And mysteriously, Beverly wasn't in the pictures. Then Missy asked me, if it was okay for Beverly to call me. And this was really funny to me. She said, it might be awhile, because she is canning tomatoes today. I thought Lord! This is country. I mean.... you know......"

Beverly looked at her and laughed. "You may have thought I was out there skinning chickens or something."

Michelle started to laugh. "I looked at my friend, and said, she is canning tomatoes."

"Or Missy, you could've told her I was outside wringing a chicken's neck."

As Byron laughed. "Yeah, snapin their necks."

Michelle said, "Then Missy was telling me how she went about asking Beverly. Said she was nervous as hell."

I walked around and put my hands on Beverly's shoulder. "Beverly looked at me funny and said, Well, I did have a baby."

Michelle seemed to get a little emotional. "Yeah! Missy said you started crying and said you didn't want to give me up. And that you named me and you was worried if I was dead or alive. She also said, that you knew my birthday just passed. It really made me cry that she would know my birthday. This is right after my birthday a couple weeks later. Beverly called me that night."

Byron said with awe. "That must've been a conversation."

Beverly started to twiddle her fingers. "I told Missy, I had to put off the call, because I had to tell Ricky first. But Ricky knew I had been pregnant back in the day. Most people did."

Excitingly Michelle said. "Oh! It wasn't a secret?"

Beverly nodded. "No! It wasn't a secret. I mean it kinda was. He just told me that was okay and that he would want to know who his child was."

Byron hit the bar with his hand. "Exactly!"

Beverly lowered her shoulders. "Later that evening he came in and asked, have you called your daughter yet? And I was just sitting there thinking what to say. I was just staring at the number, I was both excited and nervous. So I finally called and the conversation was so easy."

Byron said, "Y'all talk just alike. Fast."

"I was thinking she talked more like Jimmy. And if you heard Summer talk, she talks really fast. Oh my God! Sometimes, I just have to be like, slow it down young lady." Then Beverly went on to say. "When I first talked to Logan over here, she sounded just like Summer."

I looked over at Logan. "Beverly, now that you just mentioned that, I haven't heard a word out of Logan."

Logan raised her hand and said. "Hi!" We all start laughing.

Michelle said, "When I was on the phone with Beverly, she kept saying I can't believe I'm talking to my daughter over and over again. She even said she remembers what she was doing the day she had me. Said she was sitting there playing cards around 3 o'clock when her water broke."

Beverly responded with, "I went to the hospital and I had two little pains and you shot right out."

"That's it, huh!" as Byron slapped the counter again.

I yelled out. "Well! You're one lucky son of a bitch. My story was nothing like that."

Beverly giggled, "I was prepared for pain, but I didn't have any. You popped your little head out, just like a worm coming out of an apple."

I looked at Beverly and said. "Now you can be thankful for helping me write my book. Look at what has come out of it."

Somehow we got on the conversation of birth certificates. Beverly said that she never had one and that when she went to draw her Social Security check, she had to get work to write a letter and get it notarized. Byron looked confused when he asked. "You never had a birth certificate?"

"Nope! I was born at home."

Jimmy finally chimes in again. "Where's mine at? I had one." But no one cared and Michelle started talking about what the lady said when they wrote her back about her birth mother. I interrupted and said "Be careful!"

Michelle said, "Yeah they said be very very careful. They are some very scary people!!"

We all laughed and Beverly flashbacked. "Oh Lord! I'm still thinking about her saying she would be a little slave girl for Momma."

Michelle giggled, "I know, I know! Right?"

I pointed at her, "You are the same age as me and you could've done all the work. I still would've been looking out the windows at the neighbors."

Jimmy said, "Mom made all of us go to bed early."

Beverly said, "That's right, Jimmy. All the other kids would be out playing and we would be looking out the window waving. But Mom had nine of us kids and I can't imagine back in those days."

Michelle said "Oh yeah! Oh yeah! Tough I bet."

All of a sudden the conversation turns to chaos. Everyone is talking but Logan. Then I heard someone say, "Grandma had a heart attack with

246

just the thought of you coming out to visit."

Michelle busted out laughing and covered her face. "I know, I know, I know!

Jimmy stood up. "Look here! I was telling Charlie Bickett on the way to Louisville the other day, I will always remember when Beverly met her daughter, because momma went to the hospital that day."

Michelle uncovered her face. "That will always be in the back of my head though. I'm thinking it could have triggered something. Oh my God."

Beverly said, "I just gave them a little nun doll that I had when I was probably around 8 or 9. Momma gave it to me. I will never forget that Christmas. Marceline and Kathleen,,,,, well,,, we opened up our gifts or whatever and they had pretty ballerina dolls."

Byron laughed and said, "You got a nun doll……"

Michelle said, "I guess your mom was looking at you saying, this one is going to be a nun."

"That's believable though." As Byron nodded his head.

Beverly looked wistful. "They sent me down to the nun school. I wasn't bad, I really wasn't. I never fooled around or nothing. I got out of high school, before I did anything. My mom always accused me of everything. Sent me down to the Mount, when I was 15 and I got into trouble. I got in trouble down there all the time, because I always playing jokes, just jokes. Like smoking that Tampax. The little girl told on me. But anyway the next year, they wanted to send me back. Mom said you're going back, but they wouldn't take me back."

Byron said, "You ain't coming huh. They didn't want you? "

"Mama was mad as a wet hen about that. But I met people from all over the world. But when they left me the first day, I cried."

Then Byron and Jimmy started getting up to leave and I lost out on the rest of the conversation. I stopped them at the door. "We have to take pictures before they leave." Beverly was saying, "I hate pictures" and

247

Jimmy said, "Beverly get your ass on up here." Beverly grabbed Byron and said, "Stand in front of me. Get in here Logan." Soon as we all got situated, I was in front and let a big fart. Bryon screams, "You nasty thing you." I ran off and Jimmy said "Come on Missy, get back over here. We have smelt worse." I was laughing so hard, "I was trying to hold it, I swear." Bryon said, "well good Lord! That smell." Jimmy walked off, "see you guys. Really got to go now that Missy fumigated the house." Everybody gave everybody a hug as they were walking out. It was a very nice morning in the country.

Oh! One last story. I was showing Michelle and Logan, Summer's paintings. I was telling them about my dad asking why Summer is always painting boobs on her paintings. Like he looked really concerned about it and I was like, Daddy don't worry, she is not a lesbian. Then Michelle asked, "Is she girly, girly?"

"She is the worst of girly girls. 90 percent of her money goes to clothes and fashion. I'm gonna have to break that habit. But every time I say something to her she is like, Mom it could be worse! I could be a drug addict or a this or that. She always gets me with that. Damn! She gets me every time. She uses the excuse that artists and Virgos are the reason all her clothes are on the floor, instead of the closet."

Logan giggles as I continue with my rant. "When she was living here, I could tell when she cleaned her room, because I could hear her walking across the floor. But that was only once in a blue moon. I would yell up and say, Summer! Put all your clothes back on the floor! She wants things to be neat, but when she gets dressed she tries on every outfit and in the floor it goes. After she wears it twice, it's time to sell it. It would be different if it wasn't all expensive clothes. It's like she is walking on a million-dollar rug. If I was to take her to Hollister to shop, it would be like taking her to the Goodwill. I'm like shit! I'm never gonna get to retire. Joe Mack tells me, well you might not get to retire, but least you have a daughter who has the personality of a fat girl."

"Oh, so she is sweet?"

It had been a week or so and I hadn't spoken to Michelle since the visit. So I sent her a text. "Were we all too redneck for you?"

She replied, "No!" with a lot of ooooooooos. "You all were super sweet! I felt really blessed. Redneck would not be the word I would use at all. Country, yeah maybe. I found out Beverly raised a real live deer inside the house. Now that's country and adorable stuff."

"Yeah my second book has something in there about the difference between rednecks, country people, farmers and hillbillies."

So she asked me to school her and I did of course. You should have read all about that in my second book. So you guys already know the difference. She said that maybe Beverly was a farmer. Then I replied. "I don't really know what she is. She is pretty unique in her own way and I'm not sure what I am."

"You're very metropolitan/city to me. What is Ricky? Is he a farmer? He stayed in his man cave when I was there."

"Not really sure. He might be a country boy. I haven't hung around him enough to know exactly."

"When I think of a hillbilly, I think of that Hee Haw Show, with the harmonicas and straw hats."

"Yeah, Charlie! With his banjos and jugs." "What the hell is jugs?"

"Well, it's slang for boobs. Naw! Just kidding. You never seen people blow into them and play music?"

"I guess I don't remember. I was little. I remember guys with sideburns and overalls. What was Bo and Duke? Daisy? Boss Hog? Roscoe?

"Rebel country boys like Jimmy. Red neck girl like Amy. Boss Hog was like a guy I know that use to run the bar by my uncles and Roscoe, well there is no words for him."

My grandmother loves *Hee Haw*. She's country I guess. Most country boys are kind of sexy aren't they? Get them girls in trouble. What's Summer and Kristin's daughter?"

"My daughter and Kristin's daughter are night and day. I mean polar opposites. Summer is like *Sarah Jessica Parker* from *Sex in the City* and Kaitlin is a straight up country girl. She likes riding horses and shooting guns."

"Oh yeah, I can tell Summer is very *Sex in the City*. I didn't get to meet Kaitlyn. Summer always been like that, being raised in the country?"

"Yeah!"

"Are they close?"

"Not like me and Kristin were at that age. But they're friends." "How big is the high school?"

"Usually around three hundred people."

"My family used to play with each other and talk and watch all the cartoon channels. Now a days they stay inside on cell phones and text."

Her text kept coming in scrambled. I told her it's like working a puzzle. She said, "That's because I'm team droid."

"Well! I'm team Apple."

Which leads to a by the way that reminds me moment. A funny story that my aunt Darlene was telling the other night. She came into the café and was telling me about two other ladies. She said one lady came up to the other one and asked if she could have some money for some food because she was short on cash. So the other lady said to her, if you're hungry, why don't you eat that apple on the back of your phone?

I'm thinking I may be showing early signs of whatever Shelley Duvall has. Mentally that is. You know, the lady from the movie, *The Shining* and the one who interviewed by *Dr. Phil*. One word always reminds me of another story. What is that called? Google won't even tell me what it is. Writing this book has caused me to self diagnose myself with a lot of things. Help! Doctor! Doctor! Give me the news.

SUMMER PREVIEW

This month's preview, August 2013. Oh shit! That was a three year ago preview. But anyway, lets continue. Where do we begin with Summer? You met her when she was young, and heard a bit of her through my stories. But what is she like, you ask? Well she has entertained me all my life with her vibrant personality. At times she reminds me of *Kristen Wiggs,* off of *Saturday Night Live* and the movie *Brides Maids.* I get a kick out of her quite often.

Oh LAWD!

I myself am a scientific person, maybe not totally scientific, anything is possible. I wanted to give Summer a base, in some kind of religion, I had to lay her down some sort of guideline. I told her when she was older she could follow her own heart and that she has. She has somewhat ended up like me. She doesn't go to church on her own, but she does go with her dad when he asks, just to please him. To me, that is a good thing to do. You don't have to agree with your parents, but sometimes, it's nice just to give in and do something like that. She is very, very open minded, I mean very! I love it! Summer, has never been, like the rest of the little country girls, growing up in these here parts.. Put it this way, she isn't rough and ragged as some. Not that being a country girl is a bad thing. Just saying! I took her on one of my family's big horse and 4-wheeler rides one time and she begged me to not ever make her go again. She said it stressed her out to watch the drunk people flip their four-wheelers and act like idiots.

I just took her to get a tattoo the other day. Yes! I said tattoo. Her dad is gonna die when he finds out. Yes, we kept it from him. She decided to get an equal sign on her wrist. It's funny, as she was getting it done, she looked up with concern. "Do you think people are gonna think I'm a lesbian?" We paused, then we both laughed. Then she said, "Not that it matters." When it was finished, reality set in. "Omg! Daddy is gonna kill me."

"Summer, he won't even notice it. You're a painter and it looks like paint. Just wear a bracelet when you're around him."

Summer and I have always had a "I will tell you everything" relationship. Well, almost, more than most mother/daughter, but close enough.. It did take me a minute to find out that she had sex. Then a minute longer to found out she smoked a little weed. Caught her red handed. Glad I didn't catch her having sex red handed, not sure how that would have gone down.

I walked into the cafe one night after work. That's where her and a few of her friends would go after I left work. I let them hang there. It was a safe place. Soon as I walked in, I smelled it. You could tell they were scrambling to hide it. Then they put their hands down to their sides. I peeked over their shoulders. "Give it up ladies." They hesitated and slowly set it on the bar and I picked it up and put it in my pocket. "Thanks!" Then I nonchalantly turned to walk out. Their mouths dropped when I looked back and said, "I will enjoy this sometime in the near future."

"Mom! That's not fair!"

"Summer, don't talk to me about fair! Bye bye."

Summer's small car crash: Definitely no biggie. But I was meeting her at Panera Bread and as I was waiting, I heard a crash. I looked around and it was her. She had hit a pole when pulling into the spot. I ran to her car and said. "Are you stoned or what?"

She threw her purse over her shoulder and said. "Mom it's only noon."

"Well, how the hell did you hit that?"

"I thought the little block things were supposed to stop me."

"Omg!"

"Shhh Mom! Let's eat. I'm hungry."

I got to tell you about one other episode she had. I had given her my old Tahoe for her sixteenth birthday. So we had that one and my new one sitting in the drive. I had parked somewhat behind her and I thought about it before I went to sleep. I thought, I sure hope she doesn't back into that. Well, she had school the next morning and I heard the front door shut and one minute to follow, I heard a loud, long crunching noise. I knew what had happened in an instant. I ran outside and Summer was just standing there looking like Cindy Lou Who, with her arms out, face long and saddened eyes. I looked at the vehicles and shook my head. Mine was scarred all the way down one side and the front end of hers was smashed in. I didn't yell or anything, when I said. "Why did you keep backing up after you first heard it hit?"

"Mom, I thought I had ran over a branch."

Yep! That was her face.

Oh, and I have another one. Someone came running in the café one night and said they had seen a blue convertible hit a maroon car and then it left. And we were all thinking! Summer!!!!! What?

So I called her. "Summer where are you?"

"I'm going to McDonalds."

"Did you just hit Sandy's car?"

"Yes, but I'm coming right back."

Sometimes I just wanna knock some sense into her, and hit her in the head like Rafiki did Simba, in the movie, *The Lion King.*

Did you really say that? You better think again Mom!

Summer walked out of the bathroom the other day and said it felt like aliens were eating her belly again. "Mom, my periods are so bad. Why can't it be like that post on Facebook.. Why can't mother nature just text me and say "Whad-dup girl? You ain't pregnant. Have a great week. Talk to ya next month.""

BATH SALTS

Sometime in June, 2013, Summer and I were coming back from Louisville one day just singing our little hearts away. As I was coming down highway 49 and getting close to Mom's house I came up around a hill and a curve. There was a freaking lady sitting on the edge of the other side of the road. Summer said, "Mom, what was that lady doing? She is gonna get ran over." Her concerns were high.

"I don't know, Summer." I kept driving for a second, but my conscious immediately began to speak to me. Yes! Another delayed reaction. I turned and pulled into Mom's driveway. Summer asked, "Why are we going here? I thought you said you needed to get home to do something."

"I do Summer, but I can't let that lady sit in the road. She is gonna get killed if somebody comes around that curve from the other direction."

I headed straight back there. When I pulled in the road beside the highway to yell to her to see what was up, we could hear her almost talking in tongues. I opened my door to get out, when Summer grabbed my arm and said, "Mom! What are you doing?"

"I'm gonna go see what's up with this lady. What do you think I'm doing?"

She wouldn't let go of my arm, "don't go!"

"Why Summer?"

"BATH SALTS!"

I looked at her with laughter, "bath salts?"

Yes, Mom! Bath salts! Haven't you been watching the news? You can't go out there."

We sat there for a minute as I listened to the lady talk in tongues. So for Summer's comfort and obviously mine, I called Mom and Joe Eddie. When they arrived they realized the lady was really off her rocker. I looked at Joe Eddie and said, "before you try and handle this situation,

I hope you have practiced on sandpapering a bobcat's ass first, because that woman is full of piss, fire, vinegar and some crazy ."

REAL TIME: When I sit up here and write, I wanna punch my computer in the throat, if it had a throat. I will be trying to write and the pages start to scroll on their own, as if someone is messing with the mouse. Computer? Ghost? I will let you be the judge and jury.

CHICAGO

Summer and I had already been to Chicago several times. I started taking her when she was around the age of eight. Even at that young age, she liked shopping Michigan Avenue. While on this trip we were in a hotel room. Summer was in the bathroom as I was flipping through the channels. No sooner than I had flipped it on *Sex in the City*, there was a scene where Samantha had a man, and old old man, in bed and he was naked. Summer came strolling out of the bathroom and the man getting out of bed happened simultaneously. Summer looked up and said, "Look Mom! Someone let the air out of his butt!"

As she got a little older, her *Sarah Jessica Parker* style started coming out. Her friends and her were the young version of *Sex and the City*. I had to walk to all the shops, stand around and watch her and her friends try things on. I'm not much of a shopper, or fashion queen. She must have got the bug from her Nana. They walked into one shop, as I stood outside. When they came out, she was stunned. "Oh my God! Mom! It was like in the movie *Pretty Woman*. The ladies were staring at us, like we weren't suppose to be in there. And when we looked at the price of this coat, it was one million dollars! One million dollars."

"Summer, did you say one million dollars?"

"Yes, Mom! One million dollars!"

"No wonder they were staring at you." as I began to laugh.

258

Amanda and Summer.

I just asked Siri how to spell simultaneously because I had another brain fart. She gave me, "Sam can you sleep." I asked again and she said "Send me to teeny leap" I was wondering where teeny leap might be. I asked once more and she asked if I was ready to go to "Sammy Tennessee." Really Siri! I guess she thinks I need a vacation.

So anyway, Summer and I try to hit Chicago every year. It's our thing. She is 20 as I'm writing this and still at Bellarmine. She was on the phone with me right before Christmas, and stated to me that we should go to Chicago for Christmas. I said, "sure!" I heard her telling a friend, "OMG! I just asked my mom to take me back to Chicago for Christmas and she said sure. How easy was that?"

So we went. Not sure who went that time. Don't have any pictures to jar my brain. But here is a story about one of the summer trips.

This time we took along Logan and one of my workers, Jess. I call her Miles. As we were arriving into the city we were entertaining ourselves with some Helen Keller jokes. Politically incorrect? Yes! Sorry, but some of them are just funny. As we were laughing inappropriately, we noticed there was a big event going on down by the lake. Logan started jumping up and down in the back seat screaming, "Omg! Omg! Look y'all. What's going on over there?"

"Not sure! You guys wanna check it out?" I said. "Sure!" Everyone was agreeable.

"It look's to be a doosey of an event. Wonder how much it cost to get in?" Logan asked.

"Don't worry about it." I replied and swerved my big ass Tahoe right off the exit. It happened to be the wrong exit, so it took a minute to get back to where we were going. Summer was getting a little frustrated when she said. "I'm gonna explode like confetti, if you don't hurry up and find this place!"

"Calm your nipples, Summer!"

So we finally found a parking space and as we were walking up to the gate, some lady asked us if we were looking for tickets. We said kinda. But we still didn't know what the event was all about. Logan looked at her and asked. "What's going on in there?"

The lady replied, "They're having a big BMX event. They're filming everything for *Spike TV*. If you guys wanna go, I got four extra tickets."

"How much are the tickets?" Logan asked.

"I will give them to you for free."

"Free!" Logan said with a big grin on his face and snapped them right out of her hands. As she walked off Logan looked at me and said. "I thought maybe that bitch was gonna try and scam us."

As we walked through the gate, they were giving away all kinds of free shit. It's amazing what you think is cool when it's free. They were passing out toboggans and fans, paper fans that is, free drinks, and etc.

It was hot as balls that day. Logan was like, "What the hell? Why would they give us toboggans on a hot ass day like this? We're out here sweating like pigs, if pigs sweat. Toboggan and a fan! What an oxy moron!"

When we walked into this one tent, they were taking free pictures. So we started to model and ham it up. It wasn't your typical pictures they were taking. It made us look like we were in commercials and riding in race cars. It was pretty cool.

When we were done taking the pictures, we all walked separate ways. Summer came running back over to me, smacking me on the shoulder. "Mom, Mom! We can get on TV over there in that tent."

"For what?" I replied" I don't want to be on TV."

Logan and Summer began to beg me. "Please, please. It's our chance."

"Your chance for what? Who cares to be on TV. I don't wanna be."

"We do!" They said with excitement..

"Okay! If it makes you happy. What do we have to do?"

"Well, they're gonna be interviewing some rappers and we will just be in the audience." Summer said.

"In the audience huh?" So I complied. Wasn't much fun for me. When it aired on TV, that wasn't much fun either. There I just sat, in the crowd, sweating and waving my fan. I hate being on video, but there I sat. My five minutes of fame! Whatever! I thought. Why do people want to be on TV so much? I've had people to tell me to get on *Diners Drive-in and Dives*. I have always been like, no way! If he shows up, someone has to pretend to be me. The irony now, (we) my cafe and my waitresses are about to be filmed for a reality show. Tell ya more about that later.

After that, we got fabulous rooms at the Hilton Downtown. Soon as we got to the room, Logan started to get dressed. Summer was still in her gear from the drive and the event. When Logan walked out of the bathroom, Summer told him he looked like he was going to a wedding.

"Where are we going, Mom? Cause I don't feel like getting that dressed up. Logan, why do you look that way?"

"Uuuhhh!!! God Summer! I just want to dress up! I never get to dress up in our one horse town. I'm on vacation and I just feel like it."

"Can you two kids not worry about what each other is wearing, and just wear what's comfortable to you. We're leaving in 30, so be ready either way."

"Well, Mom, you are gonna have to buy me a new bra today."

"Why today?"

"Because I brought the wrong one and you cursed me with hard nipples." Then Summer sat down at the make up mirror and before I could reply to her nipple comment, she farts and it actually surprises her. "That's my girl! Let it out. You know they say if you hold them in, it travels up your spine and that's where shitty ideas come from."

"I know all about shitty ideas. Omg! This makeup mirror is unforgiving."

"I know it gives you a complex, don't it?"

"Yes. Look at all these blackheads. I wish I had my strips. It feels really good when you can pull out a whole colony at the same time."

"Look Summer! I was at Sephora the other day. I told the lady I was looking for some pore filler. She said your pores aren't big and I will tell you what's big. This lady that came in here the other day. Her pores were so big, I could have put my pocket change in them."

"Wow! That's big. So where are we going?"

"I think I will take us to the pier."

"Sounds like awesomeness."

As we were driving over there, we had come to a stop, when we heard Logan shout out with excitement and smacking the back of my seat.. "Omg!" Omg omg. Hey Missy! Missy! Missy! Can we PLEASE take a ride on the Segway? It will be a cool way to view the city."

As we all looked up, from the vehicle and out into the street. WHOOP! The woman riding on the Segway, bit the dust on the curb. Her face planted on North Michigan Avenue. In an instant Logan laughed and said. "Never mind! Let's keep going. I will just view the city from the safety of the truck."

"Good idea, Logan. Let's go see *Cirque du Solei.*" I said.

"Yes! Lets. I love a dramatic mix of circus arts and street entertainment."

After viewing the show, we were walking back to the truck. Summer looks over at me. "That would have been so much better on mushrooms."

I stopped dead in my tracks. My mouth dropped. "Excuse me!"

"Ha-ha-ha, Mom! You know I'm just kidding. You know, I know nothing of mushrooms."

"You better not, young lady!"

Then we headed on up to China Town. After we parked, a group of Asian kids were being dismissed from school. Logan tossed me his camera, and said, take a picture Missy. His tall ass started walking in the middle of the Asian kids.

"Find Waldo!" He yelled above their heads.

"Don't think that's gonna be too hard Logan, with your big white ass in the middle. I'm sure they think you're Godzilla."

"Hey, Mom!" Summer yelled as she was looking in the window of a Chinese restaurant. "Look at the size of that lobster."

"Omg! It's huge. Looks like something on a Godzilla movie. Let's go eat it!" Logan said.

Summer turned up her nose. "Eeeewww! It's in green water."

Logan started to laugh.

"Logan, what is so funny about a lobster?" Miles said.

"Sheeewl, I don't know. I haven't been around them long enough to know."

"Son, you are retarded." She replied.

"Let's go in?" as he rubbed his hands together. "I can't wait to eat the creature from the Green Lagoon." So we walked in. "Jesus! It smells like rotton ass up in here."

You could smell the stench of the lobster tank. Summer put her hand over her mouth and was about to gag. "Mom! I don't think I want to eat here."

"Let's give it a chance Summer. Fish never smells like roses."

As we took are seats, two Asian ladies sat in the corner just staring at us. Summer seemed uncomfortable. "What are they staring at Mom? This is weird."

Logan leans in and whispers. "I wanna go take a picture of them." So he slid over there and snapped a picture and ran back to the table. "Those two ladies were looking at me like I was an idiot."

I started to giggle and looked down at the menu. It was very extensive, but with lots of fucked up crazy shit on it. Logan wanted to try everything on the menu. He had to be adventurous, which is cool and I love it. Logan spoke with excitement, "Sheeewl! What am I gonna order? I really want something different."

Jess chimed in. "I'm staying simple. This place creeps me out."

We all passed on the lobster. After reading the menu forever, Logan opted for the quail eggs. "Oh! I've never had them." as he rubbed his hands together. He was so excited till the moment they brought them to the table.

"Sheewl, what is it?" as his face went sour. "Omg, it's the size of my thumb." Logan thought it would be something magnificent, but magnificent, it wasn't. He was so disappointed. "What am I gonna eat now?"

"Guess we can go get a hotdog at the stand." Summer said, as she started to laugh.

"No bitches! I'm hungry and I want to experience some real Chinese." So he ordered something new, as Summer ate her salad and said. "This dressing taste like Yankee candle, but in a good way."

"Like Christmas time." Logan said as he wiggled his brows. Then his other dish showed up. It was a sight for sore eyes and smelled even worse, as Logan just stared at it. "If only Ray Charles could see this shit. Shewl, this sucks. Let's blow this popsicle stand."

So, as we were leaving, it started to rain. We grabbed some newspaper out of the lobby, since we had several blocks to get to our car. So we started to run. Logan yelled and pointed, "Look at Summer." When I looked up, Summer was out front leading the pack, she was running pigeon toed, in her romper. She ran across the street and was yelling and waving while holding her little bag of goodies up in the air. "Come on you puussssiiees…" Her knees were rubbing back and forth, she turned around and yelled again. "Mom, I gotta go. Seriously! Come on you bitches! Run faster."

So we all threw down the newspapers we had over our head and darted toward the truck, splashing water everywhere. When we all jumped in the truck, we were wet as a whale. Then we started laughing and accusing Summer of pissing her pants. Couldn't really tell, because we were soaked and looked as sad as drowned kittens.

"What are you guys cackling about?"

"Summer pissed her pants! Summer pissed her pants!" Logan kept saying.

"Did not, you bitch. Shut it or I will cut you!"

"GIRL!! You wouldn't know where to start. You gonna cut me with your mascara stick?" Logan shouted back.

"I might, if you don't shut your face."

"You can't shut your face. You can only shut your mouth. So give it to me baby, ah huh ah huh."

"You're stupid!" Summer said as she rolled her eyes and laughed.

"Ok you two!" I chimed in. "What do you all wanna do after I take Summer back to change her pee clothes."

"MOM!" as she just stared at me and folded her arms and stared out the window.

"Just kidding baby!" as I reached back and rubbed her head.

"Hey Mom, turn that song up."

"Oh it's *Miley Cyrus*. I love her."

Then Logan and Summer start belting out the words to the song, *The Climb*. We were driving down Wacker Drive with the windows down and wind in our hair when Jess and I decided to join in on the fun. *"There's always gonna be another mountain."*

Jess and I turned to the back seat to see Logan and Summer air roping to the music and climbing a fake mountain. We started busting out laughing. I wasn't laughing for long. I turned back around and the light had turned red. Yep! We were pulled over. "Son of a bitch!"

"Shit Missy! Why are you always getting pulled over?" Jess said.

The officer came to the window looked around and asked some questions, that's it. He didn't give me a ticket. When he walked away, Summer yelled from the back seat. "Mom! That's not fair!"

"What do you mean Summer? How is it not fair?"

269

"When I got pulled over, I got a ticket."

"So you're saying, because you got one, that means you want your mom to get one. Plus, I paid for yours. What's up with that crazy girl?"

"I don't know Mom. Just not fair."

"Just be glad Summer." Logan said.

"I am." As she huffed and puffed.

While at the BMX event, Summer and Logan noticed one of their favorite bands were gonna be playing the next night. So that night, Logan and Summer got all dressed up. They were heading to a big concert, all by themselves. I was nervous to let them venture out on their own in the big city. I was letting the kiddos spread their wings. We told them we would meet up with them later. As were driving them there, it started to rain again. "I wonder if the concert is cancelled?" Logan asked with concern.

Summer replied, "They said it would be on, rain or shine."

I stated with concern. "Maybe you ought to make sure Summer, before I leave you here."

"Mom! I told you. Rain or shine." She can be a hard headed turd.

So they got out and off into the rain they ran. No sooner than we had arrived back to the room, the phone rang. "Mom, it's cancelled."

"Summer, I told you to check first."

"I know Mom, just stop it! Can you come get us?"

"No! Why don't you and Logan just get a cab and meet us at the sushi place down the street."

"Fine!"

Jess and I beat them there and we had already ordered. When Logan and her arrived, she wasn't speaking to anyone and looked mad as hell.

"Summer what's up?"

She sat down and folded her arms. "Nothing Mom!"

"Well something is!"

"Nothing! Just stop asking me!"

"You are about to start your period aren't you? What's wrong with you?"

"Mom, really! Just leave me alone!"

"Summer, I just want to know what's up. What do you want to eat? What do you want to do now that the concert is cancelled?"

"I'm just going back to the room." So, she jumps up and heads out the door. We all just look at each other, like. "What the hell just happened!" I looked at Logan. "What's wrong with her?"

"Well, Missy. Everything was fine and dandy, even though the concert was cancelled and we had to take a cab. We were riding down the road and then we came to a stop at a red light. Our destination was just right there. I told Summer, lets get out so the charges won't accumulate. The place we're meeting your mom is just right across the street. When I got out of the cab the light turned green. Being in a bigger city there's more traffic. So they decided to toot their horns, and that's when I started telling Summer to get out! Get out Princess, I said. She just sat there going through her purse, trying to find some ones to tip the driver. I was screaming. Let's go! Let's go! Come on Summer, people are trying to move. They just about ran over me. I yelled at her again. Come on Princess! That must have broke her. She got so mad she wouldn't talk. So here we are, and now, she has gone to the room."

I replied. "I still think she is about to start her period. Here is my card, you guys take care of the bill and I will go check on her."

She is fine.

Real Time:

I was sitting here talking to Mom and looking at pictures that I found stuffed in the attic at Kandy's house. Finding pictures is a bitter sweet moment every time. Mom said, "damn, you guys went everywhere! We couldn't even go to town without getting picked up and brought back home." Then she started telling me a story about Grandma. "I was pregnant, and Momma didn't know it. She punished me for coming in late. Made me kneel on my knees with my hands in the air. When I passed out, she knew something was up. She asked Buddy, if I was pregnant. I had already dared him to tell! But sure enough.... he did! You know what else? Mom made me go to confession on my wedding day."

Trish, me, (obviously high) and Grandma.

Let's have an update and some short stories on Grandma. I wrote a lot of these stories years ago. Grandma has changed and my opinions may have changed, because that's what happens in life when you live, learn, adapt and listen. I hope you remember *Driving Miss Daisy,* because my grandma has reminded me of her throughout the years. She has been an independent woman most of her life, especially after the passing of Grandpa. She is now 92 and she usually rocks a *Loretto Lynn* type style hair do. She drove a car all the way up until just about the past year. Mom and Beverly drive her around now. The cars on the road are thankful. Maybe she is a little more like *Shirley MacLaine (Quiser)* from *'Steel Magnolias."* A sometimes grouchy old funny southern lady, with a wit that cannot be touched. Lets just say, she is still smart as a whip. We all know about her wit! I personally love it. Which is good natured teasing back and fourth with witty remarks. Could come off as hateful to some, but of course you know the family. She is always calling me, young lady, and correcting my grammar.

If I say something that don't appeal to her, she will say, "You're not too big to have your hind end whooped. Well, that's what my momma use to tell me before I got too fat."

She treats her boys like they are still children needing to be taken care of. When it comes to all the girls, not so much. Wonder why? Guess that's where the term Momma's boy came from. Grandma has had it pretty rough, from the time she was young till now. Sometimes seems she a bit bitter, but to no blame of hers. She had two boys in prison, one of her precious daughters got murdered, and now two of her own kids are suing each other. Another story for another day.

Every day she says that she thinks the good Lord is gonna take her, then she starts to cry. Then I have to tell her. "God doesn't want her yet." The day I left for vacation, I told her. "If you die while I'm away, I'm gonna be pissed. Especially if I have to come back home for your funeral." Yes!!! It made her laugh. It was supposed to be funny, not hurtful. Just the other day when I stopped by to give her some plums, she asked me if I remember her giving me a five-gallon bucket. I stopped her right there. "Yes, Grandma, I do. You don't have to remind me. I can't believe you remember doing that."

"Well, young lady, how could I forget?" Then she started to show me her teeth and said she had just gone to the dentist. "Four cavities." she said. "Never had any in all my life. I'm wondering if I should get them fixed. I'm sure, I only got a couple more years to live. I don't know if they're worth fixing."

I kinda smiled on the inside. Why? She just gave herself a couple of years to live. She must really be in good spirits today. She likes to sit on the porch and watch cars go by and get visitors. She won't let you in her house, because she thinks it's a mess. The only thing that is a mess, is her cabinetry. It's stocked piled with canned food that dates back to the seventies. Like I told you before, she will hoard food till it grows penicillin. That has not changed. My grandma retired after 41 years of service to the community. She was a kitchen aide and one of the first to work for a program that taught people food preparation. It provided nutritional information to the community. Grandma said when she first started the program, they had to knock on people's doors, just to find people to serve. Most of the time we weren't even welcomed in, because no one knew of this new program. Grandma would always go above and beyond her job description. She said she went to a house one day, and the lady that lived there had a newborn. When she walked in, the baby was curled up next to the dog. Then she realized they had no heat. She worked endlessly, to get them help. Eventually got them a pot-bellied stove delivered. She said, "I thought good Lord, Savior above. I'll never forget that baby laying beside that ole dog"

Four generations. Not sure what happened to my nose on this one.

So the other day I walk into Grandma's and there sat ten loaves of bread on the floor. First words out of her mouth. "It's not yours young lady!"

"I know Grandma."

"Jason keeps bringing it to me."

"You giving him some on the side?" as I start to do the humpty dance and she just starts to grin.

"Missy, you know I had me a boyfriend up there where I worked? He was only 28." as she started to chuckle.

"I hear ya Grandma!"

"Oh! I'm just kidding. You know I don't want no damn man."

"Me either grandma." as we both started to laugh.

"Do you think your dad and Jimmy are lesbians? They hang around each other all the time. Your dad even gave him a TV."

"No Grandma! Don't think that's what it is. Hey do you remember Miss Gilly?"

"Well of course I do. She was a fat, short, toothless, woman that helped me clean."

"Yep! That's what I thought."

"She was a good hearted woman. She had an old sex husband. They talked about sex all the time. I never did like him."

"Are they both dead?"

"Yes they're both dead." as we stated to laugh. Not sure why, not funny.

Then Mom pulls in and walks onto the porch. Grandma asked. "You remember old Miss Gilly don't you?"

"Of course I do Momma. How could I not, when you had her down here cleaning and doing nuts all the time. You know what I remember being funny. It was when we did walnuts for ya momma."

My nose instantly turned up. "Eeeewwww walnuts. I remember those things."

"Well Missy. Momma! I don't know if you remember this or not. We had our walnuts. I had my kettle, she had her kettle. Miss Gilly that is. We had cracked all of them and brought them into the house. We were sitting at the kitchen table. Gilly is pretty slow, you know. No one should really be pulling any pranks on her. You know? Like she is missing a couple inches off her ruler. But I kinda did it anyway. Don't know if you would call it a prank. Some people would call it pretty mean. She could pull em out quicker than me. I was pretty quick myself. I guess old women were pretty good at doing stuff like that."

Grandma grinned. "Yes we are Marceline."

Mom continued. "Look, I would look at Gilly and say. look Gilly!!!! Who's looking in that window? She would have a big plate already pulled out. Then I would grab a big handful and put it on my plate."

"Did you really do that to her Marceline?"

"Yes I did Momma. She never could figure out why her bowl kept getting low. I would just take handfuls of hers. I would do it to her every time."

"Well Marceline you nut you! I always thought you was faster than her. You telling me you were stealing her nuts?"

"Yes Momma, I would always tell her to look the other way. And look Missy! Mom always said, you're faster than Gilly. And I said. well..... Yes, I am, Momma. I use to lie all the time."

"Well Marceline, I use to lie to my momma too. I told her that the teacher beat that little boy up at school"

I rolled my eyes. "Are you girls bragging about lying? I'm shocked."

Grandma blurted out, "Well I stopped when Momma caught me and came at me like a bull. I learned my lesson pretty fast."

I looked over at Mom. "What about you Mom?"

"Hey, look out the window."

So one day I'm at the cafe. I walk out the side door and there sits Grandma and Mom in her truck. "What are you ladies doing?" I ask.

"Gonna watch people walk in." says Mom.

"Hey Grandma! Why don't you come on in the cafe."

"Well no ma'am, I will not! I look like ole Mag Muff. Your mom and I have been eating ice cream. We want you to fix us a steak."

"I'm taking Momma home to the raucous spiders." As mom starts to laugh.

"You shut up Marceline! I'm not going back down there with them ole nasty spiders."

"Oh! You ought to see them." Mom says. "There's babies. There's moms and dads, grandmothers, great great grandmothers and grand daddys. Mom, why don't you stay at Missy's."

"You can!" I replied as I lifted my brows up and down.

"I ain't staying over here. Have you two lost your mind? You two are about as smart as a set of squirrel nuts."

Mom rolls her eyes and snorts. "Guess that makes us not very smart. You can just go home and sit with the spiders then." as she looks over at Grandma's belly. "Looks like you been doing that a lot anyway."

Grandma grabs her belly and shakes it, and starts to laugh out loud. "This ole thing. It took me years to make this."

"I got one too Grandma. We should be proud."

Now mind you, my grandma isn't that big of a lady. She just has a few extra rolls like most of us. About that time Kathleen came rolling in and said. "What are you two sitting in the parking lot for?"

"Well, little Miss Priss, we're waiting for a steak! And Missy is gonna give us one free." Grandma said in a smarty tone.

"Well, did your helper Danny get his work done?" Kathleen asked.

Grandma said with frustration. "No ma'am, he did not, and his girlfriend just sit at the house and smiled the whole time."

"Well, Mom, she just likes to show her teeth. I use to do that a lot. You do that when you have pretty teeth."

"Well, she sure don't have pretty legs." Grandma replied.

"Now momma be nice." my mom said.

"Well she don't. I'm not lying!"

Mom got out of the car and we all walked into the café, well not Grandma, we left her in the car. The phone rang and it was for one of my workers again. "Why are they always calling for her?" Kathleen asked.

"Drugs!" Mom replied, as she started to laugh.

"Hey, Marceline! You wanna buy a Cornbread Mafia shirt?" Amy

279

asked in her deep smoke ridden voice.

"Why would I want to do that?" replied Mom.

"Why not?"

"Why would I want a shirt when I got my two brothers in prison." as she walked out the door.

PRISON PAPER----

Speaking of prison. Mom told me the story about the day maw-maw went to visit Joe Keith and Jimmy in prison. This is Mom telling the story.

"Missy, you know, they empty your pockets and everything down there at that prison. It is strict as hell. Momma, knowing she had been down the old bar cleaning it up, should have known better than to do this. But she always wanted to go clean up for the boys, or whomever she was cleaning up for, I don't know. Who lets an old lady clean their nasty ole bar? So, anyway, she found a thing of rolling papers, and stuck them in her pocket. So, she sticks them in her pocket! Don't know who she went with to see the boys on that day, but when she got there, the guard said. "Empty your pockets" she empties them and there lays rolling papers, and that was absolutely a NO NO. I wish I had been there to listen to her explain it. I really do! She told me she got all tongue tied and everything. She didn't want to say she found them in the bar or anything. That was 20 years ago, and that's what the boys were in jail for. But they finally let her go in for her visit. They wasn't going to though. They was giving her hell. "You got rolling papers ma'am. You know this is paraphernalia." I was thinking, Momma why would you stick them in your pockets? Missy, she said she was embarrassed to death. They didn't want to believe her, that she had found them on the floor of the bar. I bet "yeah!" they were thinking. Well, you probably know what they were thinking."

I laugh, "Yeah! Grandma smokes pot. Listen! My friend and I rode down Grandma's the other day. She asked of if we were on beer or whiskey. I said we are not on either, but she is on pot." Then Grandma said, "Oh! You mean that marijuana stuff. Charlie said he is bringing me one down later. He said it will make me feel better."

Grandma in the middle in younger days. I bet she was a spit fire! Thought woman weren't supposed to show their knees back in those days. Way to go Grandma!

Grandpa and Johnny Boone

Speaking of pot, lets talk Johnny Boone. Johnny Boone! Just had to say it again. He is folklore in these parts. He is the *Robin Hood* of the Marijuana media. He has been running from the law for years. They have even written songs about him. They have also made t-shirts that says "Run Johnny Run." I even named a burger after him at my burger joint. Yes! I had a burger joint. We will talk about that later.

Johnny is on the FBI's most wanted list and made it to the world wide show known as *Americas Most Wanted*. I use to watch that show and believed everything they had to tell me. "Catch em." I would say. "Get the dirty thieves and bastards." Now! Not so much. Why? Because I know what they portray isn't always true. It disappoints me to see TV make someone look worse than they are. I mean I totally appreciate the show, and we need it, especially for murderers. But I've got a somewhat inside view of someone who seems nothing more than a big pot smoking, teddy bear. The show has now portrayed him as an unlawful, dangerous man, eluding the law. I got some beef with *John Walsh*. Yes, sirree! I do.

I first met Johnny when I went to see my uncles in prison. Down in southern Ky. Manchester, Kentucky to be exact. I must admit, I was younger then and he scared the shit plumb out of me at first. He knew who I was, because my uncles had shown him pictures. So Tessa and I were just standing there outside in the prison yard, yes, I said prison yard, waiting for them to retrieve the boys from their cells. We heard some man in a very deep voice say. "Hey girl! Hey girl come over here." We looked back over our shoulder and it was some large hairy man, that looked like Santa Clause, but his uniform was slightly different. We felt like sitting ducks, right dab in the middle of a big penitentiary. We were freaked out for a moment. Trust me, you are gonna be freaked out and like, what the fuck? I'm about to die! Then as my uncles were walking toward us they could see the fear on our faces.

"What is it?"

"That man!"

They both started laughing. Jimmy said "Oh, man o man. That's just old Johnny Boone. Come on over here and let me introduce you to him." And that was that. I didn't see him again for years, till they released him from prison. Back when Jimmy was working here, he would come to the café and set at the end of the bar around closing time. He would drink coffee and eat a salad, and of course he would be stoned. When he came to my Halloween party he just stood out by the bombfire, chain smoking his pot. He had a lot of visitors. One guy got so high, he fell in the fire!

283

Won't name no names.

Johnny used to visit my grandma a lot. People started rumors, saying she was the head of the mafia. Like on the Sopranos. I do have a picture of her setting in a winged back chair looking like some mafia wife. She is definitely not. Just the mother of boys, who had been accused and convicted. I think I mentioned that to you in my second story.

The FBI has been in this area for years looking for him. Marion Co. is very rural, and they believe Johnny, to still be around. Especially because of the tightness around these parts. When the DEA comes looking for him, no one will even give them a serious answer. Now remember Johnny Boone is a large man with a long white beard and could be in the *Macy's Day Parade*. So when someone replies, "last time I seen him, he was coming down my chimney," you might get the picture. People have given some pretty funny answers to the DEA. "He is in my tomato patch. You have a better chance of finding *Bin Laden*." Even though we have killed him since the remark, but it was a good one at the time. "He is hidden like a fat puss, watching porn." People even shout out, "Johnny Boone for president." Good luck Johnny. Have to admit he would be better than our president elect.

So let's get back to why this all happened. Marion County is and was a knob filled, winding road, with small farms kind of town. It has serene landscapes with God fearing people. When Raywick didn't grow with the times, money got tight in these parts. The young men found a new way to support their families by growing weed. Harvesting time always comes in Autumn. Around here, you're sure to know when that is. The feds bring in choppers, four-wheeler, army tanks and all. People go into panic as the choppers hover the land. They were lawless back in the day and of course it all got out of hand. The money got too good to be true and the law was ready for a crack down on someone. And they got it when they arrested my uncles and started to arrest everyone in the county, overcrowding the prisons with pot growing, non-violent people.

I hear the take down of my uncle Joe Keith was a frightening one. Beverly was telling me that back in 1989 she pulled into Joe Keith's drive and the police had the place surrounded with guns drawn and everything. She said "They asked me what I was doing there and I said I was there to clean his house. They asked me if I knew if this certain guy was in there. I told them I had no idea and asked if I could go ask my brother. Missy, I swear I was afraid they were going to shoot him."

Pot should be legal. Just don't abuse it.

285

Let's lighten up the mood. To enjoy this small story I'm about to tell you, you have to keep in mind we were high. I mean really high...and it was way back in the day, back before it just became normal routine to see dope choppers in these parts. It was back around 1994 or 5. I just moved into my little farm house. I was sitting on the front porch with Joe Mack and one of his friends. We were smoking away, laughing and giggling to no end. All of a sudden we heard tub-tub-tub-tub-tub-tub. We were confused and when we looked up, there was an army chopper, rising from behind the barn across the street at Conrad's house. It just seemed to be stuck in one spot. Our laughter turned into holy shit. Then as it slowly approached us, we were wrestling to hide the weed, our one little joint that is. The nose of it was pointed right at us, as if we were under attack. Our hair started to part from the propellers. Holy shit! Are they really gonna attack us? Then it turned and flew away. That was my first experience with a dope chopper.

NEWS ALERT: We now interrupt this program.

Damn, so many updates. Grrrrrrrr. I'm just trying to write my stories. Let me get caught up already. I'm up here writing a damn story about Johnny Boone. I get a text: "JOHNNY BOONE JUST GOT ARRRESTED IN CANADA."

Then the phone rings. It's my dad. "Watch the news. Johnny Boone just got arrested."

I got on Facebook. "Johnny Boone has been arrested. Free him, free him."

Damn Johnny! You should have hid out in Bardstown Kentucky, they have four unsolved homicides. Everyone wanted him to be free forever. Everyone except the law that is. He is looking at a life sentence which is sad. We need room in prison for real criminals, like the guy who shot the black guy in the streets of Raywick.. I'm really curious to see how this plays out. Obama has been pardoning some non-violent pot growers. I bet some of you Obama haters would like to see him give old Johnny a pardon. I'm sure Trump won't be concerned with anything but Putin.

It seems like our system would be more concerned about killers and child molesters or real criminals instead of a man living off his land. Johnny Boone has coined the phrase, "OMERTA" code of silence. In Boone's own writing, he provides to the U.S. Marshals Service. Boone described the idea Omerta as follows: "To never rat on anyone. To never hurt another person unless in self-defense. To protect women, children and the helpless. To always have a clear view of right and wrong. To do right without reserve."

I have met the man and I believe his words to be true. My uncles themselves have always been good hearted people who just decided at a young age that they would grow dope and sell it, like most young men did back in the eighties. Like I said, money was tight and not many jobs were available. Uncle Jimmy would do anything for anybody, but the judge decided when he caught them for a 2nd or 3rd time, he was going to make an example of them, and he did. 20 to 25 for growing pot. No, not murder! Pot growing!

Stated in Higdon's book: "Cornbread Mafia, the root of Johnny's support in Marion County is based on outrage toward the courts, which can justify life in prison for a victimless crime. Even ones who have not smoked can't imagine life in prison with no parole. My aunt Trish whom we all know is now deceased along with her husband, wrote an article and sent letters to the justice system over and over. She was determined to get someone one to see the light, and that her brothers didn't belong in jail for 20 years with no parole, none! They would never commit a violent crime. They are family people and would help anyone. Let the punishment fit the crime, she stated.

"If you change the way you look at things, the things you look at change" ---Wayne Dyer

LIFE INTERRUPTED-----

Found some more writings from 2013. Man-o-man how time flies. I'm just gonna put it in here like I wrote it back then. Sometime down the road, I will elaborate on some of the outcomes and situations.

The month of August, 2013 has been all but grand. It has been a tragic emotional month. I will give you a small preview, without much detail. So much shit has happened that when I ran over a skunk today and totally skunked up my car, all I could do was sing, *"I skunked my car, I don't care, I don't care, I skunk my car and... I love it..."* Not really, but point is, I'm at the end of my rope at this moment and my nerves are hanging out. It's so bad, that I think I just came down with the 'Hershey Squirts' Not that any off this stuff has happened to me per se, but it has happened all around me. Like, I have been the core of all kinds of situations, not only is the situation with Summer happening, which we will discuss on a later note, but shit just keeps coming from left to right. Momma cat just got murdered by something and Joe Eddie put her poor body in the dumpster. Can't even look at the dumpster any more. Mary's dad just died, you remember Mary, one of my girlfriends, whom now is a really really close friend. My mom is having surgery and my best friend Kandy's grandpa just died. Two of my workers just had a knock down drag out at the café. They have to be separated or fired. I'm so tired of being the referee in these situations. All I can say, is where is the camera when you want it most? More chaos you say, What a day! What a life! The gravity around me is getting heavy and I feel, that I'm about to be crushed...once again I'm exhausted. Over and out for the moment. I hope there is not much more to tell of this story except that Summer's new teeth are beautiful and that she has graduated college.

Well, readers, I didn't make it very far, now did I? Just got told by my dad, that I better get over and see Jeff, my cousin. I told you I would keep you updated and here goes. I don't want to get you too involved in this story, because it is a depressing one. There is never a happy ending to cancer. It wears the family down. Screw you cancer! You're a fucktard. So I went to visit him and I'm glad I did, but at the same time, I wish I didn't have to see, what I had seen. Jeff fought it as long as he could, he was a fighter in that aspect. We buried him a couple weeks later.

See you bitches on the other side!

When Ann and I got home from the funeral we were sitting on the couch talking and reminiscing. I was telling her how he was so much like my uncle Jimmy. Both him and Jimmy always changed the dynamics of the room and in a very, very good way. Neither of them were fighters, but if someone came up to either one of them and said, "do you wanna piece of me?" either one of them would reply with. "Well, I didn't, but now I do!"

We were also talking about her dad. He had been sick for awhile after some kind of burglary years ago and he got pistol whipped. I will fill you in on that whole story later. She got a call! We were burying him three days later. The family did not need to keep meeting this way. It was a soldier funeral and I had never been to one of those before. When the guns went off my heart about popped out of my chest.

Here lately, the Bickett side of my family has been finding long lost family and the Luckett side is losing them.

When you have a big family like mine, you have a lot of LOVE, but you also have a lot of HEARTACHE.

290

Ann and her Dad (Tommy) on her wedding day.

QUOTE_ *I am not particularly religious or spiritual; I am just an ordinary person trying to make sense of the mysteries of life."---Nelson Mandela*

QUOTE: *"The trouble is, you think you have time."----Buddha*

WALTER, IS IT REALLY YOU

No one doubts, the story of Walter. It is all too clear, that things are weird around here, especially when things start flying off walls. Like a piece of fake fruit flying off hitting Amy in the head. Amy screams, "Walter stop!" We always just tell Walter to quit, laugh and go on.

Mom and I was sitting and having lunch when a spoon decided to jump right out of the jar. Literally! No one touched it! Mom and I just sat there staring at each other. We were spooked, while amazed at the same time. Then we busted out laughing, as Logan came walking in. Then the phone rang and we told him to answer it. "Hello, this is Missy's café. May I help you?" Then he threw the phone down and ran out the door. Mom and I just looked at each other. I ran out the door after him. "Logan what is it?"

"What the hell! That phone! There was something creepy on it!"

"Get back in here."

"I will be back tomorrow. I got to go shake these chills off."

Logan has been trying to figure out if it's me or Walter. He wants to follow me around with a camera. So when he came back over the next night I asked him why? He said, "Because!!!"

Steph my waitress jumps in with, "Because!!!!! Everything always happens to you. Buy a brand new ice machine... Broke!!! Buy a new fridge, broke, buy a new this. Broke! Clean this. Broke!"

Amy jumps in, "Broke!!!"

Logan sighs. "I'm not saying everything happens to you cause you are bad luck or anything. It's just you touch something, it's done with....."

Something in your fingers... and when you touch something, it gets in em.... and makes it go terrible......I don't know, shewl..... I don't know what you call that. That's just what happens to you Missy!"

"Logan, some people would call that bad luck."

"I'm not gonna say bad luck Missy, because I've never had any bad luck around ya. But every time I come around ya, something already bad has happened to you. It's bad luck for me, because when I come around you, you are already pissed." As he laughs.

I chuckle myself, "Not as pissed as I should be."

"I know!!! Cause your use to it. Hell!!! I mean, that time your mom left you in the basement, the washer and dryer caught on fire"

I laughed at him. "That would be just the dryer Logan."

"I mean, not just the dryer. After that, every place you went into caught on fire."

"I've got other suspicions about all the fires." I gave him a wink.

"I bet you do. But damn!"

"Well I guess Logan, when life gives you lemons, eat the bitches and move along."

"I guess that's what would be your motto Missy. That's why I want to film you. Cause I'm gonna catch some shit and we're gonna be famous on U-tube. Wish I had been here when you went to ride your bike and came back with a snapping turtle in your hand. I seen the pictures and that thing was huge. How about the time you fell down *Fourth Street Lives* escalators? Or the time you ran outside and lighting about hit you. I actually seen that one. Or how about the other million other mishaps and exciting stuff that has happened to you? We would be way ahead on this reality thing."

"Yes Logan, the list goes on and on. Trust me I know. I live it everyday."

Mom peeks her head around the corner. "Logan will you help me do the potatoes?"

"Marceline! Last time I washed those potatoes for you, I raped them."

"Raped them? Logan did you get a hair cut?"

"Yes Marceline, I did. I went to Wal-Mart to get it."

"Wal-Mart? Why did you do that?"

"I had to. There was nowhere else to go, and my hair was getting rowdy."

Those tators give me nightmares.

I know sometimes these stories end abruptly. That just happens. I don't think I need to add the goodbyes and hugs at the end of every story. Goodbye!

STRANGE ACTIVITY

Gosh... It's Saturday, September 16 and the August moon has been upon us. Braino (a customer) was talking some shit at café tonight. Like spooking, howl at the moon shit. So, I'm sitting here alone on the stool at my bar at the house and I just heard the beeper that goes off when you open the door.. There is no one here! And about five minutes later, it does it again. Still, no one here. Weird occurrences happen weekly. Let's move along.

The following week I desperately needed someone to work the back room. I used to be able to con my dad into doing it as my last resort, but he quit doing it years ago. So now Joe Mack is my last resort. So I called him up and asked him to please work. He said on a scale of 1 to 10 of the worst jobs he can have, it is a 14 on the hate-o-meter. I hate people and people hate me. All I could do was laugh and say, okay. I will ask Summer.

Summer was coming to visit anyway, because it was Ham Day's weekend. She complied. We were slow, like really slow. Short night for her and no stories to tell till the next morning. When I went outside Sunday morning, the garage door was down, which is unusual because it's been up all summer. I just assumed my girlfriend at the time put it down for unknown reasons. So later that day I went outside again and the door started coming up. I looked around like, 'What the hell?' but I kept walking, then it came back down. I just stopped and stared at it. What the hell? Who is screwing with me? There is no remote to it, because it burnt up in the fire in 2008. So I walk off and it pops up again. Alrighty then, is all I could say. I went inside to tell Summer and she

296

said, "Wow, that is really weird. Have you called Patty Star yet?"

I looked at her and said, "Have you called Patty Star yet?"

"No! I've been busy."

"Exactly. Life gets in the way doesn't it?"

So I walked back out the door. The door was down. I stood there and stared at it for a moment. I was getting ready to walk off again and it went back up, it halted, then it came back down. I went in to mess with the button to no avail. So I broke out the ladder and unplugged the son of a bitch. I thought if you go down now, I am leaving this damn place. When I awoke the next morning, Summer was lying in bed with me. This was an unusual occurrence. When she woke up I asked her, what was up. She seemed a bit rattled. She said, her dog(Parker) was barking at the damn wall. The one that something always bangs on.

Wish you could see this in color.

Just a lot of strange activity leading up to the moment the transformer blew. They say spirits have the ability to create electrical disturbances to get your attention. Well there is always strange activity, just a little more that week. What the hell do they want? I got to figure this out. I can't lose another home and yes I said home, it's becoming one. I've made more memories and have found more pictures.

Occupying the same space? Hum! Yes, I believe I am. I believe we have already spoken about how spirits are the natural environment of our world. It all depends on what we are willing to accept. But when you get a glimpse, it's kinda unbelievable.

Around here, for the most part, the ghosts seem a little more rambunctious, when certain people are around. Mainly started when Crock came around. They say that when people are spiritual, they may channel that energy and awaken the spirit. Spirits are naturally drawn to and attracted to people who are highly evolved karmically. Because there is a higher chance of them being noticed. See! I on the other hand, I guess am not in tune and evolved with the spirit world. Guess I should take some peyote, like they did in the movie *Young Guns*. He was definitely in tuned with the spirit world. I didn't notice their small gestures and I guess that's why they had to burn my house down to get my attention. Well they fucking got it! Peyote or no peyote!

You can ask James how he feels about all this. He is the boyfriend of one of my workers. He has been frightened ever since we broke out the Quiji board. He believes 100 percent, that a soul is trapped here due to drama or some unfinished business. Every time the lights flicker at the café, you see him become a little unnerved. When Erin's earring flew out of her ear the other night for no reason, James said, "I'm a believer! There is no telling me any different. I am certain, I'm certain now. That son-of a gun, just knocked her earring out." I will have to tell you that story some other time also. It was a long fulfilled night. With pot and ghosts.

GRANDMAS FRONT PORCH

So I decide to stop down Grandmas today. She was on the porch as usual. Kathleen was there along with a lady named Amy, not my Amy. Soon as I walked in, her little yapping dog came at me full force.

"Damn Amy, that dog is gonna give me a heart attack. You need to leave his ass at home."

So after the dog (we will call him Cujo Junior) went back under the chair, Grandma said, "Missy, I've been taking this pill that makes me out of breath. I can't hardly get my breath."

Then I saw some onion rings setting by her. "You're gonna need a heart pill if you keep eating that. What did you say those pills are doing to you?"

Grandma said, "Well, it makes me have short breath."

I asked, "Is it taking your funnies away? You're not feeling too funny today, are you?"

"No, I can't be funny today. I'm too tired."

Kathleen while sitting in her rocking chair on the far end of the porch, starts to laugh. Grandma said, "I sang a song on Amy's phone earlier."

Amy said "She won't let me put it on Facebook. But when she dies I'm putting it on there."

I said, "Oh, we are so gonna when you pass away. We are definitely putting all this shit on Facebook." Amy and Kathleen start laughing. "We are finally gonna be able to write the truth about Coletta Bickett. These stories are gonna be all over the United States. Here is what every body is gonna say. Man! I sure wish I would have known that lady."

Amy nodded her head. "That's right! That's right!"

Grandma shrugged her head. "Yeah! Right."

I gave Grandma a big grin. "It will be, that's what they will say. How can no one not want to know you?" I grabbed the onion rings and said

"I guess I better eat these." When I looked in the box, they were burnt up. "Damn! These had to go through the deep fryer three or four times.

Grandma grabbed them. "Don't eat them damn things! Eat this sandwich! You're gonna pull your teeth out!"

"Oh! It will be alright."

Grandma said, "I need a door for my shed Missy."

Kathleen smiled, "Can you see Momma walking to the shed this winter." As Amy starts to laugh. I'm sure just picturing it was funny. Grandma randomly moves from her kitchen to the front porch chair to view the street and the bar up the street till it hits 4 o'clock and time for bed. Doors are locked at 5 for sure. I asked grandma, "What do you think about you coming outside and me hanging from that tree, that time? You don't remember that I was climbing a tree and fell and hung on my belt loop?"

Grandma said, "I don't remember."

"You don't remember fussing at me for hanging in the tree? You screamed at me. Why are you hanging in that tree for?"

Grandmas rolls her eyes, "She is remembering everything negative about me. She put it all in her first book!"

"I did not! I did not!"

Grandma said, "Yes, you did." She looked at Amy and said, "Yes, she did.

"I did not! I was talking about when I was here and I was 5 or ten years old."

Grandma seemed frustrated, "Everything was negative!!!!!"

"No! It was not Grandma. There was one story where I talked about how I didn't like getting sent to bed at six o'clock, while the kids played outside."

Grandma shook her finger at me. "All the kids had to go to bed early."

"Exactly my point. So why is that negative if you always did it?"

Kathleen shook her head like, point proven! "There you go."

300

"And in this second story, I'm writing about when Mom said she had to go to bed at 6 o'clock. So it's all good." as I start to laugh.

Kathleen said, "So what? We still go to bed before 6 o'clock down here everday."

I said, "Yeah! So why is it negative if that's what you do? If that's what you do. But I didn't like it, it's different. No big deal."

Kathleen pouted, "We didn't like it either. We would watch the kids play outside and stick our tongues out at them."

"I told everybody I liked your cooking, but I said I didn't like pinto beans."

Grandma looked straight at me, with her eyes wide open. "I like beans, young lady!"

"I hate them! But I had to give up good old biscuits and gravy for some raw ass bacon, barely ran through the pan, when I moved from here. At age ten I didn't like grapefruit and raw bacon either. But that's what Maw-maw Luckett fixed. So you know, it is what it is. So no, everything wasn't NEGATIVE! Even though I talked about having to go poop in the outhouse over here across the street."

Grandma shook her head and stared me straight in the face. "Is that not negative?"

I said, "It was a fact. I mean you can take it however you want. I thought it was a negative to have to leave the house to poop."

Amy just about fell out of her chair laughing.

Grandma grimaced. "I'm sure not laughing!" Then the Cujo Junior went off again and he crawled back under the chair. I said, "There was times I felt like the girl in the movie *Bridesmaids,* where she is trying to get across the street."

Kathleen smiled. "Yes, I've seen it."

"She starts pooping before she gets there and lays down in the road."

Kathleen said. "Yes! Yes!

I giggled "But we could do diarrhea in the commode, because it would

301

flush down. But you didn't know for sure what was gonna happen."
Grandma changed the subject. "I want a pair of Amy's glasses. Here
Amy let me put yours on." She put them on and I said, "That makes a
sexy woman, right there."

Amy wiggled her brows up and down. "You look hot!" The she looked
at me and said, "Missy, let's stay all night up at Kathleen's one night."
I laughed, "You need to just stay all night at my house."
Amy said with a shocking voice. "You got ghost, too?"
   I said, "Well duh! Did I tell you about the medium dude that showed
up at the café?"
Kathleen said, "Oh no! You didn't." as she looked interested to hear.

I said, "So Amy. You know my house burnt down. So this guy came to the café after my house burnt down. The guy across the street said that Walter died in the house. This is just a quick pro quo. The hair on my arms stood straight up! Halloween alert! Bunch of crazy shit always happening at the house. So we named our ghost Walter and my girlfriend from years ago told me I had a little slave girl ghost. That's what she felt. She's the type of person that would probably feel a presence. I have never felt a presence myself. I just stare and see the obvious. You know like the knocking." As I knock on the wall behind me. Well here came little Cujo Junior, out from under his chair again in attack mode. Grandma jumped and held her heart. "You okay Grandma?"

She breathed hard. "Yes."

"Okay! You sure?"

"Yes! I'm sure."

"Anyway, we already dubbed we had two ghosts in the house. So I'm at the café one night and this medium from Campbellsville, I don't know him from Adam, came up to the bar and asked to talk with me. I mean he approached me. I didn't call him."

Amy unsure what to think said. "He sensed something, didn't he?"

"Yes! I hadn't even written my first book. So he knew nothing of nothing. He asked, are you Missy and do you live next door, and I'm like, yeah."

Kathleen says, "I haven't heard this story."

"I told the man, yes I do. Well you already know the story about the knocking, right Kathleen?"

"Yes, yes, go on!"

"Well, he asked me if there was something over my house blinking or something. I was like, well I'm sure there is. I'm sure on the microwave or stove. I ain't never had a clock one to work over there. Ever -ever - ever."

Amy asked curiously. "How does your phone line work?"

"Well, you don't even want to ask me about that."

Kathleen made a noise, the laugh of Santa Claus or something, I'm not sure, "ha-ho-ha-ho-ha-ho."

"I was dating this girl and twice when she showed up, as soon as she hit my property, the clock on her phone stopped. We didn't know it till later that night. She looked at me and asked, what time is it, and I said like around ten. She said, "My phone says 8:30.""

Amy opened her mouth. "OOOOOO!

"So it happened to her twice. Her phone stopped on the time she got there. Not her phone, but her clock."

Amy looks puzzled. "Kathleen and I've have never heard of that."

"So anyway the medium is talking about that and he said I'm gonna walk outside. I wasn't that busy for the first time in a dick year, oops sorry grandma." When I looked at her she was half asleep. Don't believe she was feeling very well that day. So I continued with my story, but with one less listening. "So anyway, he walked out back by the dumpster and Kitty was there, and she said she remembers it plainly. If you don't believe me ask her. Which I don't know why you wouldn't, I have no reason to lie. So I followed him down there and he was like, "Ah!! I'm getting a sense of like this older man. Kind of hollow faced, but not scary, walking from down there by that lake and back up to here toward your house. He's not mean or anything. He is just, it's like he is looking for something. Like maybe his daughter or something." I mean, I look him straight in the eye. Are you telling me I have another damn ghost in my house and he was like, "no! I don't think he goes in. I don't think he is going in the house." In which, then I replied, is that the son of a bitch knocking on the wall?"

Amy starts laughing. "Trying to get in?" I giggle, "I know! Right?"

Kathleen giggled too, "Just open the door for him."

"It mostly happens to Summer, you know, when the knocking happens.

304

Even though it happened to me that night of the ice storm and Mom that one day, but mostly to Summer. She hears it on the house wall. Ask her friend Haley if you don't believe me. I was even sitting there one night when the knocking happened. We all just stared at each other in silence. Then about 5 minutes later, it happened again. My ass jumped up so fast I created a wind storm. I ran out the door. Nothing! Absolutely nothing! There is no trees, no nothing on that wall."

"Nothing?"

"Nothing! Summer is the only one who has heard the music."

"Music? What kind of music?"

"Old time music. She even text me one night and said Mom turn off your music, I'm trying to go to sleep and I was like, Hun, I'm asleep. What the hell are you talking about?"

Amy's jaws dropped, "Oh my God!"

"Yes, oh my God is right"

"Where did she call you from?"

"Upstairs."

"Where were you?"

"Downstairs." We all laughed. "Kids! She also said she has felt the presence of a man standing over top of her. But I think that's Walter."

"Right and the other guy is the other guy?"

"I told Summer, he is looking for you. He needs your help."

Kathleen mumbled, "Um-hum. How long has that been?"

"A couple years ago. Hell! I don't know. I can't keep up with time."

Amy said, "Well…. Who can?"

"You know what I mean? I mean some people can, but I can't. Hell! My house burnt down 8 years ago and it seems like two to me."

Amy asked, "Do you hear things?"

"Of course I hear things, and notice things, but I don't feel things. You know, like in a psychic way or anything. I don't have those vibes. But I do see what's in front of me and it's a lot. I tell you, it's funny when

305

someone else is there, but I tell you what! When I'm there by myself and something happens……..”

Amy's eyes grew and stopped me mid sentence. “Do you get scared?”

“Yes! Sometimes! If I'm by myself! I tell you what! I came in one night and set my phone down on the ottoman and went to the bathroom, washed my hands and everything. When I came out it clicked or dinked, whatever it does when you turn the little recorder on, and it started recording. I asked myself, self, are you high? It would make sense if I had just set my phone down. Are you hearing me? The shit just keeps adding up and adding up. Especially after I went to the court house.”

Kathleen shook her head up and down. “Um hum! There is a lot about the earth we don't know.”

“Tell me about it! Hell, that lady that lived there in 1934, left the state. She left.” as I whistled and flicked my hand away. “She was outta there.”

Kathleen looked at Amy and calmly said, “That's what Dan did. Dan left the next day.”

Amy said, “Phyllis warned me not to stay all night.”

I looked straight at Kathleen. “I think her ghosts are evil.”

“Mine aren't evil.”

“Mine are friendly with a lot of mischief and yours are evil.”

Kathleen repeated, “Mine are not evil.”

Grandma had been playing possum when she blurted out, “How do you know if they're friendly or evil?”

I pointed at Kathleen, “Hers are mean. Hers are mean.”

Grandma said again, “How do you know?”

“They just act differently. Mine act……..”

Then Kathleen cut in. “Gale got hit in the nose with something, but they never hurt me.”

Grandma twisted her mouth, “I can't believe Kathleen stays up there by herself.”

“Yours are different Kathleen. Now this is a theory. Just a theory. You just wanna play with it. You go all the way back to when I was dating Crock and she talks about the black slave girl. And when I built on to my house, she always said that little girl lived under that old staircase. She begged me and begged me not to remove that wall. All I could say was, what are you talking about, dumbass. Builders! Knock out the wall. You know what I mean? I didn't believe in that shit."

Amy shock her head up and down. "Yeah! Right! Um hum."

"She swore up and down by it, and a year and a half later, my house was on the ground. Poof! History! Dust in the wind! The girl is the mischievous one, running around all crazy and shit. Walter stuck around to keep her company. But I was talking to Crock the other day and she thinks that maybe the little girl gets on Walter's nerves."

Kathleen asked, "Have you smelt anything in your house like bacon."

"Bacon? I wish bacon! I love bacon! But I smelled an odor, a bad odor.I thought it was coming from the bathroom. Called the plumber down three different times, but he never could find anything. He just kept saying, I don't know what you are talking about. There is nothing wrong. You know what I'm saying? I always would just smell this weird smell."

"Danny and I have heard utensils and the smell of bacon. But it doesn't bother us."

"It wouldn't bother me either, if it smelled like bacon."

Amy laughed. "Missy smells like steaks."

"No I don't! That is my doing! That ain't no ghost! But it don't bother me either, unless I'm there by myself. It was a little spooky the night the radio came on and the fire alarm incident."

Kathleen asked, "When are you and your girl staying all night at my house?"

"Probably never!"

Grandma shook her head. "I sure wouldn't stay at either of your houses."

"My ghosts like guests. Kathleen's don't. Hers attack people."

Grandma said loudly. "Attack people!"

Kathleen responds nonchalantly. "Yes, like that boy that got those claw marks. But they're fine with me. I don't mind at all. I really don't."

"Here's the thing, Amy. They don't mind her cause they know when she dies she is gonna join them. And do the same thing to other people."

We all laugh hard. "They're like, we got one on the way."

"True!" Kathleen said.

"Hey Kathleen, what about the little girl in the rocking chair?" Amy asked.

"The little girl is on the bed and the mother is sitting in the chair."

Grandma asked with disbelief. "Are you telling me you've seen them, Kathleen?"

"We had the Ghostbusters. What do you call them, Missy? Mediums. I always call them ghost busters. They said the little girl is on the bed and the mother is on the chair. And the story that was told is that an old black man was in the cellar. Okay? He is in the cellar because he raped the woman. The woman had a child and she keeps him in the cellar." All of a sudden Cujo Junior came out in attack mode for no reason. Grandma about jumped out of her chair. "Whip that little dog, Amy!!!"

I smacked my hands together. "Spank his ass!! You gonna cause my Grandma to have a damn heart attack!!"

Grandma said. "I know it. Whip him!"

"Amy's gonna keep coming down here with that damn dog and Coletta Bickett, is gonna die." I pointed my finger at Amy and said, "Has Charlie been paying you to bring that damn dog down here?"

"Yeah!" She starts to laugh.

"That's gonna be the best murder ever. No one is ever gonna be able to prove that one has been planned. I'm sure Charlie is saying, take that dog down there. I'm sure it will give momma a heart attack." Then Kathleen starts telling a story. "Amy. Mother. You may remember this Missy. Charlie moved those tombstones up at the cabin.

Joe Keith said he had the worst dreams after they were moved, then he told him to put them back. When they did, he stopped having them. Now I'm thinking I might go down there and put 'em back in his yard."

Readers, that's a different story for a different day. Back to the conversation we were already having. "I've never believed in the far fetch. That's why I didn't believe Crock. I said, tear down the wall! Bring on the wrecking ball! Just didn't believe."

Kathleen jumped out of her rocker. "I do! I do!"

Amy looked at me. "But you believe now? Don't cha Missy?"

"I don't know what I believe. You know what I'm saying? I'm open to anything. Just like palm readers. I believe there are people who can vibe things, but the other 99 percent just ride the ride and get your money. I do believe there are people who can sense things. So if we believe in angels and all that type of stuff, you have to believe there are spirits of sorts."

"Of course, and demons too." Kathleen said as she sat back down.

"Spirits all around us. If we keep talking about this, I won't be able to sleep tonight." Granma said with concern.

"Well at least you don't have to go up Kathleen's with her little hags."

"What are hags?" Kathleen asked.

"Little creatures. They say it's a woman who sheds her skin and turns into vapors. She can go through keyholes or anything. She sucks the energy out of you at night and you wake up exhausted. Or you could just have a Haint, they're not uber friendly either."

Kathleen replied with a smirk, "Well, at least they didn't burn my house down!"

"You got me there! I've got the spirits, yes I do, you got hags and boo-hoo-hoo. Later ladies. Love ya Grandma!"

Just a little story.

Way back before we started talking all this ghost shit, I remember one night, way, way, back in the old farm house. I was asleep on the couch. I was woken up by the front door opening. But I didn't really get up, because I just figured it was Joe Mack coming in. You know when your expecting someone, you don't bother to wake all the way up. Well I felt a presence of someone and figured it was just him. Well a day or two had passed and I asked Joe Mack, how come he hasn't been home since that night? He said, "what are you talking about? I haven't been home all week." I thought ohhhh, peeping Tom? Ghost? Robber? Its just like when I was studying for school when all the power went out. No rhyme or reason, all the neighbor's power was on and there was no storm.

Joe Mack and Summer

310

I was at Mc Donald's today picking up Mom and Kathleen's lunch. The total on the screen said 6.66. I thought hell no!!! I'm not paying that. Right as I was getting ready to tell the lady I was gonna order something else, they added tax and the total changed. When I got to the window, I told the lady that they need to change their 3.33 menu, cause if you get two of something the total is 6.66 and that ain't cool! She laughed and said she would tell them. I was serious though, that is a stupid price anyway, 3.33. That's some bullshit. It's also bullshit that I am now afraid of the number 666 on anything. Actually I'm still scared of 66. When I turn my thermostat down, I never put it on that number, ever!!!

Later that night my phone clicked on and then everything on my phone was upside down. I kept flipping the phone around. I had it the right side up, but everything was still upside down. I called Steph telling her and asking her what she thought was going on. "Oh Miss, it's just probably Walter again" and all I could say was, Steph, shut up!! Then she replied, "Naw! It could just be your phone, but I don't know. That sounds weird with all the shit that happens over there."

So I get off the phone and I go ahead and sit on the couch and kick back. I flip on the TV and hit guide to see what was on. I was feeling a little paralyzed, wondering if I was seeing what I was really seeing. At the bottom of the screen, a set of girl's eyes, from 'Silent Hill', was just staring at me. It freaked me out, but not so much that I didn't take a picture first, for proof. Then I selected a station quickly, so she couldn't look at me. I believe it was Gunsmoke or something, and I left it there. I sure as the hell wasn't changing the station so she could pop back up again. Yes, I know it was just an advertisement, but why the hell that? And why now? After my phone ordeal. Just plain creepy and totally weird. It was very hard to fall asleep that night. Why can't my ghost just bake me a cake or something?

The next night when I went to visit Jen, I was telling her the story, about the scary face on my TV. She was kind of what-evering me. Then I showed her the picture. I swear, she about knocked me out of the bed. "That's fucking creepy!" she screamed. Then we started to laugh. I don't know why we laughed.

When I showed it to Mom, she about fell off her stool and Beverly slapped the phone right out of my hand. People freak out when I just show them a picture of her on my phone. Just her two dark evil eyes shining out from the bottom of the TV. Mind you, I have a huge TV. So huge, that when I first hooked it up, Mom came over, and there was a toll house cookie commercial on. The cookie was so big that it tripped Mom out. "Wow! "as she stepped back. "That is one big cookie!! It would take the cookie monster a year to finish that one."

Here's a little more detail about the clock on the phone stopping. Jen and I walked into the house after I got off work from the cafe.. I say she arrived at the cafe around 8:30 or so.. We got to the house around 10:30. I plopped down on the couch from exhaustion and I hear her say in a panicked voice, "Omg, omg! Missy Luckett! My phone!!!!"

"What's up with it?" as I jumped from the couch.

"It quit again when I got here. O B Jesus! Why does this happen every time I pull in the drive? The time on my phone, it just quits. This is the second time. Time just stands still soon as I arrive on the compound."

I replied with a laugh, "Well Jen, you know what I've told you about clocks around here, they never work. That rolling rock clock I gave Joe Eddie, the one that spins backwards, that is another weird situation….. There is something strange in the neighborhood. Who ya gonna call? *Ghostbusters.*"

"Did you do something to my phone?"

"NO! Why would you think that? I haven't touched it."

She looked at me and took a deep breath. "You're not fucking with me are you?"

I was still laughing, "No, Jen!! Seriously, I'm not fucking with you!

312

It's just funny, cause shit like that happens around here all the time. Did I say time? Ha-ha-ha-ha."

"I don't think I will be traveling out here much longer."

"Oh, don't say that!"

"I'm serious!!"

Later that night when we went to bed, the motion light sensor went off in my closet, and the light popped on. Jen's body came flying up out of the bed like a prairie dog. "What the fuck!" she said. "What was that? Why did the light come on? If that's a ghost I'm crawling up your ass."

"Not sure you will fit, but you can give it a whirl. It's getting ready to storm and I'm sure the little girl just wants a safe place to go." I started to laugh..

Jen was still perked up like a prairie dog. "You gotta be shittin me. Are you for real?"

"Yes ma'am I am! You might as well go back to sleep, because she will probably be in there for awhile."

She just slid back under the cover like a turtle into its shell and never peeked back out the rest of the night. She refused to visit again after she caught her young daughter, asleep in my bed, talking to someone in her sleep.

No wonder I can't keep a girlfriend. I thought it was the Café's fault, but hummm...... maybe not. I got some jealous ghost.

Some friends came to visit one day. Jyn and Liz to be exact. They had never been to my house, so I was giving them the tour. We were upstairs on the second floor, when I jumped on Summer's bed and told then they could check out the third floor on their own. A few minutes later I heard a noise that sounded like an electric razor. I yelled up, "What the hell are you guys doing?"

"Were using an electromagnetic device."

"Why?"

"You said you had ghosts!"

"Yeah, but how does that work? You guys ain't no Ghostbuster."

"It picks up their energy."

"Yeah! Yeah! Whatever!"

"It does!"

So I ran up to the third floor. "Give it to me!" They handed it to me and told me to put it close to the attic door. And when I did that sucker sounded off. I about threw it in the floor. "If you girls are messing with me, I'm a gonna kill a bitch."

"We're not." So they explained how it worked and my curiosity really started to peek. Keep in mind they knew nothing about nothing, except they had heard I had ghosts.

"Give me that thing." I headed toward the downstairs. I was gonna test a theory. The thing didn't make a peep all the way down. As soon as I got to where the old staircase door used to be, that son of a gun almost vibrated out of my hand. I looked at them. "Do you guys have a thing that's controlling this?"

"No! How would we do that?"

"I don't know. Just asking."

So I headed straight to the bedroom where Walter died. Bam! Sound off again. I was literally amazed and concerned. "Girls, follow me for a minute."

So I headed out the front door and started up the four-wheeler. "Hop on girls." They jumped on and we headed up to the barn. The barn is quite spooky all on its own. When I pulled up to the big swinging doors we all jumped off and headed on inside. There was a deafening silence and it still had some Halloween decorations hanging on the walls. I started to walk through, pushing cobwebs away from my head, but nothing was sounding off. When I got towards the end of the barn, Psycho cat jumped out from the rafters like I did New Year's Eve, and the thing sounded off again. I'm telling you! I honestly don't know what I was thinking. Are these girls messing with me right now and if so, how? How do they know when to sound it? It is like literally sounding off in every place that has had something weird to go down.

I had one last thought and one last place. "Come on girls, help me shut these big doors back and hop back on." I drove back down to the house and parked. I headed toward the garage with hesitation, because this was starting to get really, really creepy. As soon as I got to the door, not in the doors, but at the doors, it hit the highest frequency it could reach. I looked back at the girls and they just shrugged their shoulders. I walked on in and it stopped. I walked over to the electrical panel to see if it would sound off there. But nothing! Nothing at all! Nothing was coming from inside the garage, only at the entry way. The place where something or someone liked to knock. Once again, I don't know. You tell me!!!

Let's say goodbye to 2016 and wish Daddy a Happy Birthday.
HAPPY BIRTHDAY, DADDY! AND HAPPY NEW YEAR!
Aunt Peggy wished him happy birthday on Facebook, but he has no computer and still has a flip phone. We are gonna have to work on that.
Hope the New Year serves us all better. Fingers are crossed.
All I can do, is all I can do.
PEACE OUT

P.S. Hold on Betty White.